A Question of Quality?

Roads to assurance in medical care

A Question of Quality ?

Roads to assurance in medical care

Contributors: Sir George Godber,
Colin Dollery, C. J. Bulpitt, H. J. Dargie and E. Leist,
Ian McColl · Donald Irvine · Tom Whitehead,
Tony Waldron and Lorna Vickerstaff,
John Revans · Graham Wilson,
Michael Heasman · John Yates · Alex Baker,
Robert Brook and Allyson Davies Avery,
Archie Cochrane · Gordon McLachlan

Edited by Gordon McLachlan

Published for the Nuffield Provincial Hospitals Trust
by the Oxford University Press   1976

Published for the
Nuffield Provincial Hospitals Trust
3 Prince Albert Road, London NW1 7SP

by Oxford University Press, Ely House, London W1

Oxford London Glasgow New York
Toronto Melbourne Wellington Cape Town
Ibadan Nairobi Dar es Salaam Lusaka Addis Ababa
Kuala Lumpur Singapore Jakarta Hong Kong Tokyo
Delhi Bombay Calcutta Madras Karachi

ISBN 0 19 721393 6

Designed by Bernard Crossland
Printed and bound in Great Britain
by Hazell Watson & Viney Limited
Aylesbury, Bucks

Contents

Note on the origins of this book　　　　　　　　　　　ix

Working Group for the Evaluation of the Quality of Care　　xi

Introduction and perspective　　　　　　　　　1
GORDON McLACHLAN

1. The term 'quality of care'　　　　　　　　　　　3

2. The changing views on quality over the years　　　7

3. Responsibilities in quality control　　　　　　　13

4. Refining the concepts and defining objectives　　15
References and notes, 19

The analysis of professional practice

1. The Confidential Enquiry into Maternal Deaths. A limited
study of clinical results　　　　　　　　　　　　23
SIR GEORGE GODBER
References, 33

2. The care of patients with malignant hypertension in
London in 1974–5　　　　　　　　　　　　　　35
COLIN DOLLERY, C. J. BULPITT, H. J. DARGIE, and
E. LEIST
Methods, 38. Analysis, 39. Results, 41. Discussion, 46. References, 47

3. Observations on the quality of surgical care　　49
IAN McCOLL
Current practice at one teaching hospital, 53. Discussion, 59.
References, 61.

4. Contemporary professional practice. Quality in general practice 63

DONALD IRVINE

General practice in perspective, 66. Postgraduate education for general practice, 69. Knowledge, 72. Skills, 73. Attitudes, 73. Audit in general practice, 87. Towards a strategy for improvement, 93. References, 94.

5. Surveying the performance of pathological laboratories 97

TOM WHITEHEAD

The United Kingdom National Quality Control Scheme (UKNQCS), 100. Organization of the Scheme, 101. Discussion, 114.

6. The role of the autopsy in medical care 119

TONY WALDRON and LORNA VICKERSTAFF

Introduction, 121. Autopsy rates in the United Birmingham Hospitals, 123. Clinical attitude to the autopsy, 127. Prospective study, 132. References, 134.

Administrative means

7. Questions of quality arising at regional medical officer's level 137

JOHN REVANS

Introduction, 139. Quality of service and care, 146.

8. The Hospital Health Services Research Unit in the University Department of Medicine, Western Infirmary, Glasgow. Its relation to the quality of medical care 153

GRAHAM WILSON

Introduction, 155. The location and structure of the Unit, 156. Research in relation to quality of medical care, 157. Communication between doctor and patient, 163. Guidelines for management, 165. Selection and use of expensive equipment, 167. Future plans, 168. References, 169.

9. SCRIPS: Success or failure. A critical study of the Scottish Consultant Review of In-Patient Statistics 171

MICHAEL A. HEASMAN

Introduction, 173. Background to SCRIPS, 173. General reactions, 176. Types of criticism, 177. References, 185.

10. The review of hospital resources and the implication for
clinical practice 187
JOHN YATES
Summary, 189. Introduction, 189. Hesitant sparring, 191. Inquiring
curiosity, 193. Participation, 197. Discussion, 199. References, 201.

11. The Hospital Advisory Service 203
ALEX BAKER
The Hospital Advisory Service, 206. Planning and decision-making, 209.
Facts and figures, 212. Rotation of staff, 214. The future, 215.

The US scene

12. Quality assurance mechanisms in the United States:
from there to where? 219
ROBERT H. BROOK and ALLYSON DAVIES AVERY
I. A brief history of quality assessment, 222. II. Ongoing quality
assurance systems, 228. Professional Standards Review Organizations,
228. Performance Evaluation Procedure, 233. Quality Assurance
Programme, 234. HMO quality assurance, 235. Other efforts, 236. The
malpractice crisis, 237. III. Implications for continuing research in
quality assurance, 239. Hospital versus ambulatory care review, 239.
Local control, 241. Scope of review activities, 242. Type and source of
data, 242. Technique versus art of medical care, 248. Evaluation of quality
assurance systems, 248. Duplication of systems, 249. IV. Summary, 249.
References, 250.

Retrospect

13. Some reflections 255
ARCHIE COCHRANE
Addendum, Professor J. R. A. Mitchell, 263. References, 265.

Postscript and prospect 267

GORDON McLACHLAN
1. The co-ordination of the field 269
2. The over-riding principles and lessons to emerge 270
3. The changing climate of professional and public opinion 277
4. To the horizon and beyond 279
5. Epilogue 286
References and notes, 288.

Appendix

Trust activities relevant to quality of medical care   291
References and notes, 294.

A bibliography of Trust grants relevant to quality of care   295
Monitoring the service (structure and process), 295. Identification of
need and demand (objective and outcome), 296.

Note on the origins of this book

This book marks an important stage in the most recent of a long line of activities of the Trust concerned with policies in pursuit of its purpose to improve the quality of medical care. A historical note threading these is given in Appendix 1.

More than twenty years ago the observations in *Hospital and Community*[1] pointed to the desirability of studying 'outcome' in analysing the effect of medical care on the individual for whom it was designed. More recently, interest in this aspect was further stimulated by the reception given to two books published by the Trust. The first of these was *Screening in Medical Care*,[2] published in 1968, which raised questions about the effectiveness of various screening procedures in common use. The second was the Rock Carling Monograph published in 1971 *Effectiveness and Efficiency*,[3] by Professor A. L. Cochrane who himself was a member of the Screening group.

When the Trustees invited Professor Cochrane to write a monograph on his views about effectiveness and efficiency of care and its assessment, there were few clues to how the book would be received. In the event the response was remarkably sympathetic. Leaving aside the technical difficulties involved in the use of randomized controlled trials advocated by Professor Cochrane, quite clearly his general conclusion that a great deal of therapeutic practice had never been assessed scientifically as to effect, had

1. Ferguson, T. (ed.) (1948). *Hospital and Community* (Oxford University Press for the Nuffield Provincial Hospitals Trust).
2. McKeown, T., Cochrane, A. L., *et al.* (1968). *Screening in Medical Care* (Oxford University Press for the Nuffield Provincial Hospitals Trust).
3. Cochrane, A. L. (1972). *Effectiveness and Efficiency*. Rock Carling Monograph (London: Nuffield Provincial Hospitals Trust).

catalysed the anxieties of many people on this score, not just in the UK but throughout the world.

If health services are assumed to have as a major objective the effective outcome of therapy or level of care, it is that end of the spectrum therefore which must be studied.

It was to follow up the monograph that in 1972 the Trustees convened a small group under the Chairmanship of the late Lord Rosenheim to look at general questions of quality of care, and this publication is a result of the group's deliberations.

GORDON McLACHLAN

Working Group for the Evaluation of the Quality of Care

Introduction and perspective

Introduction and perspective

GORDON McLACHLAN

1. The term 'quality of care'

The term quality of care is being increasingly used often both by doctors and their potential patients. The meaning given to it is not always the same and when it is accompanied with proposals for assessment, sometimes evokes emotional responses.

In some quarters, sensitive to any encroachment on the freedom hitherto enjoyed by medicine, it is gloomily asserted that assessment of quality is likely to become part of some bureaucratic monitoring, the effect of which will be deleterious to the clinical freedom deeply rooted in the historical development of medical practice. This is an over-facile distortion of the responses to some critical questions which hang over medical practice at present. They may indeed be a threat of bureaucratic influence but it should not be allowed to obscure the realities of some of the issues. What is missing from the general debate is an appreciation that despite the elusiveness of the meaning and implication of the broad concept there are several aspects of quality which are already being measured; and that a number of authorities and bodies certain of which have statutory responsibilities are already concerned with the achievement and maintenance of standards. Indeed the complexity of all that is involved in the assessment of medical care makes it dangerous to generalize about the many roads which lead to quality assurance. For while the outcome of medical care is very personal and its quality which we tend to associate with doctor and nurse is generally evident to the patient and those close to him, on the other side, that of the institutional providers of care, the politician, the administrator, as well as the community physician have to understand the complexity of the subject before they can develop the quite different lines of approach and criteria necessary for the judgements they are severally competent to make, and for which they are accountable in their various capacities in the provision of care. It has to be appreciated above all that such approaches and criteria are quite different from those which the clinician uses daily in facing the problems presented by his patients. The confusion principally arises because tradition dies hard, since in the end and for all the division of labour in modern medicine, and for all the stake held by the public in the vast organization involved, the belief is firmly entrenched that the physician is personally accountable to his patient alone. Yet the evidence is strong and growing of a public and professional interest in the elements which constitute adequate standards of quality (1) on which the essential personal judgements of medical care can be based. Indeed, the over-all problem of what elements constitute the character of quality and where responsibilities lie in evaluating it, suggests the need for a redefinition of assumptions concerning health services operations which can be understood and appreciated coolly, by all those who have their several parts providing services, as well as in shaping opinion, both professional and public.

In the UK there now exists in the concept of the NHS an easily identifiable framework for providing health care. But within it are a series of separate operating mechanisms, all with factorial effects on the quality of care, which makes for an element of confusion in semantics and reactions to questions of quality. This fact gives a special emphasis to the need for better concepts about quality assurance which might lead to a deeper understanding of all the interrelated issues, so that the advantages of a unified system may be explored to the full.

It is interesting that it is in the United States where there is no recognizable framework of a system of medical care that the subject of quality assurance has had most attention. There the approach to understand its nature and the influences to which it is subjected has been to attempt to analyse it in three sectors (2).

1. **'Structure'** of service, ie, the level of quality which is often measurable by norms or standards or through comparisons of

'plant', equipment, organization, education, professional (specialty) expertise, etc.

2. 'Process', ie, the professionally accepted standards of practice and procedures in practice and their governance.

3. 'Outcome' of medical care as revealed by indices of effect of therapies.

Stated baldly these reveal a concentration on acute medicine, but in the total context of medical care, since 'outcome' has implications other than recovery to whatever degree, it is necessary to include additionally the concept of:

4. 'Social acceptability' (3) which has two facets:
(*a*) The level of quality and standards accepted by the community, for instance the length of waiting-lists, or for the care and maintenance of the more chronically ill who have a poor prospect in the traditional sense of outcome, such as the socially and medically deprived, the mentally ill, the mentally and physically handicapped, the aged, etc. In crude resource terms it is possible to indicate such levels by comparisons with other areas within a nation or other societies.
(*b*) The second facet is not so easily indexed, for the special component in it is not so easy to measure. It may be significant that the following observation which describes it well, emanates from a doctor staff member of the Sub-Committee on Health of the US Senate, writing in the *New England Journal of Medicine*.

The process of caring for the patient—the inter-personal, supportive and psychologic aspects of the physician-patient relation—is the component of quality that most frequently separates the fulfilled physician with a busy practice of satisfied patients from others. It is the factor that gives rise to satisfaction on the part of the doctor and patient alike, accompanying and sometimes replacing the cure. Its intensity in the doctor-patient relation is inversely related to the frequency of malpractice litigation. It is difficult to assess, most frequently ignored by health-care planners, economists, and theoreticians, and is not and cannot be addressed by mechanisms such as PSRO.* But it is not ignored by 'customers', and is certainly the most visible, easily perceived and greatly appreciated of the quality components by the patient. [4]

* Peer Standard Review Organization (see refs. 5 and 25) now being set up under a 1972 US Government Statute.

In the context of medical care in Western Society, *Structure*—in the simplest terms, the provision of 'tools for the job'—seems primarily in the area of management, which seeks to serve patient and doctor in order to facilitate the best practice for the good of the patient. This involves clinicians, management and 'trustees' for the public in the planning and monitoring process, as well as in the debate about priorities. To insert in this hypothesis that the quality of structure has an effect on 'process', emphasizes its complexity, particularly for the layman.

The quality of clinical *process* and its assessment is dependent on the establishment of what is generally accepted as good professional practice either related to an individual or for a specific risk group. It seeks to ask the question 'How well do the clinicians do what they do?' In *process* clinical staff: doctors, nurses, all who 'treat' the patient are primary arbiters since they are best able to judge the educational achievement and performance of their colleagues. In addition to the individual clinician, the universities, the Royal Colleges, and the professional associations as well as institutions with statutory functions such as the GMC, carry responsibilities as to what constitutes good practice. The politician has to encourage the forging of a relationship of trust between the professions and the legislature which decrees the structure. Management is concerned, in so far as process is an article in the contract of employment and has an obligation to provide the effective means.

The *outcome* of the totality of care involves an appraisal by as stringent intellectual and scientific procedures as are practicable, and can be along the general lines, 'Is what they do worth doing?' Obviously there is a relationship between 'process', 'structure', and 'outcome' and each of these present different problems to that of the level of service provided, which is an index of social responsibility. The indefinable component of care is largely personal and vocational.

Ultimately, structure and process have to be judged with reference to each policy decision, by establishment of the *outcome*. Where the result is not obvious, this requires the application of scientific procedures to which often it is not easy to get answers because the procedures involved in setting up experiments are subject to ethical constraints. Nevertheless a basic assumption in the debate on quality is that medical research institutions whether within or outside the NHS have a major role in developing methods and carrying out trials, and that these have a high priority for research.

The general debate, however, presumes in modern society some sort of health system with objectives, which are often confused by the complexities of medical care and therapy and the personal nature of illness.

Except in certain definable circumstances the patient decides upon an approach to the doctor and, provided he is given the proper information he is the best arbiter of any intervention proposed for him. He is also, however, a member of society requiring to conform to certain conventions and participating in certain decisions about the use of resources for social aims and levels of service. This brings in one element of *social acceptability*, ie the level provided by public policy and the level to which it is allowed to rise. Where an issue of priority arises in the allocation of resources between the claims of individual patients, and those of the whole or a group of the population of patients, arbitration comes from within the political and managerial systems, a pre-requisite for the effective functioning of which presumes relevant and precise information from the clinical professions. This poses the need not only to discuss priorities for quality assurance but the quality of the information available as an aid to decisions. This is important in the light of the increasing attention being paid to the examination of policy decisions and of the parts to be played by the public or its representatives. From the American experience, it seems that at some stage society probably demands some evidence at least of professional internal check (5).

2. The changing views on quality over the years

The early emphasis on structure

Generally in the public sector there has been over the last twenty-five years, since the inception of the NHS, increasing sophistication of the debate about what is considered important in assuring good quality of services.

At the onset, everybody was mainly concerned with the 'structure', almost the aesthetic shape of the organization as well as the physical element of services and how they were brought to those in need of them (6). To fill in the gaps, in the case of those authorities which had been brought into being for planning purposes—the hospital authorities, crude needs were established sometimes in relation to criteria developed over many years in the course of public health activities, sometimes it must be conceded mainly by assertion and sapiential authority only; the 'demand', sometimes recognized as being inflated, but always equated with 'need' was the spur to action. Often this pointed almost crudely, to the need for a major redistribution of services; hence the almost exclusive attention paid in the earliest days to the physical facilities: buildings, equipment, and the need in a National Health Service to improve organizational patterns by providing particular services, which in certain places had not previously existed in the planning areas. This is why in the beginning of the NHS planning for quality came to be mainly associated with the provision of 'plant', ie, buildings, equipment, etc., and manpower provision, following comparisons with what was available elsewhere, either in the UK or abroad. The relative efficacy of this aspect of service could be evaluated easily, especially since in the post-war period much of the 'plant' tended to be outdated; and in certain places services did not exist. The relativity of standards of service could also be adduced by comparisons of manpower and other measurable variables in services, such as for example the size and movement of waiting-lists.

These are the constituents of 'structure' which lie in the general area of management and their importance is because 'the most appropriate treatment delivered by the most devoted and trained staff will be less than satisfactory without the provision of buildings, equipment, manpower and other resources deployed in a most appropriate mix'.* It is part of the thesis that the form and

* Private Report on 'The Influence of Health Service Structure on the Quality of Care' by Scicon (Mr Frank Wellman) prepared for the Nuffield Provincial Hospitals Trust, as part of the project.

quality of structure may have a significant effect on the process of medical care which is reliant upon it and equally that the process may affect structure in the sense that choice of a particular method of treatment might either result in the use of facilities in a manner different from that originally intended or perhaps in their neglect; and therefore the interaction of structure and process can ultimately influence outcome.

There are two features of structure which are necessary to an understanding of its relation to quality. The first is that it is the most visible manifestation of care, apparent both to the patient and to the doctor, whether in the form of buildings, equipment, or health service staff. Because the acceptability of treatment is one essential constituent of quality and it is not always possible for the doctor or the patient to know of the complete process of care, let alone comprehend it, and because the outcome may also remain unknown, at any rate until after a long interval of time, judgement upon an episode of patient treatment or upon a medical policy for a whole population may often be more closely linked to an opinion about the state of facilities and manpower than is scientifically justified.

The second obstacle to easy assessment of structure is the fact that it should be based not upon the provision at one point in time of one particular resource, but upon the mix of resources and their development over a period of time.

By way of illustrating further these two features, and referring firstly to the mix of resources, it is only necessary to reflect that the element of social responsibility comes in fixing centrally the upper limit of the amount of resources available, and to secure the optimum social dividend; it is the distribution between different groups of patients with specific needs, and therefore between different medical specialties, between policies of prevention and of treatment, as well as between different geographical regions, which is a subject of assessment, as well as the quality of a particular building, item of equipment, or member of staff.

Secondly, some of the most expensive resources, whether of buildings or staff, are tied to a long time-scale. It takes up to ten years to plan, design, build, and bring into operation a new hospital which could then continue in use for up to a hundred years or more. The factors however which influence demand upon such a building, for instance, population, morbidity, or medical technology may vary on a much shorter time-scale. Many of the decisions about structure which have to be taken are of the order of difficulty associated with policy decisions about the construction of Concorde or a Channel tunnel in that they require to be based upon an assessment of trends and priorities in the future which are beyond the scope of what man can at present calculate with certainty. Less complicated but nevertheless difficult are the calculations required to assess the costs and benefits of ageing facilities in comparison with new, and the benefits of quick results of less quality in comparison with deferred benefits of higher value. Thus there may be a choice between commissioning a 600-bed hospital which will take ten years to build, and commissioning in two phases 300-bed hospitals the first of which can be commissioned earlier, but the total cost of both of which will be greater. Or the choice might be between a cardiac pacemaker costing say £300 and requiring replacement every three years, in comparison with another costing say £650 and requiring replacement every ten years. Decisions about such options at a time of limited resources are of evident complexity. The same applies in the education and training of skilled staff.

The controversy which usually surrounds any proposal to close down a hospital testifies to the importance of decisions about structure in the outlook of both the public and of health service management. The pressure group which organizes a campaign against the closure of a hospital is convinced of the value of the institution within the local system of health services; equally one must assume that health service management has been convinced that the closure is required in order to improve the local mix of resources within the funds available. Whichever side may be right, the conclusion can be drawn that decisions about the deployment of resources are viewed as crucial to the quality of care and the successful handling of such decisions is a major constituent of quality. The same point can be also developed from the recurrent debates about the quantity of resources made available for the

NHS within the national budget. The cliché that the nation will receive the quality of medical care which it chooses to pay for is too often deployed in argument, without the realization that the decisions taken intermittently and by delegation to politicians by the public about the level of resources, is dependent upon the quality of health service planning and the skill of doctors and administrators in communicating with the public. A major section of the debate about quality has therefore to do with the quality of planning and how effectively the public is educated.

Beyond structure

As more money has been made available over the years to the NHS however, there has also been an accompanying increase in demand —and sophistication leading to the realization that not only will there never be 'enough', but that developments from which much has been expected indeed the assumptions on which they were based, have to come under scrutiny for priorities (7). The emphasis in recent years has been on improving the organizational pattern, reflecting the realization that 'plant' by itself or manpower establishments are not all-important (8). Nor are statistical comparisons of utilization of much value unless related somehow to absolute standards based on accepted procedures, and to outcome of one kind or another—comparisons which are not always easy to carry out effectively. The reorganization which came into being on 1 April 1974, was intended to make the arrangements for the delivery of services more efficient in operational terms, that is to make the best use of resources in a situation where there are competing priorities, and with scarce resources. This however poses questions of quality and effectiveness of decisions, and never so acutely than at present, but without adequate answers. Quite apart from these considerations, which continually face the authorities administering services, there are of course other checks on quality which have been developed over the years. Thus there are basic educational requirements for entry into medical practice laid down in the Medical Acts, the Postgraduate awards of the Royal Colleges, the statutory appointment arrangements for the appointment of consultants in the NHS and an agreed staffing structure of sorts in the general medical services to ensure each general practitioner cares for what has been estimated to be a reasonably sized population. There are certain monitoring mechanisms which operate within the structure of health services because of legislation and statutory orders governing the regulation of entry to the medical profession and practice generally. More recently certain accreditation schemes have come into operation for the purposes of ensuring quality in higher professional training (9).

A significant spur to quality is also given through the mechanism of incentives and spurs to good practice. Merit awards are the most obvious example in this country (10); admission in the UK to lists such as the 'obstetric list' represent another kind of mechanism (11); educational allowances are a third (12).

On the less obvious side (but hardly new although the present position may worsen) the threat of malpractice suits (which in the US have reached crisis proportions) and the possibility of a revocation of contract or even of licence to practice, are spurs to the small number of doctors whose quality may be so seriously in question as to present a blatant risk to the patient. The US story of the malpractice crisis and of the legislature's response to it, is interesting and should be remembered in any general debate. It is also possible that the recent 'industrial action' in the UK may cause a rise in suits here, as part of the reaction to the possible dissolution of the 'ethos' surrounding medicine. Certainly the Press has tended to sharpen its interest in the lessons from individual disasters (13).

There was once perhaps a widespread assumption that doctors, given proper service conditions, would act according to certain codes of practice and the quality of care given to the patient would remain constantly high and only occasionally spotty. If such an assumption ever was generally held, the report of malpractice suits in the US and the crises as a result of it, and recurring public inquiries in this country have long called it to question. Indeed in certain specific fields in the UK, the series of Confidential Enquiries into Maternal Mortality (14) and the establishment of the Hospital Advisory Service (15) in the field of mental health indicate significant progress in co-operation between the administering authorities and the medical profession in the approach to monitoring the quality of care although the high quality of vital statistics in the UK as a basis for epidemiological monitoring has always been a feature of the scene (16). Indeed fundamental to the objectives behind the new organizational patterns is the assumption that the new organization will have a better capability to 'monitor' services in some vague way, presumably as to adequacy and to develop new services to meet requirements revealed as a result of the monitoring process. But questions about effectiveness of most clinical procedures tend to derive from the speculations of the independent bodies and academics interested in developing the application of knowledge in order to blaze new trials to improvements (17).

3. Responsibilities in quality control

The external pressures of a better-informed public are such that there is now some urgency to explore the relative responibility and accountability roles of authorities and individuals, within the total system with regard to the maintenance and improvement of quality generally. This includes the responsibility of clinicians *vis-à-vis* patients and the authorities designated for general responsibility for the population group, whether it is at district, area, regional, or national levels. The rationale for this is that since the objectives for individuals and groups are not of course necessarily the same, only by showing the several responsibilities of the various administrative authorities, professional groups and individuals, as well as the effect of the external regulatory constraints such as for example the courts in malpractice suits, etc., will it be possible to get a sensible perspective on a subject attracting increasing attention and in which there are emotive elements. It would also be important to sketch in the other bodies concerned, including the Social Work Services which bear on the health system but are not directly within the organization of the NHS.

In terms of public guardianship, the operating levels owing their existence to democratic election are constituted by the processes of election to Parliament and to local authorities both of which have a function of ensuring that the methods of selection for appoint-

ments to the executive statutory bodies are just and that recognized standards of behaviour by the bodies, their members and
officers are observed. The system itself through ministerial
responsibility to Parliament is self-correcting in a broad sense and
this extends to the process of 'disaster' inquiries (18) including the
Hospital Advisory Service and for complaints procedures (19)
including the Ombudsman (20) as well as much more recently for
general monitoring of local services by community health councils
(21), the constitution and future of which lie in ministerial policy.

Outside the health system itself lie the courts. Within the
organized system, at each level, there are varying statutorily
appointed authorities with responsibilities for the provision and
maintenance of standards of plant and manpower primarily. Their
charge also includes provision to ensure that there is recognition of
the educational and training standards laid down by recognized
educational bodies. The organization of such authorities may
provide for the individual institutions operating whether at
regional, area, or district level to have specific internal check
functions depending to a large extent again on ministerial policy,
for example the 'three wise men' procedures (22), death and
complications meetings within institutions, etc.

In the 'total' system there exists as a token of a free society
private bodies of both a general and specific type which may have
nothing to do with the organized system itself such as the NHS,
but which for a variety of reasons hold watching briefs over
quality. They include bodies such as the General Medical Council
which is statutory but independent of the operating authorities,
and is charged with the maintenance of educational and ethical
standards. These private bodies also include the professional
educational bodies such as the Royal Colleges, and the professional
organizations which have other objectives such as the BMA; also
non-professional organizations such as the NPHT itself (23), with
specific purposes regarding improvement and a long tradition
involving independent comment on action in health affairs. They
also include other private bodies with specific objectives. sometimes virtually pressure groups for a particular kind of patient.
Also in this broad category are the media which take a monitoring

interest in anything happening to the population as a whole and which is often the source of pressures for inquiries leading to more control.

In summary the basic hypothesis of the thesis that there has to be a comprehensive new approach to a sharper definition of objectives and a theory embodying flexibility is that the approaches to monitoring quality are different for clinician, community physician (in all his guises), administrator, politician, and public. These several approaches involve quite different institutions, groups and individuals and quite distinct objectives.

4. Refining the concepts and defining objectives

Indeed it is already evident that the debate has not yet gone sufficiently deep, and because of the implication of control it is important to analyse as many issues as practicable in order to avoid misunderstandings and to put facts into perspective. Over-simplification of the issue of quality as a whole is likely to be fatal to progress in a field in which one has to seek to influence the existing climate of opinion towards acceptance at the level of practice of self-examination, by initiatives on as broad a front as possible by research and demonstrations, etc., in which the universities, the Royal Colleges, the specialist associations as well as the professional groups such as the medical executive committees who are closest to observe and influence actual practice and especially 'divisional' structures at the clinical level (24), might be involved.

Above all it has seemed to the group that the medical profession should be persuaded to accept this responsibility for self-scrutiny because if it did not do so others would seek to enforce means of quality control which would inevitably tend to be more bureaucratic. Unless the profession is seen to understand what is possible and desirable and to institute appropriate steps it is likely a confused situation will arise which is not in the long run in the interests of either the patients or of the profession.

As a corollary it is also important from the point of view of the individual citizen that he should appreciate the complexity of

problems of health services which probably make them unique as
   totality. It must be evident by now through the public debate in
the last few years that the more technical the bases to diagnoses
and therapy, the more complex the answers must be to the more
aware patient who still wishes to reserve for himself some part in
the eventual decision about what therapy he is to undergo. It must
be recognized too, it is a far cry from the days when everything was
left to the individual doctor who acted on his own. The complexity
of the base of medical practice is now such that while the doctor (or
in hospital the clinical team) stands at the apex, many specialists
and ancillary professions may be involved in both diagnosis and
therapy. Again, in the last few years ever larger injections of public
money are being put into health care provision. The immense
responsibility of the institutional provider, which as a public body
is subject to many constraints, forces it to have a system of
accountability involving the various individuals providing services.
This picture is by no means confined to countries in which like
Britain the virtual monopoly provider is the state. Indeed one of
the significant factors in the general debate on quality is what has
recently occurred on the regulation of the medical profession in the
US where there is actually legislation requiring professional
standards, ie, 'process' and 'practice' to be reviewed for publicly
financed patients (25), and where the principle of relicensure is
now widely debated.

There are of course difficulties with terminology, particularly the
emotive term monitoring. Sir Richard Doll discussed some of the
questions this poses on the eve of the reforms of the Health Service:

As to the conditions that are required to make monitoring a success,
these are more complex. First, we must develop new methods that
measure up to the size of the task, including a national system for
linking medical records like that developed by Acheson (1967) [26] and
a system by which expensive services, whether preventive or curative,
can be subjected to controlled trial before they are introduced on a
national scale.

Secondly, we must ensure that monitoring, which is the principle
concern of the Department of Health and Social Security, is also
conducted by independent bodies. Addison argued the need for research
to be conducted independently when he introduced the Bill to set up a
Ministry of Health in 1919, giving as his reason that, 'A Ministry of

Health must necessarily become committed from time to time to particular systems of health administration . . .', while the discoveries of scientific research 'are bound to correct the conclusions based upon the knowledge that was previously available and, therefore, in the long run to make it right to alter administrative policy'. And the same applies to monitoring. It may be important, for example, to have some independent assessment of the effect of closing psychiatric hospitals, not only on the patients—who may not always be benefited (Watts, 1973)—but also on the families who have to cope with them, and more extensively on the health of the community itself.

Thirdly, the system must satisfy Himsworth's (1970) condition for the continued success of any human organisation; that it should be 'in conformity with the deep-rooted sentiments of the men who have to make it work and thus productive of the requisite loyalty and morale'. I see no reason why this should not be possible. Whatever the position in other walks of life, the long-term interests of employers and employees in the health service are the same. To make a success of monitoring within the service it is necessary only to take account of the natural human reactions of those who are being monitored. To make a success of monitoring the Health Service itself, we need the continued support of Foundations. [27]

Doll has subsequently explored further the issues of surveillance and pointed to 'three aspects—medical efficacy, social acceptability and economic efficiency—that are independent of one another and require different methods of evaluation. Moreover each aspect can be monitored in terms of the outcome achieved or the process by which the outcome is reached.' He did not separate structure, despite common usage, as it seems a part of the process by which outcome is affected. Both outcome and process demand evaluation (28).

All in all therefore, the tide is flowing ever more swiftly towards some requirements to ensure sensible assessment of performance. This has been recognized professionally; it occasionally runs even faster in certain directions because of the opening of the debate into the public domain, because of malpractice. The Professor of Surgery at Cambridge University has expressed this recently:

It is anomalous that the day a man ceases to be a senior registrar on his appointment as a consultant marks the beginning of a period, extending to retirement age, in which professional criticism from his colleagues is most unlikely, unless his malpractice is so blatant as to involve a suit for damages. Such immunity from criticism is unusual in other professions and occupations. First-class and very bad surgeons tend to be known by their colleagues, particularly their junior staff. Yet a surgeon may spend his whole life making poor judgements and operating badly with an unacceptably high morbidity and mortality, and remain unaware that his work is below par. If no-one else will criticise our work objectively, then we must judge ourselves and attempt to correct recognisable faults. [29]

The whole question however begs the need for a framework for a sensible development and approach. The fact that the NHS is a recognizable system in itself makes it probably however, somewhat easier to develop concepts for a better appreciation of what 'control' means in the sub-systems operating within the framework of the NHS and with direct effect on it. This involves all the facets of postgraduate education in which the service element is inextricably entwined with that of further education both graduate and continuing. It is thus inseparable in fact from the administrative system which however is mainly concerned with the service requirements of professional practice.

The practical line of advance seems first the establishment of a better atmosphere than hitherto towards more systematic self-evaluation of the quality of care by the individual clinician. In this respect the emergence of the specialty of community physician, particularly that group within the specialty concerned with the development of epidemiological skills and techniques could be an important factor if it was also accompanied by a deliberate policy designed to create the right atmosphere of understanding and to develop techniques of self examination.

The particular objective of this publication is primarily to bring a better perspective to the debate to help persuade the profession of the value of studies of quality and of the wide variety of activities involved. The collection of essays which follows indicates the many faceted sides of quality studies and together gives some clues to how the establishment of a sympathetic atmosphere to the general approach of monitoring quality may be accomplished.

Inter alia these show the variety of ways in which the challenge to scrutinize practice has been taken up. Sir George Godber's review has to do with initiative by a clinical specialty supported by the Department of Health; Dollery's with an individual initiative supported by a foundation; and Whitehead's with an acceptance of responsibility by a Royal College. McColl and Irvine carry the demonstration further. There are probably many other examples of analysis which exist. These are not reported only because of restriction upon the size of this volume.

There are also a number of reports upon the capacity of official and academic authorities to back up the clinician with effective organization and information. The essays by Revans, Heasman, Wilson, and Yates are but single examples of several instances which might have been reviewed. To these is added the cautionary study by Waldron of an apparent decline in the use of the traditional mechanism of autopsy. To broaden the picture by looking at what is happening elsewhere the current American scene, the lessons of which will be ignored at peril, is reviewed by Brook and Avery. Despite the lack of a unified system, there is no lack of will in the USA to assess quality. Perhaps Cochrane's conclusion is of all the most immediately pressing for without the will scientifically to assess the results of therapy, the study of facilities and practice is without a base. Too little work has yet been done in recording and correlating the sum of effort put into clinical trials.

This mosaic of quality assessment set out by these essays will it is hoped be a signal contribution to the continuing debate by the medical profession in the confident hope that it may prepare the way for Doll's third and fundamental condition of success, that the assessment of quality may be seen to be 'in conformity with the deep-rooted sentiments of the men who have to make it work'.

References and notes

1. Over the last two years there have been numerous references on this subject in the medical press as well as in the press generally, although in the UK there has been nothing to equal the series of articles in the *New York Times* between 26 January and 1 February 1976.
2. DONABEDIAN, A. (1966). 'Evaluating the quality of medical care, Part 2', *Milbank Meml Fund Q.* **44**, 166–206.
3. DOLL, SIR RICHARD (1974). *To Measure NHS Progress*. Occasional Paper 8 (Fabian Society).
4. CAPER, P. (1974). *New Engl. J. Med.* **291**, 1136–7 (NN21).
5. COMMITTEE OF FINANCE, US SENATE (1972). *Background Material Relating to PSROs* (Washington, DC: US Government Printing Office).

6. 'Hospitals and the State', Acton Society pamphlet, 1955–7.
7. Sir Keith Joseph's foreword to CMND 5055 (London: HMSO, 1972).
8. *Management Arrangements for the Reorganised NHS* (London: HMSO, 1972).
9. Most of the Royal Colleges Faculties now have schemes for the accreditation of training posts.
10. Circular RHB49 (115) BG49(99).
11. Circular ECL81/60.
12. Health Services and Public Health Act, 1968. S.63.
13. DOYLE, CHRISTINE (1976). *The Observer*, 1 February.
14. ARTHURE, H. (1975). 'Confidential inquiries into maternal deaths', *Br. med. J.* (8 February), 332. See also Chapter 1 Vol. 1.
15. See Chapter 11.
16. See CMO's Annual Reports.
17. COCHRANE, A. L. (1971). *Effectiveness and Efficiency*, Rock Carling Monograph (London: Nuffield Provincial Hospitals Trust). See also Chapters 2 and 13.
18. *Report of the Committee of Inquiry into allegations of ill-treatment of patients and the irregularities at the Ely Hospital, Cardiff*, March 1969, Cmnd. 3995 (London: HMSO).
19. DHSS (1973). *Report of the Committee in Hospital Complaints Procedure* (Davis Committee) (London: HMSO).
20. NHS Reorganisation Act, 1973, Part III, S.31–39 (London: HMSO, 1973).
21. NHS Reorganisation Act, 1973, Part I, S.9 (London: HMSO, 1973).
22. Circular HM (60) 45.
23. See Appendix 1 for an indication of the range and variety of approaches.
24. *Organisation of Medical Work in Hospitals*, First Report of the Working Party (London: HMSO, 1967).
25. Act of October 1972. PL92.603 (US).
26. ACHESON, E. D. (1967). *Medical Record Linkage* (Oxford University Press for the Nuffield Provincial Hospitals Trust).
27. 'Monitoring the Health Service', Nuffield Lecture at the Royal Society of Medicine, 1973.
28. DOLL, SIR RICHARD (1974). 'Surveillance and monitoring', *Internat. J. Epidemiol.* **3**, 305.
29. CALNE, R. (1974). 'Surgical self-scrutiny', *Lancet* (30 November), **ii**, 1309.

The analysis of professional practice

1

The Confidential Enquiry into Maternal Deaths

A limited study of clinical results

SIR GEORGE GODBER

DM, FRCP

Formerly Chief Medical Officer
DHSS

The Confidential Enquiry into Maternal Deaths

A limited study of clinical results

The National Health Service is a system for giving access to medical care for all on the criterion of need and not of ability to pay. It does not have, but badly needs, a system for the study of outcome of medical and allied care. National or regional morbidity and mortality statistics tell us a little about the health of the population and nothing about the effects of particular clinical methods. The Hospital In-Patient Enquiry and Hospital Activity Analysis provide some material from which comparisons can be made. The Oxford Record Linkage Study begins to approach the area we need to study more closely, as do regional cancer registers and psychiatric registers like that in Camberwell. Some specialist units make a close study of their own results and there is growing interest in such studies. The Confidential Enquiry into Maternal Deaths (1, 2) is the only example of a national continuing outcome study mounted within the NHS. It has operated for more than twenty-three years in little changed form and the three-year reports derived from it have been widely read. Its genesis, progress, and possible development are due for review.

The present Enquiry was introduced in 1952 and replaced a more limited study which had continued after the special study undertaken by Mr Arnold Walker and Mr G. F. Gibberd for the Departmental Committee on Maternal Mortality during the four years preceding that committee's report in 1932. The then Ministry of Health continued to obtain confidential reports from medical officers of health for the ensuing twenty years, and maternity units made statistical returns to the Ministry in limited form but recording morbidity as well as mortality. The quality of both kinds of report varied widely and there was not an effective review of the clinical care of individual patients. Some maternity units produced their own annual reports in detail on lines recommended by the Royal College of Obstetricians and Gynaecologists and Sir William Fletcher Shaw compiled regional statistics for the Manchester Region including much detail that an inquiry related only to deaths did not include. The change which was introduced in 1952 for the first time tried to bring in information from all the clinical services for analysis by independent experts at both regional and national levels and an assessment by them of the presence or absence of avoidable factors.

The method used in this inquiry is not necessarily reproducible in any other. The study related only to fatalities which even in 1952 occurred only once in more than a thousand deliveries. Pregnancy and childbirth are normal physiological processes and maternal deaths are only the worst outcome of some abnormality which required professional intervention; there must be a far larger number of occasions when the outcome was not fatal, but the course might have been less hazardous had the professional intervention been better managed if it was sought by the patient at all. Nevertheless at the outset it was a reasonable assumption that best current practice could reduce the mortality substantially and further that a study of those cases in which the worst result had occurred could point the way to improvements in service.

The original suggestion of a new inquiry was made to Sir Wilson Jameson just before his retirement by Sir Eardley Holland who had been prompted by a comment made at an international conference of which he had been President. It fell to me to undertake the discussions with the various interested groups with whose help the scheme was devised. The RCOG was involved from the first through successive Presidents, Sir William Gilliatt and Dame Hilda Lloyd. Mr Arnold Walker and Mr A. J. Wrigley advised on the scope of the reports to be obtained and on the actual draft. Consultations took place with MOHs, SAMOs of regional hospital boards, and the General Medical Services Committee of the BMA. The Royal College of Midwives was kept informed, as were the medical defence organizations. The most difficult problem was the guarantee of confidentiality, since complete frankness in reporting could only be expected if there was reasonable certainty that the reports would be treated as privileged and never to be disclosed to anyone other than the professional staff involved in the Ministry. Within the Ministry no report was ever used for any purpose other than the inquiry; if a complaint was received in the Ministry about a case on which a confidential report already existed the complaint was handled as if there was no knowledge of the case within the department. It is hardly surprising that the preparations took almost two years.

The basis of the Enquiry was understood to be voluntary and its objects did not include action by any outside authority on evidence of action or inaction in any case where there were adjudged to be avoidable factors. It was intended from the beginning to rely upon the effect of review by the individuals concerned of their own course of action if it had failed to save a life. It might have been impossible to secure any other result by a different course of action, but the very fact of discussion among themselves could lead the professionals to a fresh appraisal of their own practice. The idea of the reports came later.

The registration of a death related to pregnancy was the starting point for action. The MOH of every county or county borough normally saw the registered causes of deaths in his area by arrangement with the Registrar. His part was to pick out all deaths due to or associated with pregnancy and to collect any information available from his own services or from the general practitioner, and then send the four-part form on to the local obstetrician involved. The obstetrician then obtained the full clinical information by personal inquiry from anyone concerned and sent the report to a regional assessor, a senior obstetrician invited to undertake this work by the Chief Medical Officer after consultation with the PRCOG. The regional assessor reviewed the information, made supplementary inquiry if any information was lacking and sent on the report to the CMO with his assessment as to the existence of avoidable factors. In the Ministry one doctor experienced in obstetrics held the reports which were all then examined by the two consultant advisers in obstetrics who made a final assessment. When it became apparent that there was a substantial number of cases in which anaesthesia could be the cause of death, the consultant adviser on anaesthetics, Dr A. D. Marston, was asked to review those cases.

So far all this procedure was intended to secure improvement by the local review of cases, but it was soon apparent that avoidable factors were too often present in antenatal and intranatal care for the opportunity of central remedial action to be ignored. The inclusion of a few paragraphs and tables in the CMO's Annual Report would be insufficient. It was quickly seen that reduction in deaths due to toxaemia of pregnancy and to haemorrhage would bring about the greatest improvement. One direct contribution could be made by administrative action; obstetric flying squads already existed in several centres and if generally available would help to eliminate one practice which the Enquiry quickly revealed as associated with too many deaths. Patients with retained placenta after delivery at home were often put into ambulances and removed to hospital before either transfusion or manual removal of the placenta, only to be found moribund on arrival. All regions then organized flying squads after a discussion with SAMOs and with the help of the regional assessors and the policy of treatment before removal was generally introduced. In the first three-year series there were 53 such deaths with 89 per cent having avoidable factors; in the next three-year period there were only 24 deaths in this group, though 48 per cent of them still had avoidable factors, and haemorrhage dropped from the highest place as a cause of death.

Toxaemia of pregnancy or pre-eclamptic toxaemia was nearly as large a cause of death as haemorrhage in the first series and there was no direct administrative action which RHBs could take. It was clear from the examination of the first year's reports that improved antenatal care offered the best hope of reducing the toll. The Standing Maternity and Midwifery Advisory Committee was therefore asked to consider a memorandum on antenatal care related to the prevention of toxaemia drafted in consultation with the consultant advisers with their knowledge of the failings recorded in some of the reports. The Committee revised and adopted the memorandum and recommended its circulation to general practitioners and obstetric staff. The memorandum was in no sense a directive but it certainly led to more intensive antenatal supervision and in ten years the deaths due to this cause were halved.

The action on both these subjects was initiated before the question of reports had been considered, but it was clear that the consultant advisers and Dr Katherine Hirst of the Ministry, who worked with them, had collected much information about the ways in which things went wrong and the possibility of avoiding them. The regional assessors were therefore given a resumé of the information and invited to a meeting to discuss its use. All agreed that the three should attempt to draft a report, that they should have the help of an experienced statistician in the preparation of the figures and that Dr Marston should be asked to prepare a chapter on the unexpectedly large number of deaths attributed to anaesthesia. The drafts were discussed at two subsequent meetings of assessors and the first report was published, for the years 1952–4, in 1957, over the names of Messrs Walker and Wrigley, Dr Hirst, Dr Marston, and the statistician, Dr Martin.

The decision to publish seemed at the time adventurous and some thought that its open admission of failure to provide fully satisfactory professional care in so high a proportion of patients who died would arouse sharp public criticism and cause alarm unnecessarily to many women. No such reaction occurred and the report was immediately successful among the professions concerned and was widely read abroad. Similar studies were later introduced in Northern Ireland, Scotland, New Zealand, and some Australian states.

In the first and all the subsequent reports the most commonly observed departures from optimal practice were described in such a way that individual cases would not be identifiable either by relatives or by professional colleagues, though there was increasing realism in the reports which may sometimes have made at least close analogies apparent to some of the doctors concerned. The clinical situations and the moments for decision when mistakes could occur were identified with growing clarity in each succeeding report. The crucial decision about place of confinement at a time when one-third of deliveries occurred at home gave one of the most common occasions for misjudgement. Criteria for selection for home confinement were emphasized with growing certainty. The special problems of anaesthesia in advanced pregnancy were studied by regional anaesthetic advisers. The fact that most abortion deaths were the result of illicit intervention was clearly exposed. The special need for autopsies to be carried out by pathologists experienced in this work led to consultations with the Coroners' Society. But the objective throughout remained the same, to collate and present for the professional staff concerned how often and in what way things went wrong, not stigmatizing any individual or any professional group but providing them with examples which they could see for themselves and seek to avoid. The reports were merely the indication of the much more important process of self-examination which should have occurred locally.

What happened locally probably depended more on the influence of the regional assessor with his colleagues than on the reports. Naturally the assessors varied in their approaches and some pursued their inquiries further than others in the early years. But the regular meetings with the consultant advisers and the Ministry medical staff concerned made it possible to ensure a more uniform standard of assessment. The final appraisal always lay with the consultant advisers.

Participation in the Enquiry was voluntary on the part of three different branches of the profession. In the sixth three-year period 89 per cent of the cases known to the Registrar General were the subject of reports, but information supplied by coroners revealed that there was a small additional number in which the relation to existence of pregnancy was not mentioned in the registration particulars. Nevertheless the Enquiry was so nearly complete in its coverage that it can be held to give a reliable picture for the country. It is unlikely that this degree of completeness could be expected on a national scale for any other condition, since the combination of manageable numbers and the legal requirement of registrations of both births and deaths is unique. Other inquiries have dealt with much smaller numbers, as for instance major adverse reactions to vaccination against smallpox or to other immunizations, and still been incomplete; or they have been selective as in the British Association of Anaesthetists' inquiry into post-anaesthetic deaths or the local inquiries into post-neonatal deaths.

During the first three-year period there were 1,094 maternal deaths directly due to pregnancy or childbirth and there were 2,079,275 births; in the sixth period there were 455 maternal deaths and 2,484,004 births. The maternal mortality excluding abortion had fallen from 0·54 per thousand births to 0·15 between 1952 and 1969 and the mortality from abortion from 0·13 to 0·04. By 1973 these rates had fallen further to 0·10 and 0·02. The Enquiry had called special attention to toxaemia as the largest single cause of maternal deaths and to the need to deal with certain causes of haemorrhage more effectively. These two causes were much more rapidly reduced than the other two leading causes, pulmonary embolism and abortion. Abortion deaths were decreasing slowly until the Abortion Act and thereafter were sharply reduced. Pulmonary embolism as a cause was reduced more slowly, but hopefully was responding to some of the general measures suggested in the various reports. There is no doubt of the reduction since the Enquiry began but it cannot be certain that the improvement was due to the Enquiry.

Scotland's Enquiry started later, but the maternal mortality fell more rapidly in Scotland and was lower there until 1970, possibly because the relatively larger resources available to Scotland under the NHS made possible a more rapid increase in the proportion of births taking place in hospital. The same effect occurred in Wales and possibly for the same reason. But the explanation may be more complex because the best provided regions did not have the lowest rates. Perhaps the most striking result was in the Liverpool Region where the number of deaths fell from 103 in the first period to 14 in the sixth. Other countries may have used their own systems to equally good purpose, 6 out of 15 listed in the last three-year report (2) had lower rates than England and Wales in 1968 or 1967, though not as low as the rate now reached here. Nevertheless it is a reasonable conclusion from the way in which the improvement developed that it was at least influenced by the Enquiry, both by the local review it brought about and the way the collated information influenced obstetric policy.

It would be comforting to be able to report that deaths with avoidable factors became a progressively smaller proportion. This did not happen, but as the sixth report explains standards became more stringent as policies largely arising from the Enquiry became more sharply defined. The total of deaths in the Enquiry series in 1967–9 was actually less than the number adjudged to be without avoidable factors in 1952–4. Since 1959 illicit abortion has been greatly reduced, at least as a cause of maternal death, and this will have improved the position materially. Subjectively there was clear evidence of improved standards in the reduction in number of the truly grievous errors. Nevertheless it is still clear that maternal mortality could be further reduced and a rate below one in ten thousand births is to be expected.[1]

Successive reports drew attention to particular factors large and small. The necessity of a close watch for signs of toxaemia and quick reaction if they occurred was one of the first. Special care in selection of place of delivery is less a preoccupation now that 90 per cent of deliveries take place in hospital, but there are still voices raised in favour of the small maternity unit, which is clearly less safe on the evidence of the Enquiry. The need for a better anaesthetic service and the special risk of inhalation of vomit (Mendelsohn's syndrome) caused the relevant specialist groups to examine the problem and to

1. The seventh report now published reveals that three regions had rates (excluding abortion) ranging from 5·9 to 9·7 for the period 1970–2.

make recommendations which have not yet been fully implemented for lack of staff.

The Enquiry is now more searching and the reports are more outspoken than in the early days, but the main purpose of the Enquiry is still to promote local review. Since deaths are now so few, the Enquiry touches a progressively smaller part of the obstetric services of a district. The average district now will have a maternal death perhaps once in two or three years instead of two or three a year. A general practitioner with a list of 2,400 at current rates would expect about thirty-one births in the practice each year. With the likely maternal mortality rate of the next ten years a group practice of ten doctors might expect that one maternal death would occur in their combined practices in thirty years. A local review of deaths only is not likely to be very educational for them. In fact the Enquiry by its very success has shown up its own inadequacies. Unless there is a systematic review of the practices used locally and their outcome, the maternal deaths' inquiry will become a diminishing force for improvement. It can remain an important piece of background work for the on-going review of practice which should become part of the year's work in every health district and with the participation of all the relevant disciplines, medical and other.

The lessons from this twenty-four-year-old survey are that the professions will undertake an open review of mortality in a way that may present starkly to one or more of them real shortcomings in their own work, provided this is conducted with complete confidentiality and without disciplinary intent. The knowledge that such a study is undertaken and the fact of publication of general conclusions do not lead to public recriminations or loss of confidence. The outcome can be clearer definition of clinical policies and consequent administrative action in support, as instanced by the improved provision for in-patient treatment of toxaemia and the organization of flying squads. The fact that in ranking with other comparable countries in mortality statistics we stand higher in this respect than in almost any other, apart from anaesthesiology, seems more likely to be attributable to this country-wide effort than to anything else.

The inquiry method is peculiar to the circumstances of obstetric practice and is not likely to be applicable nationally to other fields. It would not be possible to handle the problems of reducing neonatal or post-neonatal deaths in the same way at the national level, because of the numbers involved. But the review at district level which has been stimulated in some places and which covers the whole field of obstetric work and not merely mortality could be applied to paediatrics and in other clinical fields. Local Maternity Liaison Committees grew out of the Enquiry; other such developments are possible in many fields. It is time we stopped preening ourselves on the Enquiry and started to plan for them.

The Enquiry benefited greatly from continuity in the individuals involved. The two young obstetricians who had undertaken a special survey for the Departmental Committee twenty years earlier, Mr (later Sir) Arnold Walker and Mr G. F. Gibberd took part in the new Enquiry in 1952 as consultant adviser and regional assessor. Six of the regional assessors who took part in the first three-year report were still involved in the sixth. The two original consultant advisers were joint authors of the first four reports. Altogether the effort put into this study by leading obstetricians and the steady support of their Royal College provided its real foundations.

References

1. *Reports on Public Health and Medical Subjects*, nos 97 (1957), 103 (1960), 108 (1963), 115 (1966), and 119 (1969) (London: HMSO).
2. *Reports on Health and Social Subjects*, nos I (1972) and II (1976) (London: HMSO).

2

The care of patients with malignant hypertension in London in 1974-5

COLIN DOLLERY
BSc, MB, ChB, FRCP
Professor of Clinical Pharmacology

C. J. BULPITT
MSc, MD, BS, MRCP
Honorary Lecturer in Clinical Pharmacology

H. J. DARGIE
MB, ChB, MRCP
Senior Registrar,
Department of Clinical Pharmacology

MRS E. LEIST

Royal Postgraduate Medical School
Hammersmith

The care of patients with malignant hypertension in London in 1974-5

Efforts to improve health services have been concentrated upon the provision of an adequate range of facilities accessible to the people who need them. A definition of adequate facilities in terms of personnel and equipment is no easy matter but even if they can be agreed and provided there is no guarantee that the manner in which they are used will be satisfactory. Measurement of the quality of care is difficult and relatively few attempts have been made to do it. There are two main reasons. The first is the difficulty of agreeing what constitutes a good quality of care and the second is to find means of collecting the information and causing some action to be taken when deficiencies are found. There are several possible indices that can be used to measure the quality of care. The firmest is the measurement of outcome. If there were a significantly greater morbidity and mortality after treatment of the same condition in similar patients in two centres there would be a presumption that the quality of care was higher in the centre with the lower morbidity and mortality. The difficulty with this approach is that it will be rare indeed that a single GP or hospital consultant looks after a sufficient number of patients with a single condition for a significant difference to be found. Two possible alternatives are patient satisfaction and studies of the process of care. Patient satisfaction is very important because the great majority of patients need comfort and reassurance rather than active treatment. Surveys of patient satisfaction suggest that most patients are fairly well satisfied with the care they receive. However in many instances the patient may be a poor judge of the quality of care as opposed to kindness and consideration with which they have been treated. For example the waiting time at a clinic might be short which would be regarded favourably by patients but inquiry might show that the short wait was because patients were rarely examined or did not have a proper history taken of their illness. Thus there is an argument for research into the process of medical care in some common conditions where there is evidence that treatment may have an effect upon outcome. The present study was undertaken to look at the process of medical care in patients with malignant hypertension who died and the choice of this condition and this method of case-finding needs explanation.

Malignant hypertension is an uncommon but serious variety of high blood pressure. It arises mainly in middle-aged people usually when the pressure has risen to a high level relatively quickly. It is characterized by progressive damage to small arterioles leading to leakage of plasma and blood into their wall with eventual obliteration of the lumen. In the retina this leads to formation of cotton-wool spots and papilloedema, in the brain to focal ischaemia and oedema and in the kidney to loss of functioning nephrons. The most common cause of death is kidney failure. Prior to 1950, when the first effective antihypertensive therapy was introduced, 90 per cent of patients with this condition died within one year of diagnosis (1). Since drug therapy has been available the life expectancy has increased steadily so that one-third to one-half of the patients can expect to survive for five years (2, 3). This research project has the objective of evaluating the process of care in patients with malignant hypertension who died and had the condition mentioned on their death certificate.

Methods

The investigation was made possible by the co-operation of the Office of Population Censuses and Surveys (OPCS) who agreed to provide a copy of the death certificate of anyone dying in Greater London whose death certificate mentioned malignant hypertension. Usually the certificate arrived within three weeks of death. The doctor who signed it, usually a junior hospital doctor, was contacted by telephone to ask the name of the consultant in charge. The consultant received a detailed letter explaining the aims of the project and promising complete confidentiality. The letter requested the loan of the case-notes. In no case was this refused although in several instances hospital rules forbade notes leaving the hospital so that they were consulted on the premises. The name of the GP was obtained from the case papers or directly if he had signed the death certificate. A similar letter was sent and again there was a very good response although sometimes with greater delays (Table 1). To date fifty-two death certificates have been forwarded by the staff of the OPCS.

TABLE I. *Death certificates received to 23 June 1975*

Number of death certificates received	52	
Number of hospital records received	47	
Number of hospital records not received including five recent cases	5	52
Number of GP records received	43	
Number of GP records not received including six recent cases	8	
One visit to GP	1	52

Once the notes are obtained a number of particulars are abstracted into special forms. They are as follows:

1. Administrative particulars of the patient's age, sex and race, address and date of death.

2. The date and the criteria used to diagnose malignant hypertension.

3. All blood pressure readings with their dates, and body position.

4. All blood urea readings with their dates.

5. All visits to hospital, including admissions, and general practice visits with their dates.

6. The drugs used with their doses.

7. A few other particulars such as values of blood lipids, smoking history, etc., were transcribed on to forms.

8. A general review of the patient's progress by reading all of the relevant documents, especially the GP notes in sequence with the hospital ones.

9. Some important documents such as discharge summaries were photocopied.

Analysis

The analyses so far conducted are incomplete but a number of points have been looked at in detail in forty of the case-records.

BLOOD PRESSURE CONTROL

The blood pressure readings were averaged in three-month periods. The average for a year was calculated from the average of the three-month blocks recorded in that year and the over-all average from the average of the yearly averages from the data of diagnosis of hypertension.

This method neglects the effect of body position and may be unfair to those who used drugs such as guanethidine, bethanidine, and debrisoquine that lower the blood pressure to a markedly greater extent in the standing position than in other positions. However the body position of blood pressure readings was frequently not specifically identified and it appeared more accurate and possibly more meaningful to average all readings.

RISE IN BLOOD UREA

Two factors seemed important, the rate of rise and the period when the blood urea first rose from normal to above 60 mg per 100 ml. The latter is of crucial importance as this period often coincided with loss of control of blood pressure and this was a major determinant of death from renal failure at a later time.

VISITS

The over-all frequency of visits has been calculated but the most interesting finding was the infrequency of blood pressure readings per visit in general practice. A separate calculation was made of the total number of visits to a GP and the number of those visits on which the blood pressure was recorded. It was relatively uncommon for blood pressure not to be recorded on a hospital visit after the diagnosis of malignant hypertension has been made.

SOCIAL AND PSYCHOLOGICAL FACTORS

Many factors may affect compliance with long-term drug therapy and these have been evaluated by counting the number of patients who were recorded as living alone, suffering from mental illness, excessive intake of alcohol, mental retardation, etc. As the death certificates forwarded included a surprising number of recent immigrants to the UK a separate count was made of these. In all these instances the counts may be incomplete as they could only be abstracted if a positive record of a feature was made.

DRUGS

The method of analysing the drug prescription data is still under discussion. The analysis is planned to take into account the dose and number of drugs used in relation to the efficacy of blood pressure control.

AVOIDABLE FACTORS

The final review of the file concentrated on the question of avoidable factors. Some deaths clearly could not have been avoided by any reasonable standard of care. Examples of unavoidable deaths include the following.

1. Presentation with a fatal cerebral haemorrhage in a patient who is not known to be hypertensive or who has not consulted a doctor for a long period.

2. Death from myocardial infarction in a patient with good blood pressure control.

3. Death from an unrelated disease.

4. Eventual death from renal failure after a lengthy period of good pressure control in someone who presented with renal failure.

Avoidable factors include the following.

1. Death following poor pressure control in a patient with near normal renal function at presentation.

2. Failure to take blood pressure for long periods during follow-up of a patient with malignant hypertension.

Results

Forty of the fifty-two patients' records have been analysed in some detail thus far and the present report deals with these patients. They all died in the Greater London area in 1974 or 1975.

DIAGNOSIS

The clinical diagnosis of malignant hypertension is normally based upon the presence of papilloedema on the retinal examination, which is due to the hypertension. The pathological diagnosis of malignant hypertension rests upon the presence of fibrinoid necrosis in arterioles or onion-skin proliferation of the intima. Scrutiny of the records of

the forty patients showed that many did not strictly fulfil these diagnostic criteria. In some instances there were no notes of retinal
examination and one patient was blind so that this examination was
unhelpful. In only nineteen was there unequivocal evidence of papilloedema that had no other explanation. A particular problem were
patients who presented with cerebral haemorrhage and papilloedema
with no earlier record of retinal examination. The disc oedema might
have been due to the acute rise in intracranial tension following the
bleed into the skull. In the end it was decided to accept all the
patients for analysis as examples of very severe or malignant hypertension, as many had renal failure although there was no record of
papilloedema.

CAUSE OF DEATH

The principal causes of death in the forty individual patients were as
follows: renal failure, 17; cerebrovascular accident, 14; heart failure,
3; myocardial infarction, 3; sudden death at home, 2; carcinoma of
bronchus, 1.

Thus all save one died a cardiovascular death. The high proportion
of deaths due to renal failure or cerebrovascular disease, almost entirely cerebral haemorrhage, is a measure of the severity of the hypertension and poor control of blood pressure. Recent reports suggest
that many well-controlled hypertensives still die a cardiovascular
death, but mainly from myocardial infarction (3).

AGE AT DEATH AND SEX

The mean age at death was 53·9 years with a range from 27 to 77
years. There were ten women and thirty men.

BLOOD PRESSURE CONTROL

A brief review of all the case records in this group of forty patients
suggested that twenty had poor control of blood pressure with most
diastolic readings above 125 mmHg. In thirteen there were insufficient readings to draw a conclusion. All save one of the remainder had diastolic readings that lay mainly between 110 and 125
mmHg diastolic.

Full analysis of blood pressure control has been made in eight
patients who were followed up for at least one year. The results in
them are shown in Table 2.

TABLE 2

Number	Average of yearly means (mmHg)	Period of follow-up (years)	Number	Average of yearly means (mmHg)	Period of follow-up (years)
009	219/136	2	036	213/148	1
010	177/117	3	037	226/131	1
015	223/132	5	041	195/120	6
030	199/117	6	044	197/140	1

In no case can the blood pressure control be regarded as good and in only two was it anything other than poor. Many patients had poor control of blood pressure for long periods and in some instances few steps seem to have been taken to try and restore the situation.

The mean yearly pressures in one patient were 209/125, 209/130, and 213/127 mmHg in the first three years of treatment. During this period a serious deterioration occurred in an initially normal blood urea. During most of this time drug treatment consisted of a diuretic and almost the lowest commonly prescribed dose of an adrenergic neurone blocking drug. In another patient the quarterly mean pressure during the first three years of treatment never fell below 200/117 mmHg. This state of affairs was not improved by referral to a hospital. The next quarterly mean was 250/140 mmHg and the patient was then admitted to hospital dying of a cerebral haemorrhage.

VISITS TO GENERAL PRACTITIONERS

A substantial part of the care given to these patients with malignant hypertension was provided by their GPs. Even when the patients were attending a hospital clinic they usually saw their GP more often than they attended hospital. The frequency of follow-up appeared to be satisfactory but it was noticeable how few blood pressure readings were recorded. Data from nineteen GP notes has been analysed covering 869 patient visits. Blood pressure readings were recorded on only 215 (24·7 per cent) of these. This figure has been arrived at after including remarks such as 'blood pressure ISQ' and 'control inadequate' as evidence that the pressure was taken although not recorded. It is quite possible that more readings were taken than were written down and there was a considerable variation between GPs. The range of frequency of recorded pressures per visit was from zero to 75 per cent in visits after the diagnosis of severe or malignant hypertension had been made. The infrequency of recordings of pressure may have been because the GP knew the patient was attending a hospital and saw his role mainly as a provider of prescriptions. However in instances when the patient refused hospital referral or was referred back to his GP the average result was similar.

One patient who was being looked after by his GP had a blood pressure recorded of 210/140 mmHg six months after treatment began. Over the next twenty-two months the patient attended eighteen times for repeat prescriptions but no reading of blood pressure was recorded. Altogether this patient attended ninety-three times and had blood pressures recorded eleven times. The average of these readings was 229/133 mmHg.

SOCIAL AND PSYCHOLOGICAL FACTORS

A major determinant of outcome in any disease which requires prolonged treatment is the patient's willingness to adhere to it despite side-effects and other inconveniences. It was striking how high a proportion of these patients had social or psychological situations which may have modified their willingness to comply with therapeutic advice.

Twelve of the patients had been born outside the UK and of these eight were black. It has been suggested that black people are prone to suffer a particularly severe form of malignant hypertension and it is a common experience that immigrants are less willing to tolerate drug side-effects although there is no firm data on the latter point.

Among the remainder there were five with severe mental illness that antedated hypertension, two who were mentally retarded, and one who was blind. Two were noted to drink heavily and two lived alone.

The effect of non-compliance upon outcome was obvious in several instances. One patient who lived alone was admitted to hospital eighteen months prior to death and was established upon an effective regime. For the next ten months he failed to attend either his GP or the hospital out-patients' department. Over this time his blood urea rose from 40 to over 100 mg per 100 ml and he died in renal failure four months later.

AVOIDABLE FACTORS

An avoidable unfavourable outcome might occur as a result of suboptimal management in the medical, social, or administrative sphere.

This study has concentrated upon medical factors but the high proportion of patients in whom social factors appear to have been important suggests the need for action in this area as well.

Failure to achieve an adequate control of the blood pressure was the most important single failing. We cannot say whether it would have been possible to control the pressure of these patients by means of larger doses of drugs or better chosen regimes but we suspect that in some instances it would have been. It was puzzling to find prescriptions for moderate doses of drugs being renewed without an increase in patients with diastolic pressures persistently above 130 mmHg. Several patients were sent to specialist clinics late in their illness, usually after they had become uraemic. It seems likely that a specialist clinic would have done better in some of these severely hypertensive patients, if they had been involved at an earlier stage. The lack of blood pressure readings recorded in the GP notes appears also to have been an avoidable factor contributing to an unfavourable outcome, in some cases.

There were a few instances where easily recognizable errors of judgement by the doctor had a directly unfavourable effect upon outcome. One patient was treated with great energy upon presentation to hospital and his death was precipitated by pulmonary oedema following intravenous fluid overload when he had been rendered oliguric as a result of rapid pressure reduction. Another patient with good pressure control on a multi-regime was admitted to hospital for another reason and during bed rest it was possible to withdraw almost all the antihypertensive therapy. The drugs were not restarted upon discharge and a period of six months of very high blood pressure followed during which renal function rapidly deteriorated.

Failure of patients to take medicines or to keep appointments was a much more common problem than these medical misjudgements. Some case-records contained letters making it clear that determined efforts had been made to trace and restart treatment in these defaulters but they were a minority. An efficient registration follow-up and recall system for patients with very severe hypertension would almost certainly save some lives. It was also disturbing to note the lack of continuity in hospital care. Many of the longer-term survivors had been admitted to more than one hospital during their treatment with a lack of continuity in management. It was chastening to realize that we, with all of the hospital notes and GP records before us, had a far more complete appreciation of the patient's problem than it is likely any one team of doctors had during the patient's life.

Discussion

The project is unfinished and the analysis of the existing patients has not been completed. It must also be remembered that a study based upon individuals who died is biased towards those who suffered disasters and may not be typical of the generality of patients with malignant hypertension. However some cautious conclusions are possible.

The first is that a project of this kind which depends upon the willingness of GPs and hospital consultants to make available, in confidence, their case-notes is feasible. The only comparable investigation in the UK, the Confidential Enquiry into Maternal Mortality, has a less difficult task in that it looks at events spread over a much shorter span of time. It is a great credit to the openness and desire for improvement in services of the doctors who co-operated in this study that they gave their help so willingly.

The results to date suggest the need for some improvements in care of patients with malignant hypertension on the medical, social, and administrative fronts.

The main medical problem is the need to achieve better control of blood pressure. Very bad control of blood pressure is likely to lead to disaster, and this needs to be more widely appreciated. It will involve more determined use of existing drugs and more frequent recordings of blood pressure as opposed to visits purely to renew prescriptions.

The problem of patient compliance with treatment is a difficult one. In a few patients with mental retardation or severe mental illness it is doubtful whether application of a very complex multi-drug treatment schedule is practical. In other patients better co-ordination of social and medical action might improve clinical attendance and compliance.

The administrative failings can only be appreciated if one has read the whole of the records of a patient who has been under the care of several hospitals and his GP. On a month-to-month basis no one may have an over-all view of what is happening to the patient. The records are orientated to institutions not to individuals. A document that travelled with the patient that specified his blood pressure readings, his treatment, and a few major risk factors such as the blood urea might help. In the case of these very severe hypertensive patients there appears to be a need for a register of patients to be maintained in the area concerned so that they do not become lost to follow-up as a result of forgetfulness either on their part or their doctors.

This study is intended to be a prototype to illustrate the opportunities for studying medical care by clinicians using relatively simple methods. Other conditions that might be studied in a similar way include deaths following general anaesthesia or blood transfusion, deaths following gastro-intestinal haemorrhage, etc. Any condition in which there are reasonable grounds for feeling that medical or surgical management has a favourable effect upon outcome would be suitable for this method of study. Although the present investigation was undertaken from a single centre, the ideal arrangement might be for a group of specialists and general practitioners within a defined geographical area to share the responsibility and the work.

Medical care will never be perfect, but studies to determine the reasons that lie behind the successes and failures probably offer the best chance of raising the general standard closer to that which has been achieved under optimal conditions. Establishment of professional study groups working in a similar manner to that described in the present investigation could make a substantial contribution to that end.

ACKNOWLEDGEMENTS

This work was supported by the Nuffield Provincial Hospitals Trust. Grateful thanks are due to the staff of the Office of Population Censuses and Surveys and to all the doctors in both hospital practice and general practice who helped with the provision of records and information.

References

1. KEITH, N. M., WAGENER, H. P., and BARKER, N. W. (1939). *Am. J. Med. Sci.* **197**, 332–43.
2. SMIRK, F. H. (1957). *High Arterial Pressure* (Oxford: Blackwell Scientific Publications).
3. BRECKENRIDGE, A. M., DOLLERY, C. T., and PARRY, E. H. O. (1970). *Q. Jl Med.* **39**, 411–29.

3

Observations on the quality
of surgical care

IAN McCOLL

MS, FRCS, FACS

Professor of Surgery
Guy's Hospital

Observations on the quality of surgical care

This chapter opens with a brief review of some important attitudes which have a bearing on the assessment of quality of care in surgery, and then deals with what has already been done at one teaching hospital in attempting to create an environment where clinical appraisal becomes accepted. Finally, it outlines for the future a possible system of clinical appraisal which is based on explicit criteria, is conducted cheaply and confidentially, and supplies the clinician with acceptable and compelling information which fires his enthusiasm to improve his work.

The dearth of means of assessing the quality of surgical care in this country is no accident. It derives from a long tradition of clinicians avoiding acrimony and open criticism, morbid introspections of their work and defensive surgery, all of which are potentially harmful to the patient.

Before the Second World War, the Teaching Hospital was run by a handful of consultants who were close friends. They held their committee meetings after dinner at the home of the senior clinician, who sat at the top of a well-defined hierarchy. Their close friendship and loyalty precluded open criticism, but did not prevent them from having a quiet and friendly word in the ear of an erring member of the group. This close-knit friendship and loyalty were clearly of great importance in the smooth running of the hospital and in maintaining a high standard of clinical care. When a surgeon removed a stone from the common bile duct left behind by another surgeon at St Elsewhere's Hospital, he might remark that this was not an occasion for pride as the other surgeon was probably removing stones which he himself had left behind in another patient. This tolerance and lack of open criticism were complemented by insight and humility. All this combined with a close working relationship among the surgeons to give, under ideal circumstances, an atmosphere conducive to providing the best care possible at a time when the field of surgery was advancing slowly and keeping up to date was not a serious problem.

Morbid brooding over the results of his surgery was likely to curtail the career of the surgeon in the pre-antibiotic days when anaesthesia was poor and rapid operating essential. Surgery was not for sensitive souls who looked too closely at their mortality figures. The enthusiastic extroverted surgeon knew that time takes the pain out of memory and there was little purpose in putting it back. There was little interest in recording over-all mortality figures. Nightingale (1) proposed that a register should be kept for surgical operations including the outcome and Groves (2) made a similar plea for registration of operation results. He conducted a survey of fifty hospitals in the United Kingdom compiling operative mortality figures. As Brook (3) has emphasized, the renewed interest in quality assessment in the 1940s was no longer concerned with the end results of care but rather examined what the doctor did for his patient, a change from outcome studies to process studies. Unfortunately, the mortality and morbidity figures which are published tend to be only the best. The unpublished series are often much more instructive.

The surgeon should 'fear for his patients, fear for his shortcomings, fear for his own mistakes but never fear for himself or his professional reputation' (Samuel I. Mixtter). This old tradition survives so long as hostile and unbridled criticism remains absent. If an abrasive kind of medical audit were introduced the surgeon would, naturally, fear for himself and his reputation and consciously or unconsciously might tend to operate only on low-risk patients and deny those who are at high risk who might be well cured by surgery. For instance, a 60-year-old 100-kg man with a carcinoma of the rectum and two previous coronary thromboses might have his abdomen explored and pronounced inoperable for tenuous reasons which would not be open to further examination. The real reason for not embarking on resection might well be the reluctance of the surgeon to risk his own reputation.

This tradition of avoiding acrimony, open criticism, and defensive surgery should not lightly be thrown overboard in favour of a system of audit which is unproven in the USA and may be so unsuitable in the UK that it actually lowers the standards of patient care.

Current practice at one teaching hospital

We believe that medical audit or clinical appraisal should be a teacher rather than a policeman; that it should be confidential, educative and interesting, non-abrasive, cheap, and not disruptive. With these principles, we have tried to create an environment in which clinical appraisal is accepted and welcomed by the clinician and in an integral part of the process of continuing education. We have tried to tackle this with five different approaches:

1. Death and complication meetings.
2. Problem-orientated medical records.
3. Special surveys.
4. Patient questionnaire.
5. Review of resources.

DEATH AND COMPLICATIONS MEETING

These meetings have been established for many years in the USA but are rare in the UK. For the past five years, it has been our practice to conduct death and complication meetings at 8 am every Friday of the year except public holidays. The five surgical firms in turn present all the deaths and complications of the previous five weeks. This makes for a more cohesive meeting having one firm responsible for a single meeting rather than all five firms contributing every week.

The meetings are friendly and full of interest. The identity of the surgeons responsible for the cases under discussion is not usually known. In this atmosphere, the participants are usually frank and the meeting has an air of a general confession. All semblance of a witch-hunt is avoided because it is thought that this would breed the type of doctor who is expert at wriggling out of embarrassing situations rather than learning from them, but would tend to destroy the more sensitive person who had learned the lesson from his mistakes weeks before the case was discussed at the death and complications meeting.

The success of this venture is largely due to the enthusiasm of the registrars who enjoy more security and freedom in this particular training scheme, which accepts the principles of medical audit as a natural and educative part of their professional life.

These meetings promote the early detection of problems which might otherwise remain hidden. For example, each firm might have a complication which on its own would be unremarkable, but if a death and complication meeting revealed that all the firms had had the same experience at the same time, the problem would thereby be highlighted earlier.

Administrative muddles are frequently brought to light as the cause of clinical problems and highlighted. An attempt can be made to rectify them at an earlier stage.

This is a painless, interesting, and cheap method of audit and its main emphasis is educational. It offers an *in situ* refresher course which is immediately relevant to all the participants and costs virtually nothing; which is more than can be said of many of the expensive refresher courses attended which are as far removed from their site of work geographically as in content. The accelerating advance of medical science and the technical and organizational complexity of modern medicine are presenting the clinician with an increasing problem. It is difficult for him to keep up to date. The death and complications meetings help to that end and introduce clinical appraisal in a cheap, unobtrusive, and profitable way. In 1974, there were only two hospitals in the UK conducting such meetings. Why are other hospitals so shy?

PROBLEM-ORIENTATED MEDICAL RECORDS

Two years ago, problem-orientated medical records were introduced into the surgical unit. No attempt was made to persuade the rest of the hospital community of their advantage, but within three or four months the system was working well enough to attract its use in other departments. To our surprise, the whole hospital decided through its democratic machinery to adopt the system. Some of the most ardent supporters were the oldest clinicians. The system has stimulated a great deal of interest and has improved the quality of medical records. It remains to be seen whether it has improved the quality of patient care and a study is currently in progress to evaluate this point. In another pilot study, the house surgeons and physicians are being scored for the quality of their notes. Although this information is confidential, the junior staff compare their scores and this element of competition is also contributing to the improved performance. As Laurence Weed originally intended, we are currently trying to audit the logic of the students and our own records, and are finding this a rewarding way of teaching.

An improvement in the medical records system is yet another way in which a favourable atmosphere can be created which encourages the clinician to appraise his own work, and in fact is a necessity before any real evaluation can take place.

SURVEY OF CLINICAL PROBLEMS

The death and complications meetings often bring to light a complication or clinical problem which is increasing. This can be dealt with by instituting a controlled clinical trial or if that is unacceptable, a simple prospective survey. Two years ago, the incidence of burst abdomens seemed to be increasing but the suggestion of a controlled clinical trial was not feasible because no agreement could be reached on the protocol. The problem was resolved by undertaking a survey. Each surgeon performing a laparotomy over a period of one year was asked to complete a questionnaire at the end of the operation. Data such as name of procedure, duration of operation, quantity of blood transfused, type of incision, etc., was recorded. Patient factors such as nutritional state, presence of malignant disease, jaundice, or steroid therapy were noted since previous studies have shown these factors to correlate with a high incidence of wound dehiscence. There followed a detailed description of how the wound was closed. Whether or not the wound dehisced was also recorded before the patient left hospital. No attempt was made to influence the manner in which the surgeon closed his incisions. In order to have some comparison, the rate of laparotomy wound dehiscence on the gynaecological firms was tabulated from the operating theatre casebooks and used as a control, since they were not included in the questionnaire survey. During the period of study, 460 laparotomies were done. During the six months before the survey was undertaken, the percentage of wounds which dehisced was 6 per cent. Of the first six months of the survey it was 7 per cent but during the second six months of the survey the rate had fallen to 0·6 per cent. During this eighteen-month period, the dehiscence rate of the gynaecological firms remained constant at 0·7 per cent. There was no obvious difference in the type of operation, duration, or transfusion requirements, or technique used in sewing up abdomens between the dehiscence group and the other patients. As these figures were not published and no action whatever was taken, it is reasonable to conclude that merely looking at the problem like abdominal wound dehiscence is likely to reduce the problem considerably. This is another example of a cheap, effective, and painless type of audit.

PATIENT QUESTIONNAIRE

King Edward's Hospital Fund (4) produced a useful questionnaire which was sent to 2,171 patients discharged from ten hospitals. Of the 62 per cent returned, most were favourably disposed to the hospitals apart from the usual dissatisfaction with the toilet facilities. Of 5,000 distributed in the Radcliffe Infirmary, Oxford (4), 85 per cent were returned and told much the same story. This has also been our experience during the past year. In addition, there have been frequent complaints about too much food being supplied. We are experimenting with different methods of conducting these surveys in different wards for limited periods of time. The distribution and collection is carried out by ward receptionists in order to encourage the patients to be frank in their comments. This kind of 'market research' (5) is not only an important public relations exercise, but gives early warning about defects in the service and increases the chance of earlier remedy.

REVIEW OF RESOURCES

There is an ever-increasing problem of acute surgical and medical beds being occupied inappropriately by chronically sick and geriatric patients who cannot be placed in more suitable accommodation without an inordinate delay. At one stage, 70 per cent of the orthopaedic patients had completed their surgical treatment and were waiting to be transferred to more appropriate accommodation. In order to try and improve the situation, a committee was set up to review all patients who had been in hospital for more than two months. This is not a critical or punitive exercise but simply designed to help the clinician and the patient and it has made a modest start. As it gains in experience and confidence it could extend the terms of reference to patients who have been in hospital for shorter periods. This procedure is bringing to light many constraints which exist in the system which have been an irritation to the clinicians but have never been systematically tackled before, and has underlined the importance of early social evaluation of elderly and orthopaedic patients.

All the processes mentioned so far are simple, cheap, and effective ways of helping the surgeon to appraise his own work. They could be included among the requirements for accreditation of surgical training programmes, but some of the Royal Colleges are still reluctant to accept this idea.

POSSIBLE FUTURE DEVELOPMENTS

Clinicians now realize the need to look more closely at what they are actually doing to their patients and the way they set about it. Hospital Activity Analysis may be of some value to hospital administrators but it is virtually unused by clinicians because:

1. Relevant clinical information is missing.

2. No attempt is made to summarize the voluminous computer output in order to enable the individual clinician to relate his performance to that of his colleagues.

In practice HAA ignores the first principle of an information system which is to communicate salient facts to the people who are in a position to act on them. Length of stay, numbers and kinds of operations, length of time on waiting-list, and date of first operation depend on clinical decisions. Improvement in the use of these and other hospital resources will only occur where clinicians see the need for change. Similarly, the decision to act in such a way as to improve the management of patients rests on the clinical recognition that improvement is required. One of the primary functions of a medical information system could or should be to supply the kinds of data which will allow clinicians to make their own evaluations of the quality of care that they are giving.

Basically there are two methods for developing this information base:

1. Numerous precise measurements can be made in all aspects of process and outcome. This requires the collection of data by teams of clinicians who re-examine patients, validate laboratory results, repeat clinical judgements, and follow-up patients after discharge. The expense of this limits the number of cases studied. The ironic consequence of this method is usually that there are too few cases to substantiate the findings, and the extent to which these results can be generally applied is severely limited.

2. The second method employs the two components described by Donabedian: 'one that sifts large numbers of cases and identifies those most likely to contain defects of management, and a second that subjects questionable cases to detailed and definitive profes-

sional evaluation'. The second component is self-explanatory. The sifting component depends upon collecting information from pre-existing documents such as medical records and regrouping them to create new data on large numbers of people. This method relies on the principles of statistics. Findings are based on the probabilities that: data are entered correctly in the original source document; that false negative and false positive and laboratory results are randomly distributed; that rogue or intuitive behaviour (the 'art' side of medicine) is similarly random among clinicians; that the more patients one studies, the closer one comes to identifying the behaviour pattern of the practitioner or disease. Errors in specific individual cases are offset by the ability to isolate gross deviance from mean behaviour.

Performance Evaluation Procedure (PEP) is an example of this method which is being developed by the Joint Commission on the Accreditation of Hospitals in the United States. Simple criteria are specified for medical and surgical diagnosis seen most frequently in hospital. For each diagnosis one set of criteria is formulated which is used to screen for cases appropriately and inappropriately admitted to in-patient care. Another set is applied to assess minimum standards of the outcome of that case. For gallstones as an example, the criterion for justifying the hospitalization is: a positive histology report of acute or chronic inflammation; gangrene or calculi. Criteria for assessing the outcome or patient status at discharge are: (*a*) the patient was afebrile; (*b*) was tolerating a soft or normal diet; and (*c*) wound healing with no drainage.

These pieces of information are taken from case-notes by trained medical record personnel and returned to a clinical committee for assessment. The committee then reviews in detail the cases where the criteria were not met, discusses them with the consultants concerned, and monitors his cases for change.

We do not believe that this system can be applied directly to hospital medicine in Britain because:

1. The organizational structure for taking sanctions against consultants who do not conform does not exist as it does in the United States.

2. The review of individual cases is physician-intensive and probably a wasteful and expensive use of this scarce manpower resource.

3. Criteria for disease management may be different in the two

countries. The technique of screening cases for a few elements associated with good management, however, merits closer examination.

The Scottish Consultant Activity Review may be said to sift large numbers of cases but leaves the consultant to identify areas in which further clinical investigation might prove rewarding. The information is the same as that in the HAA, for example, age, sex, marital status of patient, principle and secondary diagnosis, length of stay, days before first operation, days on waiting-list, number and kinds of operations. Unlike HAA, however, statistics on each consultant's cases and the averages of all other consultants with similar cases are returned to him to allow him to compare the length of stay, time on the waiting-list, etc., for his patients with the combined experience of his colleagues' patients.

Summarizing these data and returning them with comparative statistics clearly makes more appropriate use of the information than the HAA system. It should be noted, however, that these are primarily variables on the use of hospital resources, for example, bed use, use of the operating room. While they may affect clinical management indirectly, utilization of structural resources is not the primary concern of clinicians. Change will not occur until a more direct relationship is established between the use of these resources and the quality of clinical performance and considerable work remains to be done in devising incentives to help bring this about.

MEASURING THE QUALITY OF CLINICAL PERFORMANCE

We are studying the changes in the quality of care following the introduction of problem-orientated medical records at a teaching hospital. To accomplish this we are quantitating differences in the use of resources and clinical management between 1972 and 1975 at that hospital and at two control hospitals where POMR are not used, using a multiple regression statistic especially tailored for this research. Approximately 4,600 patients with three surgical and four medical diagnoses are being studied. Nothing can be known as yet about the main study hypothesis, since we are only at the mid-point in the data collection.

Discussion

We contend that feeding back this information to surgical staff could prompt relatively simple remedial action. These findings might be discussed by consultants in an attempt to devise agreed standards, thus bringing all consultants up to the standard of their more skilful colleagues and fulfilling an important educational function for junior staff.

As mentioned earlier the noticeable response of house officers to the feedback about their use of POMR is encouraging evidence of the efficacy of this technique as a stimulus to change. Feedback in this project is of two kinds: the weekly return to each house officer of a structured questionnaire evaluating his use of POMR with a case selected at random and monthly return of statistics showing his performance in relation to house officers on the other medical or surgical firms.

In both medical and surgical groups there is a consistently significant difference among house officers' monthly scores in the use of POMR which in turn correspond with academic sign-up scores in medical school, for example, the house officers with the best academic records score highest in their use of the POMR format. Although the research team preserves the identity of the scorers in strict confidence, the house officers invariably compare POMR scores and recognize the relationship between these scores and academic standing. Feedback of a comparative sort makes use of the tendency of the excellent to remain so and the tendency of the less excellent to strive to match the standards of the former. It is our belief that the combination of professional pride and the forces of natural competition in a highly selected group can be enlisted to improve the standards of medical care.

One of the most important results of our experience with the POMR projects has been to demonstrate that key information on clinical performance can be abstracted accurately and efficiently by non-medical personnel. A continuing random review of the complex material taken from the notes by the staff shows an error rate of less than 0·5 per cent and an accuracy superior to that of the POMR registrar and a consulting surgeon. The fact that this staff was drawn from the medical records department of Guy's suggests that, with training and precise specification of data requirements, this type of manpower is the logical resource for collecting the data in a medical information system.

Our present aims are:

1. To identify data which could be routinely collected to provide the basis for continuing evaluation of medical care in hospitals.

2. To develop a system of feedback of this information which would be educational, non-threatening, and useful.

3. Our efforts will concentrate on defining the kinds of data that can be included in a medical information system at reasonable cost, how central tendencies may be clearly summarized and demonstrated, and through what mechanisms these results should be returned to clinicians. A formal demonstration of the techniques will be mounted to test their effectiveness in improving the quality of clinical care.

References

1. NIGHTINGALE, F. (1863). *Proposal for Improved Statistics of Surgical Operations* (London: Savill and Edwards).
2. GROVES, E. W. (1908). 'A plea for a uniform registration of operation results', *Br. J. Med.* **2**, 1008–9
3. BROOK, R. H. (1974). 'Quality of Care Assessment Policy and Relevant Issues'. From the Carnegie Commonwealth Clinical Scholar Program of Johns Hopkins University.
4. RAPHAEL, W. (1969). *Patients and their hospitals* (London: King Edward's Hospital Fund).
5. DOLL, R. (1974). *To Measure NHS Progress.* Fabian Occasional Paper 8.

4

Contemporary professional practice

Quality in general practice

DONALD IRVINE

MD, FRCGP
Family Doctor
Ashington

Contemporary professional practice

Quality in general practice

It is difficult to imagine a more sensitive moment to take stock of the professional practice of family doctors in Britain. Today there are deep divisions amongst GPs of all ages about the future direction and responsibilities of their branch of medicine. Yet unlike previous upheavals which have been defensive, essentially about finding the resources and carrying out the restructuring necessary for survival, the open debate which these divisions is now provoking is about standards of professional competence and patient care. This is a refreshing sign of vitality, an indication that at least one section of general practice is feeling sufficiently confident to embark on the searching internal reappraisal of clinical practice, postgraduate education, and standards of competence it considers necessary if the discipline is to cope effectively with the primary care needs of patients in the next decade.

I should declare the boundaries of my essay before going further. Following a note intended merely to place contemporary general practice in perspective, and so bring a sense of history to current events, I have concentrated on two overlapping areas which together are the focus of reappraisal and innovation in professional practice. The first is about education, at least those aspects which are making us think more carefully about the nature of our clinical practice, ways in which we can improve its quality now and about standards of professional competence on entry to general practice. I have given this section most attention because it is very important now and will be for the rest of this decade. Until we can guarantee to the public that we are at least offering it family doctors who have been well trained and have achieved demonstrable standards of competence on completion, further consideration of audit and of the application of other methods for improving primary care will remain for all practical purposes of academic interest, for enthusiasts only. The second area is about the next generation of problems which the advancing edge of general practice is now beginning to explore. Important amongst these is the need to elaborate on the work of general practice; to formulate criteria on which to base acceptable working standards wherever possible and to find means of applying these in everyday practice; and to develop and validate measures of outcome in primary health care. I have not extended my horizon to compare British general practice with systems of primary medical care in countries of similar economic status and social organization in Western Europe and North America, because in the UK the general political decision has been taken that general practice should predominate in this field for the foreseeable future. Nor have I entered the debate on the availability of such resources as time, adequate medical, nursing, and ancillary manpower, properly equipped buildings, and readily accessible laboratory and other treatment services. I can only acknowledge that these are important factors which can and do influence standards of professional care, but they are primarily questions of health services management.

General practice in perspective

In 1950 Joseph Collings, an Australian graduate at Harvard, reported on his 'reconnaissance' of general practice in Britain (1). His account makes compelling reading even today, and it is a timely reminder that major changes often span generations. He said that general practice has no generally accepted standards: 'what the doctor does, and how he does it, depends wholly on his own conscience'. In the summary of his *Lancet* paper he noted,

my observations have led me to write what is indeed a condemnation of general practice in its present form; but they have also led me to recognize the importance of general practice and the dangers of continuing to pretend that it is something which it is not. Instead of continuing a policy of compensating for its deficiencies, we should admit them honestly and try to correct them at their source.

The report spurred the medico-political organizations of general practice into a predictably defensive response, which achieved nothing. Fortunately, more thoughtful family doctors considered its implications dispassionately, and they concluded that general practice would indeed have to alter radically to meet patients' changing needs. They began to co-ordinate their efforts through the new College of General Practitioners which they founded. Their aim, and that of the new College, was to set standards of good general practice where none existed, to promote education and to encourage research, and to provide a fellowship of like-minded men and women. Their efforts are reflected in the early literature of general practice; here are the first attempts to describe morbidity, to show differences in the structure and organization of practices, and to indicate quite simply many of the ways they set about their clinical work. These enthusiasts also began to experiment with different methods of working; grouping together, attaching nurses to their practices, and introducing appointment systems are typical examples. Quite quickly these ideas began to interest other doctors some of whom adopted them. The most important were steadily moulded and shaped into a new policy developed in a partnership between government, the RCGP and the BMA which has become the framework for the modernization of general practice, an undertaking still substantially incomplete today. There were six elements to the policy: to encourage group practice; to rehouse GPs in properly equipped, purpose-built premises; to help individual practitioners develop a viable organization; to give family doctors access to the hospital-based diagnostic services they need for their work; to redistribute some clinical work by introducing nurses and other health professionals to form functionally integrated primary care teams; and to provide better postgraduate education. The 'Charter' (2) for general practice injected additional finance to help implement the policy throughout the country. Most elements, indeed all except rehousing, have been accomplished to the extent that the opportunities and facilities are now there for doctors who want them. However, since there has been no obligation on every doctor to use all or even some of the new facilities, general practice of increasing diversity has emerged. Indeed it is diversity which is *the* most striking characteristic of the general practice of our time. Thus, for example, although money is now readily available to provide the staff for an effective practice administration and organization some doctors have decided that these are unnecessary. The evidence on the use made of diagnostic radiology and pathology services has been examined (3) and shows substantial variations. And at a time when much better arrangements have been made for postgraduate training there is evidence (4) that considerable numbers of doctors are becoming principals with minimal supervised clinical experience following full registration.

The over-all effect of this idiosyncratic approach to the use of new resources has led to a patchiness in the pattern, and thus possibly the quality, of general practice which is becoming more obvious. The public has noticed. Complaints about poorly run appointment systems, principals who are invariably unavailable for emergency care out-of-hours and failures to visit, contrast with the satisfaction recorded about practitioners giving a capably managed personal and comprehensive service (5, 6, 7). On the question of clinical competence the lower level of public complaint is of little comfort because lay people find it difficult to comment on technical matters. However, hard evidence from the MRCGP examination (8, 9) prescribing patterns (10–12) and the content of medical records in general practice (13, 14) adds to the subjective observations of clinical colleagues in hospital that there are variations in the clinical practice of individual family doctors which are, to say the least, unquestionably wide.

It is important to follow what is happening. General practice is in a period of transition in which two concepts, which are quite different at their extremes, are existing side by side. For many doctors, young as well as old, their general practice is still diffuse in its aims and therefore its functions other than to serve as the first medical staging post for people who become patients in our Health Service. They still regard it as 'the sum of a number of specialties practised at a fairly superficial level' (15); thus they see no need for postgraduate training and very little for continuing education, and they tend to seek protection from the scrutiny and criticism of their peers by encouraging professional isolation. The more recent concept of general practice has evolved from the best of the old and has thus retained an emphasis on the primacy of people, but there the similarity ends. Though founded on 'whole person' medicine there is a growing recognition of the need to apply scientific method wherever possible to all dimensions of diagnosis and management, social and behavioural as well as physical. Indeed it is the very use of this approach which is moving general practice towards a stage where the general boundaries of a discipline can be discerned, as morbidity is more carefully categorized, the processes of the consultation in this setting are unravelled and a beginning is made to look at outcomes of diagnosis and management, so to set standards. It is hardly surprising that family doctors belonging to this school are guiding general practice towards the mainstream of medicine, because they recognize that professional isolation is the barrier to the fostering of higher professional standards and creative thinking.

This ambivalent situation will probably last for some time because evidently long-established attitudes change slowly, especially in those people who have understandable reasons for feeling threatened by the modern movement. Nevertheless, the incorporation of the new concepts and knowledge into the training of family doctors is moving us inexorably towards a turning point at which minimum standards of competence are bound to be set for new entrants. This step, the traditional regulator used by the specialties in Britain, could have far-reaching effects if experience in other fields is any guide. It is also a necessary preliminary to any attempt formally to review the clinical competence of doctors who are already established. The change will not be premature. The NHS is evolving on a pattern of very local health care units which can provide first contact, continuing and terminal care complemented by highly specialized services available to patients when necessary, in order to cope with the predicted pattern of the main health care problems which we will encounter in the remainder of this century. General practice, nominated by the community as the main provider of primary care, can thus hardly avoid its substantial responsibilities if it is to retain credibility in comparison with alternative systems.

Postgraduate education for general practice

As the new organizational structure took shape in the 1960s, the RCGP began to turn its attention to the next stage of development, namely, to provide relevant postgraduate training and continuing education. Perceptive doctors had become aware of two related problems: their basic medical education did not seem to have equipped them to recognize and treat properly many of the illnesses which patients brought to them; and the diet of postgraduate courses served by specialists did not always help in the diagnosis and management of undifferentiated conditions which often presented at an early stage in their natural history. The BMA made the first attempt at specific postgraduate training with the introduction of the trainee GP scheme. The aim was simple and the intention sound, to attach a young doctor to an experienced practitioner for a year so that he could learn how to practise well. The scheme fell into disrepute over the years for a number of reasons, the main one of which, in retrospect, seems to have been that the educational aims and objectives had not been worked out because the basic research into the content of general practice had not been done at that time. Thus the criteria on which GP trainers were chosen, questionable in educational terms and doubtful even as a basis for a vocational apprenticeship, were applied haphazardly when placed in the hands of local medical committees. No objective assessments were used; trainers and trainees had only to report to their local medical committees what they thought of each other. In the 1960s recruitment to the scheme, never high, fell away as increasing numbers of young doctors perceived no compelling educational or career advantage to offset the financial attraction of entering general practice as a principal as soon as possible after obtaining full registration.

The profession learnt from this lesson and another start was made by the then College of General Practitioners, which put forward new proposals to the Royal Commission on Medical Education (16). These proposals were accepted in the main (17) and in the past ten years preparations have been made to implement them. The College and the Councils for Postgraduate Medical Education suggested five years' vocational training following full registration but in the event three-year programmes comprising two years in selected hospital specialties and one year in a carefully chosen general practice were accepted as an interim measure, largely because of the extensive and difficult logistic problems involved in finding suitable posts for an annual intake of over a thousand doctors. It is still the College's intention to add two more years of supervised work in general practice in the future, though how this will be done has not been described. The second period would be the equivalent of higher training in other specialties.

A number of experimental schemes have blossomed in the past ten years, and the national programme is now well advanced. This year sufficient training places have become available to accommodate every future general practitioner. Discussions are now in hand between the BMA and the health departments to find ways of ensuring that, after 1980, principals in the NHS will first have completed a recognized programme of training.

Vocational training programmes for general practice now have the potential to differ significantly from the earlier trainee scheme in a number of important respects. The College has produced aims and an outline of content which seem to have gained general acceptance amongst those concerned with teaching although there is evidence (18) that they have not been adopted in every programme. The statement of aims has led to a clearer view of the kinds of experience to which the learner should be exposed, and to the introduction of new methods of learning. It has also focused on the need for GPs to learn about modern practice in higher education, since general practice has no history of involvement in medical education. These developments have led to another important difference, that is, the construction and application of methods of assessment and evaluation which will show whether a learner has acquired relevant knowledge and skills, and whether programmes are achieving their objectives.

The present position is that some trainees are completing vocational training programmes in organized schemes which are adopting the aims and methods to an admittedly varying extent. But others, we do not know the proportion but suspect it is substantial, are arranging their own rotations of posts, and may or may not attend supplementary courses of lectures, demonstrations, and discussions increasingly regarded as important by the College.

THE AIMS OF TRAINING

Several morbidity studies (19–25) have demonstrated the categories of disease the family doctor meets in his practice in very general terms, and other investigations (26–31) have broadened our understanding of the consultation in this setting. These data have enabled the College to describe five main areas of content (32) in a discussion document to help teachers. Of the five areas, three are concerned with clinical practice. The first, on health and disease, is about health and health education, the prevention of diseases and the process of diagnosis and treatment in individual patients. The second area is about human development, a knowledge of which is important to the GP's aim of helping individual patients in his care to obtain optimum development as a whole person. The third clinical area is human behaviour in which the GP has a special interest. The family doctor, more than most clinicians, is compelled by the nature and setting of his work to be interested in how people behave when they are ill, how they seek medical care and how they accept it. He learns that behaviour has many variations and that neither diagnosis nor prognosis has much value unless they are taken into account. The fourth area, on medicine and society, is about the organization of man and groups and the way in which the characteristics of these groups affect individuals. It deals, therefore with class in relation to illness, diseases of civilization, the uses of epidemiology, the organization of medical care in this country and a comparison with other countries, the relationship of medical care in the UK to other institutions of society, and historical perspectives of general practice. The last area is about the practice itself, and concentrates on the principles of management.

The aims of training proposed by the College (32) and later revised at a recent European conference on the teaching of general practice (33) are derived from a job definition advanced by Byrne (34). This job definition has served as a useful starting-point since it takes account of the content of general practice and the main trends in the way the family doctor works. It will need to be modified in time as a clearer picture of work patterns based on task analyses of critical incidents becomes available (35).

The general practitioner is a doctor who provides personal, primary and continuing medical care to individuals and families. He may attend his patients in their homes, in his consulting-room or sometimes in hospital. He accepts the responsibility for making an initial decision on every problem his patient may present to him, consulting with specialists when he thinks it appropriate to do so. He will usually work in a group with other general practitioners, from premises that are built or modified for the purpose, and with the help of paramedical colleagues, adequate secretarial staff and all the equipment which is necessary. Even if he is in single-handed practice he will work in a team and delegate when necessary. His diagnosis will be composed in physical, psychological and social terms. He will intervene educationally, preventively and therapeutically to promote his patient's health.

The statement of aims consists of three groups involving knowledge, skills, and attitudes, all of which are important and are reproduced below. At the conclusion of training the doctor should be able to demonstrate:

Knowledge
1. That he has sufficient knowledge of disease processes, particularly of common diseases, chronic diseases, and those which endanger life or have serious complications or consequences.

2. That he understands the opportunities, methods, and limitations of prevention, early diagnosis, and management in the setting of general practice.

3. His understanding of the way in which interpersonal relationships within the family can cause health problems or alter their presentation, course, and management, just as illness can influence family relationships.

4. An understanding of the social and environmental circumstances of his patients and how they may affect a relationship between health and illness.

5. His knowledge and appropriate use of the wide range of interventions available to him.

6. That he understands the ethics of his profession and their importance for the patient.

7. That he understands the basic methods of research as applied to general practice.

8. An understanding of medico-social legislation and of the impact of this on his patient.

Skills

1. How to form diagnoses which take account of physical, psychological, and social factors.

2. That he understands the use of epidemiology and probability in his everyday work.

3. Understanding and use of the factor 'time' as a diagnostic, therapeutic, and organizational tool.

4. That he can identify persons at risk and take appropriate action.

5. That he can make relevant initial decisions about every problem presented to him as a doctor.

6. The capacity to co-operate with medical and non-medical professionals.

7. Knowledge and appropriate use of the skills of practice management.

Attitudes

1. A capacity for empathy and for forming a specific and effective relationship with patients and for developing a degree of self-understanding.

2. How his recognition of the patient as a unique individual modifies the ways in which he elicits information and makes hypotheses about the nature of his problems and their management.

3. That he understands that helping patients to solve their own problems is a fundamental therapeutic activity.

4. That he recognizes that he can make a professional contribution to the wider community.

5. That he is willing and able critically to evaluate his own work.

6. That he recognizes his own need for continuing education and critical reading of medical information.

Although these aims are general, and some obviously apply to all clinicians, the imaginative and resourceful teacher in general practice will find a wealth of material in his surgery and at his patients' bedsides to clothe, illustrate, and give a living form to them.

The aims and five areas of content form the basis for the selection of suitable posts for practical experience and for choosing appropriate teaching methods. They are also, therefore, central to assessment and to programme evaluation.

METHODS OF LEARNING

We have already noted that there may be two main parts to vocational training. First, there is in-service experience in general practice and relevant hospital posts which everyone is required to do. Secondly, supplementary courses, usually based on small groups, to cover areas of knowledge not always most effectively dealt with in the former, are offered as a requirement in some schemes, an option in other programmes.

Hospital experience. Experience in specialties other than general practice can be helpful in several ways. For example, the hospital environment can provide for the close supervision of clinical work; and it offers opportunities to demonstrate clinical research, and to learn the use of technical investigations.

The relevance of hospital experience is currently being reconsidered as the RCGP becomes less concerned with the nature of the specialty posts chosen by trainees and much more interested in their educational value. The implication of this approach is that there will be more flexibility in the range of specialties recognized as suitable for vocational training in general practice, but at the same time greater strictness in the selection of individual posts.

Learning in the practice. The most important learning situation is in the practice because it is in this setting that the trainee is exposed to the work of his chosen career. It is recognized that a trainee learns in three main ways in this situation: first by having responsibility for the care of patients who are in the environment of their homes and work; secondly by exposure to the clinical practice and the attitudes of the trainer and his partners; and thirdly, by being in very regular contact with a teacher who can understand his educational needs, excite inquisitive interest, and stimulate sustained application and effort.

This ideal combination does not appear to exist in all training practices today. There is evidence (36–39) from several studies of some variation. The main problems identified are: the doubtful quality to the trainer's clinical work; an inability on the trainer's part to grasp the educational significance of the period; ignorance of one-to-one teaching methods; and unexplained discrepancies between the time teachers say they make available for teaching and the time trainees say they get. To a large degree these variations seem to reflect the adequacy of regional trainer selection policies and the extent to which teachers meet together to improve their own knowledge and skills.

In two regions, Northern and Oxford, trainers have agreed to meet together regularly to take part in group teaching, and actively to help with curriculum development especially of the general practice year. In schemes where this happens regularly these meetings inevitably raise questions about clinical practice. The very need for trainers to clarify content, and the skills trainees should acquire, is thus forcing them first to review the nature of their own work, the adequacy of their own knowledge and skills, and the organization and general management of their own practices in a way and to an extent that has simply not happened hitherto (40, 41). In the Northern Region the importance of this activity has been given formal recognition (42). There, trainers are asked, and have readily agreed, to make available a minimum of thirty sessions per year for audit and related tasks, in addition to their time spent supervising trainees in the practices and attending to their own continuing education. They work at these sessions mainly in the evenings so that patient care is not unreasonably disrupted. This commitment, it has been found, is generating both the interest and opportunity to think about standards of clinical practice based on peer review.

Small group learning. One of the major differences between general and hospital practice is the relative isolation of the GP in his everyday clinical work. There is no routine mechanism through which his everyday hypotheses about diagnosis and management can be critically tested as happens, for example, on well-conducted ward rounds and in the normal course of consultation between one specialist and another about clinical problems. Thus far no generally useful way of overcoming this difficulty in the surgery has been found; group practice does not necessarily provide an answer, as one study has shown (43). It is for this reason that GPs have shown great interest in small group methods of learning.

The advantages of small groups are that they encourage participation by all learners; they provide a framework for assessment by the learner and for informal peer review; and they give the leader a window on the strengths and weaknesses of individual participants. Small groups now form the basis of most supplementary courses of half-day release for trainees in general practice and have largely replaced the lecture.

Unquestionably it is the stimulus of vocational training which has led to such a striking expansion in the use of the small groups, and thus to the variety of techniques modified or devised to meet the needs of family doctors. The first successful example was the London Teachers Workshop (44) which had its roots in the earlier Balint courses and which brought together a group of doctors who were or wanted to become teachers, to learn about their patients and themselves through the many facets of the consultation. More recently (1974), in the North of England, the Royal College of General Practitioners has been trying another approach using a group comprising trainers, other principals and recently qualified trainees (45). Here the main aim was to sensitize doctors to the need to meet regularly to review their clinical work, to learn to accept criticism without being hurt and to give it without offence and ultimately to modify their individual behaviour in a direction the group considered desirable. The methods used are interesting. The records of patients who died during a three-month period were reviewed by a records working party, and cases where diagnosis or management might have been better were later discussed by the group as a whole with the doctor concerned. Another working party examined a randomly chosen selection of records from the practice of each participant with the object of seeing whether the group, from their study of these records, could then formulate any general criteria about minimum content. On other occasions doctors presented cases where they knew things had gone wrong. And throughout the course, members began to explore the population diagnosis and management of hypertension; working criteria were devised and agreed, and attempts to put these into practice will be checked by record sampling in each practice. The group is to continue its work on an on-going basis, meeting regularly throughout the year. Interest in the experiment and thus in audit, has spread. In October 1975 almost a hundred principals enrolled on similar courses beginning throughout the Northern Region. These developments are extremely encouraging because they may be providing part of the foundation on which more formalized audit procedures can be built if it is shown that they are desirable in the future. Certainly they are important in providing that measure of confidence in the profession without which a major extension would be simply blocked and rejected.

The provision of capable teachers in general practice, and in particular of leaders for small groups and schemes is a major problem which must be solved if the next generation of family doctors is to practise at a higher over-all level of competence than their predecessors. The need to teach the new trainers at least the elements of curriculum construction, to introduce them to one-to-one and small group teaching methods, and to familiarize them with the methods of assessment and evaluation already available for use in general practice was coupled with the sobering realization that this would not be achieved, other than in one or two progressive regions, without a substantial, centrally directed effort which could make most efficient use of the limited resources of skilled people available. The RCGP has been fortunate in gaining support from the Nuffield Provincial Hospitals Trust and the health departments to provide such a central course the aim of which is to help train a key group of teachers who are already local leaders in various parts of the country. These doctors have attended the course at intervals for a total of six weeks spread over a year; and whilst at home they have provided local courses for trainers and trainees, an important part of their task. These field exercises have thus, indirectly, been under central supervision. When this Nuffield Project is completed in 1977, a hundred doctors will have been through it and they in turn should have influenced and helped train about seven hundred trainers in their own regions.

The provisional results of the first course are very encouraging. Each participant was subject to very extensive assessment which included taking the MRCGP examination. Interestingly, the scores achieved in this examination rated all members of this leadership group as very high achievers with almost all at distinction level. And this assessment was carried out against a level of anxiety created in the group which far exceeded that normally encountered in the examination itself.

Although the course is primarily about medical education, all participants have found that they have acquired greater insight into their own strengths and weaknesses in clinical medicine to a degree that they had not experienced before. The influence of this new expertise is beginning to be felt in at least some of the regions.

ASSESSMENT, ACCREDITATION, AND SPECIALIST REGISTRATION

There is general agreement in the profession that young doctors who wish to become principals in general practice should first undergo a period of specialist training. There is also general support for the view that individual trainees who wish to have their knowledge and skills assessed should be encouraged to do so by taking the MRCGP examination. However, at the time of writing, there is a serious division in general practice on the critical question of whether or not doctors who seek principal status should now be required to demonstrate that they have first attained a minimum standard of professional competence at the end of training. Discussions are now taking place between the BMA and the RCGP to try and find common ground. Since it is probably not an understatement to say that the nature of the outcome of these discussions will have far-reaching consequences for the quality of professional practice in the future, it is worthwhile considering the methods of assessment in current use, and the results they have shown so far, in some detail.

ASSESSMENT

The RCGP and the Department of General Practice in Manchester University are the two sources of data, the former through its

Membership examination, the latter through a study designed to evaluate vocational training.

THE MRCGP EXAMINATION

The RCGP introduced the examination as a requirement for membership seven years ago and the College regards it as indicating the minimum standard of competence required of a GP. Admission can be gained without examination in exceptional circumstances. However, since the College made the examination the usual pathway of entry only two doctors have been admitted using other criteria. One was already an examiner and had thus demonstrated his knowledge and skills on several occasions in the course of validating papers; the other was a Nepalese doctor whose academic credentials were well known and who had written an outstanding thesis on leprosy.

Initially the examination was taken only by established principals since there were no trainees. Now the number of vocationally trained candidates is increasing as schemes get underway.

The examination is designed to test knowledge, skills, and to some degree attitudes in general practice. The questions relate to the five areas of content already described and their proportion by subject reflects as closely as possible the spectrum of illness the practitioner is likely to encounter in his everyday practice. The methods used have been chosen or developed to test important areas of knowledge and skills. They include:

1. A multiple choice question paper (MCQ) which tests factual knowledge recall in those clinical subjects shown by the morbidity studies to be most relevant to general practice.

2. A modified essay question paper (MEQ) which presents an unfolding clinical problem and which is designed to test problem solving skills as well as factual knowledge recall and attitudes.

3. A short essay question paper (SEQ) which tests the candidate's factual knowledge recall and his ability to conceptualize and express himself in the management of clinical problems, preventive medicine, aspects of development and behaviour of clinical importance, and practice management.

Candidates whose performance in the written paper is satisfactory go on to two oral examinations of thirty minutes each; in the first a log diary of the candidate's own practice and a series of his own

patients is discussed; the second is about the diagnosis and management of clinical problems presented by the examiners.

There are two important criticisms of the examination. There is
no practical clinical component; and, since it is an endpoint assessment of specialist training, it gives no indication of the candidate's
performance in his training posts. Nevertheless, it is regarded by the
College as an increasingly reliable assessment of competence since
the written and oral components are validated on each occasion by
a panel of examiners who are themselves active clinicians in general
practice.

INFORMATION FROM THE MRCGP EXAMINATION

In its evidence to the Merrison Committee (8) the College noted

in three recent examinations, whose candidates were obviously drawn only
from a group of practitioners who wanted to become Members and who
were therefore prepared to be assessed, 188 out of 289 doctors passed, a
65 per cent over-all pass. Certain trends emerged; (*a*) for young doctors
who had completed three-year vocational training programmes for general
practice (44) the pass rate averaged over the three examinations was 89 per
cent; (*b*) for established principals who received their undergraduate training in the United Kingdom (196) the averaged pass rate was 75 per cent;
(*c*) for graduates of universities overseas (49 but none from Eire), nearly all
of them principals in the N.H.S. the averaged pass rate was 6 per cent.

The College later furnished Merrison and the GMC with con-
solidated figures for the Membership examination from spring 1972
to autumn 1974. There were 1,010 candidacies. The over-all pass
rate for 869 doctors who received their basic medical qualification in
the UK or Republic of Ireland was 82 per cent. The pass rate for the
remaining 141 who had an overseas basic medical qualification[1] was
21 per cent. Of the 141 candidates who received their basic medical
qualification overseas, 100 were principals in the NHS at the time of
taking the examination. Of these 100 principals, 19 passed the
examination.

In 1975 the College published the results of examinations held in
the year 1974/5 (9). There were 454 candidates with a pass rate of
71 per cent; 122 (27 per cent) of these were vocationally trained, and
these doctors achieved a pass rate of 88 per cent; the remaining 332

1. Ninety-three from India, 15 from Pakistan, 7 from Sri Lanka, 5 from Burma, 5 from
South Africa, 3 from Singapore, 2 each from Bangladesh, Greece, Kashmir, and the
West Indies, and 1 each from Egypt, Malta, New Zealand, Nigeria, and Norway.

were established principals and they attained a pass rate of 68 per cent. Although numbers of vocationally trained doctors taking the examination are still small, and they are unevenly distributed across the country, there were interregional differences which will be important in future in the evaluation of programmes. Furthermore, because all eligible trainees in the Northern Region have taken the examination in the past year, and, with one exception, all have passed comfortably, that Region has now introduced accreditation for the moment on the basis of educational experience gained and successful performance in the examination. This is an important step particularly since it has been shown (34) that the trainers in this Region do not differ significantly in their knowledge and skills from those in three other parts of the country.

Taken over-all, the examination has identified several categories of candidate:

1. A small group of very high achievers at distinction level.

2. A large group of high scoring candidates (currently increasing in size).

3. A majority with satisfactory marks.

4. A small borderline group, normally discussed in detail at the examiners' conference.

5. Within this group, a small proportion of candidates whose marks in retrospect did not justify their oral examination.

6. Doctors who failed the examination by a significant margin.

Doctors in the borderline category are now given a more structured oral examination which focuses on their knowledge of the diagnosis and management of common clinical conditions in an attempt to sharpen the assessment of their clinical competence, to be as objective as possible in deciding whether they pass or fail.

THE MANCHESTER STUDY

Freeman and Byrne (34) have just completed a detailed evaluation of early vocational training programmes in four centres. Knowledge, skills, and attitudes in a cohort of 80 trainee GPs who received their basic medical qualification in the UK were assessed on entry, during and on completion of training; and the trainees' characteristics were compared with a volunteer group of 112 GPs, some of them already trainers. The areas of knowledge and skills assessed were similar to those covered in the MRCGP examination and some assessment methods used were of the same type (that is the MCQ, MEQ, and SEQ papers).

An attempt was made to develop a method of in-course assessment using a modification of the criteria applied by McGuire to orthopaedic surgery (35). The nine criteria used on the twelve-point rating scale were: 1. Information gathering; 2. Problem-solving; 3. Clinical judgement; 4. Relationship to patients; 5. Continuing responsibility; 6. Emergency care; 7. Relationships with colleagues; 8. Professional values; 9. Over-all competence.

On the scale, which was used for each criterion, ratings of 1–3 were classed as poor, 4–6 marginal, 7–9 as good, and 10–12 as excellent. Progressive rating gave high correlations with the other general assessments and proved particularly helpful in the recognition of educational deficits or of a falling off in performance during training. But it has not proved to be as fine a discriminator as the combination of MEQ, TEQ, and MCQ. The authors' claim that although the method has value as a predictor of outcome, its use would be enhanced if taken in conjunction with the wider spread of methods employed in the MRCGP examination, which seems prudent given the skewed sample of trainees studied.

ACCREDITATION AND SPECIALIST REGISTRATION

The Merrison Committee (46) accepted the evidence of the RCGP that GPs require specific knowledge and skills and that general practice should therefore be recognized as a specialty on the specialist register which is proposed. Both the College and the BMA accept this recommendation. More controversial, however, was Merrison's interpretation of what specialist registration for general practice would mean. The report went on to say 'it follows . . . that the standards of general practice ought to be maintained in the same manner and to the same degree as other specialties' (para. 129). This proposal has been endorsed by the Council of the College (9) but sidestepped by the Conference of Local Medical Committees at its meeting in June 1975 (47). There are three parts to the present argument. First the question of whether assessment is an integral and therefore necessary part of the educational process; secondly, if it is, what methods should be used; and thirdly, which body will be recognized by the new General Medical Council to accredit individual doctors completing specialist training in general practice if specialist registration is adopted. It is helpful to summarize the present position in relation to each of these parts to introduce as many facts as possible on a highly emotive subject.

The College and Merrison are at one that the assessment of individuals is, by definition, an integral part of any competent educational programme. Indeed the consequences of not assessing the competence of individuals, in the context of accreditation and specialist registration, were enunciated recently (48) and are difficult logically to refute.

Without assessment [it was said] individual trainees will not know how or whether they benefit from their training; teachers will have no clear idea of whether or not their programmes are relevant or of the required quality; the profession will be unable to tell the public which young doctors completing training are competent general practitioners; and Government cannot know whether its investment of the taxpayers' money is being spent wisely or squandered.

The Conference of Local Medical Committees (47) has taken a different view '. . . the satisfactory completion of a recognized course of vocational training is not to be determined by the individual assessment or examination of the trainee'. This statement is extremely confusing for in the use of the word 'satisfactory' there is the clear implication of a measurement of quality, yet the means to determine this is specifically to be denied. The likelihood is that this topsy-turvy policy, which means neither one thing nor another, will change at least to admit the principle that assessment is an integral part of education.

This brings us to methods. The methods used in the MRCGP and the standard the examination reflects are endorsed by the Councils of Postgraduate Medical Education for those trainees who wish to be assessed. Progressive rating is an additional method though not yet validated as another option. For the immediate future, perhaps ten years, progressive rating or any other form of continuous assessment is likely to prove unreliable if used unsupported by end-point tests. It would prove impossible to achieve a uniform UK standard when it is known that the competence of the assessors both as doctors and teachers varies widely and that trainees are undertaking programmes of considerable variation in content.

Resolution of the question of whether or not there should be a minimum standard of entry based on assessment may therefore turn on the adoption of two levels of competence in general practice. It was the Merrison Committee which recommended that the new GMC should be required to promote excellence in postgraduate medical education as well as to set minimum standards for each specialty. In the context of general practice, a branch of medicine with over 20,000 doctors, this approach would make good sense, since two separate needs have already been recognized; to raise the general standard of competence of all new entrants to general practice; and to select from those already in post a proportion, up to one-third according to some estimates, who would become teachers in their practices or who would take up academic appointments. It would not be difficult to devise a combination of continuous assessment and endpoint examination which would distinguish the safe from the incompetent, so achieving the main aim of specialist registration. This combination could then be used as the first part of a more comprehensive and searching assessment for those wishing to gain the MRCGP qualification which would recognize the subgroup of high achievers who, as we have already seen, comprise a very substantial and increasing minority of those passing the existing examination (49).

The RCGP is believed to be examining the technical and professional implications of this concept at the moment. There are several attractions. For example, it would relieve the BMA of its two main objections to the MRCGP examination today, namely, that the standard is already too high to be reconciled with manpower requirements, and that there are doctors who do not want to be committed to an ongoing association with the College. Even more importantly, it would leave the College free to establish its higher qualification as the normal requirement for such career groups as principals who wish to become trainers as well as others who simply want to know that they can do well, whilst enabling it still to conduct the lower-level assessments for accreditation and specialist registration on behalf of the Regulating Body. This mode of development could bring general practice closer to the other specialties in Britain, which have the problem of reconciling the requirements for specialist registration in Europe with the standards normally required as a precondition of consultant appointments.

PROGRAMME EVALUATION AND RECOGNITION

All specialties have now recognized the need to pay more attention to the quality of training programmes which means looking at their educational content, posts, and supporting educational facilities available. The Joint Higher Training Committees are doing this for senior registrar posts, and the Royal Colleges for junior appointments in hospitals.

The College established its Postgraduate Training Committee with a similar function. Recently this Committee has been replaced by the new Joint Committee on Postgraduate Training for General Practice. The Joint Committee comprises representatives of the College, the General Medical Services Committee of the BMA, the National Conference of Regional Advisers in General Practice, the Conference of Postgraduate Deans, the Armed Services, the Society of University Teachers in General Practice, and trainees. It stands in a similar relationship to the College as does the Joint Committee on Higher Training for Medicine to the Royal College of Physicians of London and the other Colleges of Physicians (9).

The Joint Committee has two functions:

1. To advise the Councils for Postgraduate Medical Education and the regional postgraduate committees of the standards required for vocational training programmes in general practice.

2. To recognize vocational training programmes furnishing an educational experience of the required standard.

It has just begun its work. Now that sufficient training programmes are available a major effort is being made to raise the overall standard of teaching practices. The College's initial criteria have been revised recently and tightened by the Committee, and are to be published. Visits to teaching practices in the regions are being carried out, partly to develop ways of assessing individual trainers, and partly to verify information gained from previously circulated questionnaires about the characteristics of these practices.

It is now recommended by the Joint Committee on Postgraduate Training for General Practice that doctors wishing to become or to remain trainers should be assessed by the regional postgraduate organizations' appointments committees under several heads: the applicant be asked to demonstrate his desire, experience, and ability in teaching; that he is clinically competent; that he has time for teaching; that his practice and its organization are suitable; and that he is willing to have his work assessed. These criteria are regarded by the Joint Committee as the minimum which should be used by regional appointments committees. But firm encouragement is given to those individual regions which have already advanced beyond the minimum criteria and are anxious, therefore, to maintain their own high standards, on the grounds that the establishment of such standards in progressive regions will lead by example and by competition for good trainees to a more general improvement. One region, for example, now asks trainers to take part in peer review and other auditing procedures as well as to show that they have reached the MRCGP standard by passing the examination.

Mention has been made of important variations in trainers and practices already appointed, a finding borne out by visitors from the Joint Committee conducting on-site reviews. However, these are early days and the Postgraduate Joint Committee is proceeding with caution and care; since trainers must be reviewed before reappointment, after a period of five years, there is considerable scope to influence, persuade, and thus effect changes in the future.

The only really objective measure of the quality of training is to show whether the majority of learners in a programme consistently achieve what they are supposed to do. Hence we return to the critical importance of assessing individuals. Freeman and Byrne (34) provided outcome data on their cohort of eighty trainees. They showed that in the course of training over-all scores of factual knowledge were raised and problem-solving skills improved very significantly. The attitudes of individual trainees appeared to change in the general direction of those held by their trainers and less precisely to reflect those of the teaching group as a whole. Over-all clinical competence was improved sufficiently to suggest that in general terms the period of vocational training had been valuable for this highly motivated group of trainees. Supportive evidence is beginning to come from the MRCGP examination. One region and another scheme, both known to have highly sophisticated and well-conducted training programmes, are producing trainees a large proportion of whom fall into the high achiever groups of those passing the examination. By contrast another region has had a substantial failure amongst its candidates. This feedback data is important to medical educators and indeed has already prompted several regional advisers in general practice to ask the College for general analyses of the performance of their candidates to see if areas of weakness or deficiency as well as of relative strength can be identified. The College is thought to be considering how best it can make general outcome data available for use by university organizations responsible for training, whilst preserving confidentiality in respect of the performance of individual candidates.

CONTINUING EDUCATION: AN UNDEVELOPED AREA

This account of contemporary postgraduate education for general practice has centred largely on postgraduate training. It is therefore worth restating an important effect of vocational training which is now becoming evident. Apparently GPs who have become trainers and are now exposed to small group work are having to think hard about the nature and quality of their own clinical work, to try and improve on their knowledge and skills, to accept criticism from their peers, and so reconsider their behaviour, in response to external and self-generated pressures to become more effective teachers. These are new steps in continuing education which should have relevance to all GPs, but they have yet to be extended to the 95 per cent of doctors who are not trainers. This will not be possible in the immediate future for, even if the majority of GPs wanted to take part in such activities there are insufficient numbers of doctors experienced in small group methods to go round. Good small group teachers in general practice are at a premium; and as their numbers increase they will be used first more securely to underpin vocational training.

There are weighty implications of this practical constraint for those who envisage clinical audit in general practice. Put bluntly, it would be difficult if not impossible to introduce audit on a widespread scale until the postgraduate educational foundation for the whole of general practice is recast along the general lines now being adopted in vocational training.

Audit in general practice

It is against the background of a long, slow haul in postgraduate education that we have to view the first tentative steps in the direction of audit as a means to improve quality of care in general practice. To help place audit completely in context, it is useful first to indicate some of the more general problems besetting the measurement of quality in this field.

Donabedian's classification (50) of care into three components is usually used as a basis. The three parts are: (*a*) the structure of care —for example, the setting, qualifications of the providers, administrative arrangements and policies of general practice; (*b*) the process of care—the diagnostic, therapeutic, and preventive actions taken by the providers; (*c*) the outcomes of care—the change in the health status of the recipients of care. It is now recognized that the relationship between structure/outcome and process/outcome is not nearly as predictable as an indicator of quality as was once thought. Knowledge of the ideal clinical management of many conditions is deficient so that more research into process/outcome and structure/outcome relationships is needed before standards of quality can be set. Just how difficult the problems are in the context of general practice was shown at a recent RCGP meeting sponsored by the Rockefeller Foundation (51). Background papers (52–55) stressed the following points:

1. In definitions of primary care, emphasis is usually placed on availability, accessibility, continuity, and the co-ordinating function.

2. Non-medical factors, both personal and environmental, have a strong influence on health and may often be more important than medical care.

3. The outcome of preventive and therapeutic actions against chronic diseases is usually not clear for many years; hence there is a need for record linkage if process and outcome are to be related.

4. Studies of quality relating the outcomes of care in general practice must consider the objectives of general practice. Providers and consumers have different implicit objectives which are not necessarily symmetrical or reciprocal, and no two providers or consumers are likely to have exactly the same range or order of objectives.

To illustrate the difficulty of measurement further, one group at the meeting specified eight elements of outcome in seeking the ultimate criterion of quality. In terms of the individual patient these were:

(*a*) Prevention of disease or control of the disease process.

(*b*) Improvement or preservation of the patient's level of function in his family, at work and in his social activities.

(*c*) Relief of the patient's symptoms, distress, and anxiety, and avoidance of iatrogenic symptoms.

(*d*) Prevention of premature death.

(*e*) Minimizing the cost of illness to the patient and his family.

(*f*) Giving the patient satisfaction with his care.

(*g*) Relieving or at least clarifying the patient's interpersonal problems.

(*h*) Preserving the human integrity of the patient from an ethical point of view.

The Conference recognized that another group might have produced a different list and would have argued about the relative importance of individual items. And it was clear also that had consumers been asked to provide such a list it might have been quite different.

Ginzberg (56) reminds us that the use of outcome measures to evaluate quality in illnesses which are self-limiting or for which no effective therapeutic action is possible, would be unreasonable. His point, if applied to general practice, would remove a substantial part of content from the area of measurement. He has suggested that it may be more fruitful to focus on known problem areas which in general practice would presumably include therapeutics, especially adverse drug reactions, the effectiveness of health care maintenance and rehabilitation (57), and the availability and accessibility of the providers. Such an approach would ignore another group of problems encountered in general practice, namely, those which have a substantial social or behavioural component. Whilst it is important not to neglect this group because of difficulties in classification and assessment, it may be nevertheless more productive to concentrate on solvable questions in the first place.

There is another general point. Quality of care measurement in general practice cannot be considered as an entity solely concerned with the work of family doctors, although obviously they have a key role in the system. The actions of the other health professionals who now comprise part of the clinical team in general practice as well as the work of receptionists and other supporting staff have to be taken into account. And general practice as a local system of care cannot be assessed in isolation from the service provided by nearby hospitals, social and other agencies which may also be concerned in the management and care of individual patients.

To come down to a level of more direct interest to the average practising doctor, he may well begin to wonder how he can improve the quality of care in his practice. Maintaining his effectiveness, as judged against working criteria rather than ideal measures of outcome is perhaps the most fruitful avenue for him to explore. These working criteria, based on the 'conventional wisdom' of medicine, can be used to formulate clinical and operational standards which

will reflect the best that the profession can do with the knowledge
and resources available.

AUDIT

Mourin (58) in a comprehensive review of audit and evaluation in
general practice, found it helpful to clarify the distinction between
these two terms by suggesting that audit comprises the whole process
of enumeration and the making of value judgements, whilst evaluation might be better restricted to the making of value judgements.
Perhaps it is simplest to consider audit as comprising three components (59), setting standards, assessing performance, and modifying clinical practice.

Setting standards. There are two main ways; the use of externally
generated criteria; and criteria internally derived by individuals or
small groups after evaluation of all available data. The former has
been favoured in North America whilst the latter is attracting most
interest in general practice in the UK. Whilst there is clearly a place
for both methods Crombie (60) has pointed out that it is only
occasionally that value judgements can be supported scientifically
a priori although when they can their use is not only justified but
mandatory.

The place of the small group, meeting together over an extended
period of time, is the favoured mechanism for promoting the cycle of
standard-setting, evaluating performance, and modifying behaviour
in general practice at present for a number of reasons. Perhaps the
most compelling is that of active participation in a peer group. As I
noted earlier many GPs find this experience stimulating because they
spend more time than doctors in the specialties consulting alone. To
be involved in the working out of reasonable criteria of performance
with like-minded colleagues is itself an educative process, the effects
of which are reinforced by normal group pressures when the question
of implementation and subsequent assessment arises. There are,
however, certain factors which it seems may be critical to the
effectiveness of the process (45); it appears that the group needs to
be well led if objectivity is to be maintained; to meet often enough
to maintain a momentum and cohesion; to have access to and use
expert resource when necessary; and above all, to have easily available data from the participant practices which is reliable, and
capable of true comparison with data from practices elsewhere.

Records. The gross inadequacy of existing general practice records to meet the main requirements for auditing the quality of patient care has already been mentioned. Several proposals for improving their structure and format have been made (61–63) although the most important of these, the A4 folder, has become a casualty of the recent economic recession. The use of the problem-orientated record is being examined (64, 65) as a further index of morbidity (66), as an indicator of 'critical events' (67), and in the use of 'delay pattern analysis' (68). These individual studies and others of a similar nature are very interesting but until there is a general movement to accord records a higher priority, and to recast systems to become compatible for use in patient care evaluation, there is little prospect of real progress. Dr F. A. Boddy (69) has suggested broad criteria which a record system should possess to gain general acceptance. These criteria are that:

(*a*) There be a clearer definition of the uses of records than exists at the present which should be reflected in design.

(*b*) While maintaining a standard format, records should be compatible with the needs of different clinical settings and the kind of activities they undertake.

(*c*) The basic format should be sufficiently flexible to accommodate the needs of individual doctors.

(*d*) Records should be used in a variety of data systems.

(*e*) Records should be susceptible to automatic data processing.

(*f*) Records permit the aggregation of data within and between data systems (for example between local, regional, and national systems).

(*g*) There is preservation of privacy and confidentiality.

(*h*) Records are orientated towards future needs.

Two other studies, in the early stages of development, are worth mentioning in connection with providing individual participants with comparative information about their practices. In Nottingham (70) eighty-one doctors in the catchment area of the two teaching hospitals are taking part in a study designed to furnish more data about doctor/patient contacts on a sampling basis as part of a longer-term objective to devise a computer-based model of health services for planning purposes. These doctors have already been enthusiastic about the comparative analyses of data they have received in a preliminary run. In the second study the RCGP Postgraduate Training Committee is examining the feasibility of an information

system to give data on the general characteristics of teaching practices in the UK. Analyses of important structural and process
differences between individual practices would be fed back to
individual teachers and regional general practice advisory committees
for educational purposes, as well as for use by the Committee for
recognition.

PROFESSIONAL INCENTIVES

In the main general practice has relied on the conscience of its
individual doctors to prepare themselves for their work and thereafter to keep up-to-date. However, some specific incentives have
been tried, mainly financial. For example, the obstetric list was
introduced to try and ensure that as far as possible family doctors
who provide midwifery services have first gained further experience
in obstetrics. The list identifies these doctors to the health service
authorities so enabling them to claim higher fees than others who
are not registered. Seniority payments were linked with a minimum
attendance at postgraduate courses in an attempt to stimulate the
minority of doctors who seemed to take no interest in keeping
abreast of recent advances. More recently, an allowance has been
made to doctors completing vocational training, partly to offset their
financial disadvantage over contemporaries who become principals
immediately after registration, and partly to encourage those most
in need of training, and perhaps least motivated to choose it, to alter
their behaviour. It is interesting that no assessment of the individual
has been conducted as a condition of making any of these payments.
The doctor wanting to be placed on the obstetric list merely has to
indicate his completion of an approved obstetric post; his colleague
seeking his seniority payment has to show that he attended the
minimum number of postgraduate sessions, not that he learned anything; and the doctor undertaking vocational training has only to
serve his time to receive his money though he can be assessed
through the MRCGP examination if he chooses to do so. In cost/
benefit terms these payments cannot be justified since there is no
evidence that they achieve their implicit aims. One has to resort,
therefore, to the questionable value judgement that they are worthwhile if, in the words of an anonymous health service administrator,
'a little bit of something rubs off somewhere'.

The time may soon be ripe for a change. If vocational training becomes a normal precondition of appointment as a principal in the

NHS the vocational training allowance will disappear. And there is a strong case for abandoning the unpopular link between education and seniority. If financial incentives to promote the maintenance of competence are still required, as I believe they will be especially when audit becomes a reality, there will be much to be said for devising a specific educational allowance the criteria for which would include assessment of the individual.

It is perhaps encouraging to recall that not all incentives are financial. The desire to teach, and to lead a richer professional life, has been the motivation of a sufficient number of doctors to enable the principle of academic selection to be introduced into general practice for the first time. And there are now indicators from some regions that training practices are beginning to look more critically at the professional and academic qualities of young doctors seeking partnerships. Since some of these practices are in under-doctored areas, the fact that they seem able to attract suitable candidates is a useful pointer in the right direction.

Towards a strategy for improvement

In drawing the threads of my paper together, I suggest it is possible to indicate several factors which will have an important bearing on the improvement of quality in general practice. These are to:

1. Sustain the effort to rehouse and re-equip general practice especially in areas of the country where an effective primary care service is proving difficult to maintain, far less improve.

2. Introduce postgraduate training as the normal precondition of appointment as a principal in the NHS immediately.

3. Introduce specialist registration and recognize general practice as a specialty on the Register as soon as possible.

4. Ensure that doctors seeking specialist accreditation leading to specialist registration are assessed, to show that they achieve minimum standards of competence.

5. Generate working criteria of good clinical and operational practice in key areas, based on further research into the content, processes, and intermediate outcomes of care in general practice.

6. Improve practice records, and devise acceptable information systems which will permit local, area, and interregional comparisons of essential data with reasonable economy.

7. Promote high standards for teaching practices in the regions by:
(*a*) Insisting that the criteria for recognition are based on what can be achieved over most of the country, rather than be indexed to the region furnishing the lowest common denominator.

(*b*) Encouraging regions which want to set more exacting standards to do so, to foster competition.

8. To encourage the use of small groups as an integral part of postgraduate education and as the basis for clinical audit for all GPs.

9. Test methods of audit suitable and acceptable for use in general practice; and similarly, consider methods to encourage and control ongoing competence to practise.

10. Collaborate with other specialties in medicine, and related health professions, to establish more substantial measures of outcome.

In such a large branch of medicine as general practice this will be a very formidable task indeed. The question is whether we can measure up to it?

References

1. COLLINGS, J. S. (1950). 'General practice in England today: a reconnaisance', *Lancet*, i, 555–85.
2. BRITISH MEDICAL ASSOCIATION (1965). *A Charter for the Family Doctor Service* (London: BMA).
3. ROYAL COLLEGE OF GENERAL PRACTITIONERS (1973). *Present State and Future Needs of General Practice* (3rd edn), Reports from General Practice no. 16 (London: RCGP).
4. McINTYRE, A. D., and PARRY, K. M. (1975). 'Career attainment—chance or choice', *Br. J. med. Educ.* 9, 70–77.
5. VARLAAM, M. D., and JEFFERYS, MARGOT (1972). 'Patients' opinions of their doctors —a comparative study of patients in a central London borough registered with single-handed and partnership practices in 1969', *Jl R. Coll. Gen. Practit.* 22, 811–16.
6. KLEIN, R. (1973). *Complaints against Doctors* (London: Charles Knight).
7. CONSUMERS' ASSOCIATION (1975). 'N.H.S.: how well does it work?', *Which* (August), 232–40.
8. ROYAL COLLEGE OF GENERAL PRACTITIONERS (1974). 'Evidence of the College to the Committee of Inquiry into the Regulation of the Medical Profession', *Jl R. Coll. Gen. Practit.* 24, 59–74.
9. —— (1975). *Twenty-Third Annual Report* (London: RCGP).
10. PARISH, P. A. (1971). 'The prescribing of psychotropic drugs in general practice', *Jl R. Coll. Gen. Practit.* 21, Suppl. no. 4.
11. HOWIE, J. G. R., RICHARDSON, I. M., GILL, G., and DURNO, D. (1971). 'Respiratory illness and antibiotic use in general practice', ibid. 21, 657–63.
12. PETRIE, J. C., HOWIE, J. G. R., and DURNO, D. (1974). 'Awareness and experience of general practitioners of selected drug interactions', ibid. 2, 262–4.

13. CORMACK, J. J. C. (1971). *The General Practitioner's Use of Medical Records*, Scottish Health Services Studies no. 15 (Edinburgh: SHHD).

14. DAWES, K. S. (1972). 'Survey of general practice records', *Br. med. J.* 3, 219–23.

15. BRITISH MEDICAL ASSOCIATION PLANNING UNIT (1970). *Primary Medical Care*, Report no. 4 (London: BMA).

16. COLLEGE OF GENERAL PRACTITIONERS (1966). *Evidence of the College to the Royal Commission on Medical Education*, Reports from General Practice no. 5 (London: CGP).

17. ROYAL COMMISSION ON MEDICAL EDUCATION (1968). *Report, 1965–68* (Todd Report), Cmnd 3569 (London: HMSO).

18. ROYAL COLLEGE OF GENERAL PRACTITIONERS (1974). 'The accreditation of vocational programmes' (unpublished data).

19. LOGAN, W. P. D., and CUSHION, A. A. (1958). *Morbidity Studies from General Practice: General*, Studies on Medical and Population Subjects no. 14, vol. i (London: HMSO).

20. —— (1960). *Morbidity Statistics from General Practice: Occupation*, Studies on Medical and Population Subjects no. 14, vol. ii (London: HMSO).

21. COLLEGE OF GENERAL PRACTITIONERS (1962). *Morbidity Studies from General Practice: Disease in General Practice*, Studies in Medical and Population Subjects no. 14, vol. iii (London: HMSO).

22. FRY, J. (1966). *Profiles of Disease* (2nd edn) (Edinburgh and London: Livingstone).

23. HODGKIN, K. (1966). *Towards Earlier Diagnosis* (2nd edn) (Edinburgh and London: Livingstone).

24. MORRELL, D. C. (1971). 'Expressions of morbidity in general practice', *Br. med. J.* 2, 454–8.

25. OFFICE OF POPULATION CENSUSES AND SURVEYS (1974). *Morbidity Statistics from General Practice. Second National Study 1970–71* (London: HMSO).

26. BALINT, M. (1964). *The Doctor, His Patient and the Illness* (2nd edn) (London: Pitman).

27. BROWNE, K., and FREELING, P. (1967). *The Doctor–Patient Relationship* (Edinburgh and London: Livingstone).

28. HOWIE, J. G. R. (1972). 'Diagnosis—the Achilles heel?', *Jl R. Coll. Gen. Practit.* 22, 310–15.

29. —— (1973). 'A new look at respiratory illness in general practice', ibid. 23, 895–903.

30. —— (1974). 'Further observations on diagnosis and management of general practice respiratory illness using simulated patient consultations', *Br. med. J.* 2, 540–3.

31. BALINT, E., NORELL, J. S., et al. (1973). *Six Minutes for the Patient: Interactions in General Practice Consultation* (London: Tavistock Publications).

32. ROYAL COLLEGE OF GENERAL PRACTITIONERS (1972). *The Future General Practitioner: Learning and Teaching* (London: BMJ for RCGP).

33. SECOND EUROPEAN CONFERENCE ON THE TEACHING OF GENERAL PRACTICE (1974). *The General Practitioner in Europe: Statement by the Working Party* (Netherlands: Leeuwenhorst).

34. FREEMAN, J. and BYRNE, P. S. (1975). 'The assessment of postgraduate training in general practice', Final Report on DHSS Project no. J/R127/78 (to be published).

35. McGUIRE, C. H. (1967). *An Evaluation Model for Professional Education: Medical Education* (Chicago: College of Medicine, University of Illinois).

36. IRVINE, D. H. (1972). *Teaching Practices*, Report from General Practice no. 15 (London: RCGP).

37. —— RUSSELL, I., and TAYLOR, G. (1974). 'The recognition of vocational training programmes—results of a pilot survey', *Jl R. Coll. Gen. Practit.* 24, 617–29.

38. HORDER, J. Personal communication.

39. DONALD, J. B. (1975). 'The trainee year: critical appraisal', *Br. med. J.* 1, 672–5.

40. REGIONAL GENERAL PRACTICE ADVISORY COMMITTEE (1974). *Annual Report: Postgraduate Education for General Practice* (Northern Regional Postgraduate Organization for Medicine and Dentistry).
41. HASLAR, J. (1975). Personal communication.
42. REGIONAL GENERAL PRACTICE ADVISORY COMMITTEE (1975). *Annual Report: Postgraduate Education for General Practice* (Northern Regional Postgraduate Organization for Medicine and Dentistry).
43. IRVINE, D. H., and JEFFERYS, M. (1971). 'B.M.A. Planning Unit survey of general practice', *Br. med. J.* 4, 535–43.
44. MARINKER, M. (1972). 'A teacher's workshop', *Jl R. Coll. Gen. Practit.* 22, 551–9.
45. IRVINE, D. H., and CARR, R. (1975). 'Audit in general practice: preliminary report on a course using peer review' (in preparation).
46. COMMITTEE OF INQUIRY INTO THE REGULATION OF THE MEDICAL PROFESSION (1975). *Report*, Cmnd 6018 (London: HMSO).
47. CONFERENCE OF REPRESENTATIVES OF LOCAL MEDICAL COMMITTEES (1975). *Minutes* (London: BMA).
48. IRVINE, D. H. (1975). 'William Pickles Lecture 1975, 1984—The Quiet Revolution?', *Jl R. Coll. Gen. Practit.* 25, 399–407.
49. ROYAL COLLEGE OF GENERAL PRACTITIONERS (1972). Board of Censors Paper no. 100 (unpublished).
50. DONABEDIAN, A. (1966). *Milbank Meml Fund Q.* 44, part 2, no. 3, 166–206.
51. BUCK, C., FRY, J., and IRVINE, D. H. (1974). 'A framework for good primary care—the measurement and achievement of quality', *Jl R. Coll. Gen. Practit.* 24, 599–604.
52. BUCK, C. (1974). 'Working paper to the Conference on the Measurement and Approvement of Quality in Primary Health Care' (typescript).
53. FRY, J. (1974). Ibid. (typescript).
54. JEFFERYS, M. (7974). Ibid. (typescript).
55. LEE, P. (1974). Ibid. (typescript).
56. GINZBERG, E. (1975). 'Notes on evaluating the quality of medical care', *New Engl. J. Med.* 292, 366–8.
57. MARINKER, M. (1975). *The Doctor and His Patient* (Leicester University Press).
58. MOURIN, K. (1974). 'Auditing and Evaluation in General Practice, A Report on an Upjohn Travelling Fellowship 1973–74' (typescript).
59. ROYAL COLLEGE OF GENERAL PRACTITIONERS (1974). 'Working Paper of the Education Committee to Council' (typescript).
60. CROMBIE, D L. (1975). 'Clinical audit by self-evaluation', *Jl R. Coll. Gen. Practit.* (in press).
61. HAWKEY, J. K., LOUDON, I. S. L., GREENHAULGH, G. P., and BUNGAY, G. T. (1971). 'New records folder for use in general practice', *Br. med. J.* 4, 667–70.
62. HODES, C. (1973). 'A new medical records system for general practice', *Lancet*, ii, 897–8.
63. HARDEN, K. A., McG. HARDEN, R., REEKIE, D., and JOLLY, L. (1974). 'New approach to information handling in general practice', *Br. med. J.* 2, 162–6.
64. TAIT, I., and STEVENS, J. (1973). 'The problem-orientated medical record in general practice', *Jl R. Coll. Gen. Practit.* 23, 311–15.
65. TAIT, I. (1975). Personal communication.
66. CLARK, E. M. (1974). 'Disease coding in a problem-orientated general practice', *Jl R. Coll. Gen. Practit.* 24, 469–75.
67. METCALFE, D H. (1975). Personal communication.
68. HODGKIN, G. K. (1973). 'Evaluating the doctor's work', *Jl R. Coll. Gen. Practit.* 23, 759–67.
69. BODDY, F. A. (1975). Personal communication.
70. METCALFE, D. H. (1975). Personal communication.

5

Surveying the performance of pathological laboratories

TOM WHITEHEAD

PhD, MCB, MRCPath, FRIC

Professor of Clinical Chemistry
University of Birmingham
Director of the Wolfson Research Laboratory
Queen Elizabeth Medical Centre

Surveying the performance of pathological laboratories

A basic role of the clinical laboratory is to provide reliable data on the composition of specimens obtained from patients as an aid to the diagnosis and treatment of disease.

The results of all scientific observations are subject to variance and this includes observations in clinical laboratories.

There is abundant evidence both from the UK and from many other parts of the world where portions of the same material have been analysed by a number of laboratories that the variance in the results obtained indicates a situation which is unacceptable on the basis of both clinical and analytical criteria.

Techniques to reduce discrepancies in laboratory results are generally described as quality control techniques. Many of those used in industry have been adapted for clinical laboratories. These techniques are more readily applied to quantitative data so that the disciplines of clinical chemistry and haematology have been in the forefront of such developments. Their use in bacteriology, serology, and blood transfusion is increasing; histopathology poses special problems. Routine clinical chemistry laboratories in the UK normally practise some form of quality control.

There has been growing interest in the subject in recent years.

Questions on the use of quality control techniques in routine clinical laboratories feature prominently in the Royal College of Pathologists examinations and in international conferences of clinical chemistry. The World Health Organization is, at the present time, organizing courses on quality control for laboratory workers from the less developed nations.

Two different controls are involved. In the first, portions of the same material are put through an analytical process, say daily, on several occasions and a 'spread' of results is determined. Such internal quality control systems are now routinely practised by many clinical chemistry laboratories.

In the second, the same material is presented to a number of different laboratories, some using the same analytical methods, some using different analytical methods. A spread of results is determined within and between methods. Surveys involving quality control are playing an increasing role in clinical laboratory science and it is this aspect of quality control which is discussed in this article.

Surveys of clinical chemistry, haematology, and bacteriology laboratories in the UK have been sponsored by the DHSS. The UK National Quality Control Scheme in clinical chemistry is used to illustrate the approach. The scheme is operated from the Department of Clinical Chemistry, Queen Elizabeth Medical Centre, Birmingham. It is financed by the DHSS; the present annual cost is approximately £9,000 per year. The over-all policy of the scheme is guided by the Standards and Quality Control Sub-Group of the Laboratory Development and Advisory Group of the DHSS. The Department receives reports on the over-all performance of laboratories but does not have access to the performance of individual laboratories.

The United Kingdom National Quality Control Scheme (UKNQCS)

The main objectives of the Scheme when it started in 1969 were:

1. To send at fourteen-day intervals a portion of the bulk human serum and, on occasions, non-human serum, to all those hospital laboratories in the UK which perform clinical chemistry analyses.

2. To assess results from fifteen of the more commonly performed analyses. A laboratory which did not routinely perform all of the fifteen analyses, would not necessarily be excluded from participating in the Scheme.

3. To return results from participating laboratories to the organizing laboratory quickly; the results from all laboratories to be available to the participants within ten days of the specimen arriving in the participating laboratories.

4. To make participation voluntary and preserve anonymity.

5. To present the results in a manner that would enable the

participants to make judgements of their performance, particularly in relation to the analytical method used.

6. To assess the role of automation, analytical methods, laboratory workload, and other factors possibly affecting the variance of results.

7. To determine whether any improvement in precision and accuracy in the hospital laboratories of the UK occurred as a result of such frequent surveys.

Organization of the Scheme

The Scheme has been in operation for six years, during that time the number of participating laboratories has doubled. The distribution of serum specimens to 200 laboratories in the UK began in July 1969; at the present time the participants number 420. There is reason to think that the vast majority of laboratories within the NHS performing clinical chemical analysis have entered the scheme and approximately 90 per cent of participating laboratories return the results for each distribution of serum. At the present time the survey regularly includes fifteen different chemical determinations. These are serum sodium, potassium, chloride, urea, glucose, calcium, phosphate, iron, total protein, albumin, bilirubin, alkaline phosphatase, cholesterol, uric acid, and creatinine. Not all fifteen substances are required to be assayed for each distribution of serum. A group of eight tests alternates with a group of seven but occasionally all fifteen tests are surveyed in a particular serum. Surveys of blood lead, thyroid function tests and certain enzymes have also been carried out. The IBM 1130 computer in the author's laboratory has been programmed to perform virtually all the clerical tasks involved in the scheme and the survey involves approximately four hours of computer time each fortnight.

SERUM PREPARATION

In the operation of the scheme obtaining sufficient material of suitable quality is a problem. A variety of non-human and human material has been distributed both lyophilized and liquid. Liquid human serum is ideal and has been provided from excess test specimens obtained from hospital laboratories or blood transfusion centres. Approximately 4 litres of serum are required for each distribution. Occasionally chemical constituents are elevated by additions to the serum. Every effort is made to exclude specimens from patients with hepatitis, but all participants are warned to treat the specimens as potentially contaminated.

TIMETABLE OF DISTRIBUTION OF SERA AND RESULTS

Labelling for distribution is facilitated by the computer line printer which draws on a disc file of addresses and code numbers of the participating laboratories. The computer is also programmed to punch a card with the code number and the date of the serum specimen for each participating laboratory; the specimen of serum and the appropriate punched cards are packed in a protective polystyrene box.

All packs are posted on a Saturday and almost without exception arrive in the participating laboratories early on the following Monday morning (day 1). The laboratories perform the analyses listed on the punched card and return the results before the following Monday (day 8). On day 8 all returned cards have the written results punched into them and following verification they are analysed by the computer on the Tuesday (day 9). Photocopies of the computer printout of results are posted to the participating laboratories on the Wednesday (day 10). This timing of distribution enables at least 90 per cent of all participating laboratories to be included in the printout prepared on day 9. The preparation of the serum and any production of all results takes approximately 38 hours of labour each week; most of the labour is unskilled.

FORMAT OF REPORT TO ALL PARTICIPANTS

The following is a description of the information provided in the computer printout. The computer lists the results attributed to each laboratory so that they may be checked for clerical errors by the participating laboratory. The mean, standard deviation, and coefficient of variation for each determination is calculated and printed. After removal of all results outside three standard deviations either side of the mean, these statistics are recalculated, and these are termed the recalculated mean and standard deviation. A copy of this portion of the printout is shown in Fig. 1. This technique eliminates those results which are probably due to random mistakes. Following the statistical calculations, there are printouts of histograms of the reported results for each determination. An example of such a histogram is shown in Fig. 2. The range of the histogram corresponds to

	URIC ACID	CREATININE	BILIRUBIN	TOTAL PROT.	ALBUMIN	ALK. PHOS.	CHOLESTEROL	
NO.OF RESULTS	274	248	0	323	301	307	292	0
MEAN VALUE	3.58	3.77	0.000	5.83	3.65	5.45	172.67	0.00
STD.DEVIATION	0.478	10.293	0.000	0.412	0.340	4.043	18.350	0.000
COEFF.OF VAR.	13.352	272.903	0.000	7.065	9.336	74.179	10.627	0.000

RECALCULATED RESULTS EXCLUDING THOSE OUTSIDE 3 S.D. IN THE ABOVE CALCULATIONS

	URIC ACID	CREATININE	BILIRUBIN	TOTAL PROT.	ALBUMIN	ALK. PHOS.	CHOLESTEROL	
NO.OF RESULTS	270	247	0	319	295	302	289	0
MEAN VALUE	3.58	3.11	0.000	5.83	3.64	5.01	173.35	0.00
STD.DEVIATION	0.379	0.534	0.000	0.318	0.300	1.738	14.294	0.000
COEFF.OF VAR.	10.601	17.134	0.000	5.452	8.261	34.641	8.245	0.000

PLEASE NOTE THAT THE RANGE OF THE HISTOGRAM APPROXIMATES TO A TWO STANDARD
DEVIATION INTERVAL EITHER SIDE OF THE MEAN AS GIVEN IN THE SECOND CALCULATION.

358 LABS. PARTICIPATED IN SCHEME THIS WEEK

FIGURE I. An example of the statistical calculations given in the computer print out.

the recalculated means, ± 2 SD. A result within the limits is shown by a cross and a result outside these limits by a dot. These limits are not 'limits of acceptability' but are a convenient method of presenting the results, which enables each participant's results to be related to all other results.

```
HISTOGRAM DISTRIBUTION FOR  CREATININE

LT. MIN    7  '.........
    2.1    3  'XXX
    2.2    1  'X
    2.3    0  '
    2.4    2  'XX
    2.5   12  'XXXXXXXXXXXX
    2.6    4  'XXXX
    2.7   14  'XXXXXXXXXXXXXX
    2.8   17  'XXXXXXXXXXXXXXXXX
    2.9   27  'XXXXXXXXXXXXXXXXXXXXXXXXXXX
    3.0   23  'XXXXXXXXXXXXXXXXXXXXXXX
    3.1   29  'XXXXXXXXXXXXXXXXXXXXXXXXXXXXX
    3.2   36  'XXXXXXXXXXXXXXXXXXXXXXXXXXXXXXXXXXXX
    3.3   17  'XXXXXXXXXXXXXXXXX
    3.4    8  'XXXXXXXX
    3.5   10  'XXXXXXXXXX
    3.6   13  'XXXXXXXXXXXXX
    3.7    4  'XXXX
    3.8    3  'XXX
    3.9    1  'X
    4.0    4  'XXXX
    4.1    2  'XX
    4.2    2  'XX
GT. MAX    9  '..........

NO. OF RESULTS WITHIN HISTOGRAM LIMITS = 232
ASTERISKS OCCUR WHERE THERE IS INSUFFICIENT SPACE
```

FIGURE 2. An example of the printout of histogram for a particular determination. Each cross ($\times$) represents a result from a participating laboratory. A dot (.) also represents a result but one which is outside ± 2SD of the mean.

The computer disc file contains information regarding the analytical methods in use in the participating laboratories for each determination and the results are classified according to the methods in use. These are presented as statistical summaries. Only results used in the calculation of the recalculated mean are included. The mean, standard deviation, and coefficient of variation of the results of each method are calculated and a summary is typed and included in the report received by each participant. Table 1 illustrates the format used for the presentation of the results according to analytical method, calcium is used as an example.

TABLE I. *An example of the information provided to participants regarding the results obtained by laboratories using different methods*

Analytical method	Auto-Analyser reduction	Auto-Analyser glucose oxidase	Manual: folin and Wu	Manual: other copper reduction	Manual: glucose oxidase
No. of values	148	40	19	19	59
Mean	110·64	114·30	114·47	116·68	113·13
SD	9·02	10·18	13·82	11·77	10·20
CV	7·48	8·90	12·07	10·99	9·01

CALCULATION OF THE VARIANCE INDEX

If external quality control schemes are to play a part in improving the performance of the participating laboratories then certain objectives are essential.

The over-all performance of individual laboratories must be communicated to those laboratories as simply as possible. It is the laboratories which need most help which have the greatest difficulties in interpreting complex statistical calculations.

The performance of individual laboratories should be compared with the performance of all participating laboratories. This means that all laboratories should know what the best laboratories are capable of. Mere declaration of the percentage of laboratories achieving results within a certain acceptable coefficient of variance does not communicate such information. Performance in any individual laboratory and in all laboratories taking part in a scheme will alter with time, knowledge of the magnitude of such changes is also important.

Laboratories in External Quality Control schemes should be provided with information indicating quantitative relations of performance of individual laboratories to methods, apparatus, workload, staffing, etc.

It is for these reasons that the variance index was devised; its calculation and use is described in detail.

CALCULATION OF THE VARIANCE INDEX (VI)

The VI is calculated on the results obtained from the participating laboratories for a particular determination. First, the mean value obtained by laboratories using the same method is calculated. Previously the type of analytical methods used by participants for

individual determinations have been classified and those using the
same or similar methods are grouped together for calculation of the
method mean. The participant is required to agree to such classification. For some determinations participants may use methods which
cannot be classified in this way and their results cannot be used in
VI calculations. More than 90 per cent of the 420 participating
laboratories use methods which can be used for VI calculations.

The calculation only uses those values which fall within the mean
$\pm 3s$ for all results returned by participants. This is to avoid incorporating results which are random mistakes, such as those occurring in clerical transcription into the method mean calculation and
thus falsely distorting the value.

The method mean $(\bar{x}_m)$ is subtracted from the result of an individual laboratory (x) and the percentage variation from the method
mean calculated.

$$\% \text{ Variation} = V = \frac{x - \bar{x}_m}{x_m} \times 100 \text{ (The sign is ignored)}.$$

The VI is calculated from this figure by dividing it by the chosen
coefficient of variation (CCV) given in Table 2. To avoid decimal
points this figure is multiplied by 100.

$$\text{Variance Index} = VI = \frac{V}{CVV} \times 100.$$

Obviously, the lower the VI, the closer the result is to be method
mean. The CCV values shown in Table 2 are the lowest CVs obtained for particular determinations during the first two years of the
scheme. They are kept constant so that improvements in the performance of laboratories can be detected.

Because the coefficient of variation and not standard deviation is
used in the calculation of VI when the mean value falls outside the
limits listed in Table 3 the VI is not calculated. It is particularly
important to avoid VI calculations on low mean values for serum
determinations with a high variance such as bilirubin, alkaline phosphatase, and iron.

A formal definition of variance index is 'the difference between
the result obtained by a participant and the calculated method mean
expressed as a percentage of the mean, divided by a chosen coefficient of variation for that determination; the resultant figure is multiplied by 100'.

TABLE 2. *Chosen coefficient of variation used in VI calculations*

Determination	Coefficient of variation (%)	Determination	Coefficient of variation (%)
Sodium	1·6	Uric acid	7·7
Potassium	2·9	Creatinine	8·9
Chloride	2·2	Bilirubin	19·2
Urea	5·7	Total protein	3·9
Glucose	7·7	Albumin	7·5
Calcium	4·0	Alkaline	
Phosphorus	7·8	phosphatase	19·6
Iron	15·0	Cholesterol	7·6

TABLE 3. *Range of values used in the VI calculation*

Determination	Low	High	Units
Sodium	110·0	160·0	m mol/l
Potassium	1·5	8·0	m mol/l
Chloride	65·0	130·0	m mol/l
Urea	2·5	66·7	m mol/l
Glucose	0·8	22·2	m mol/l
Calcium	1·0	4·0	m mol/l
Phosphorus	0·6	3·9	m mol/l
Iron	3·6	53·6	μ mol/l
Urate	179·0	893·0	μ mol/l
Creatinine	62·0	1770·0	μ mol/l
Bilirubin	9·0	342·0	μ mol/l
Total protein	40·0	100·0	g/l
Albumin	15·0	60·0	g/l
Alkaline phosphatase	6·0	100·0	KA units/100 ml
Cholesterol	1·3	12·9	m mol/l

TABLE 4. *Running over-all mean VIS for laboratories with different workloads (the figures in brackets are the number of tests performed each year)*

All laboratories	73·6	Size 3 (101–185,000)	66·8
Size 1 (50,000)	91·5	Size 4 (185,000)	60·6
Size 2 (50–100,000)	70·9		

VARIANCE INDEX SCORE (VIS)

The performance of an individual laboratory in several analyses of different material for the same substance may be expressed as the mean variance index. In the UKNQCS we use the term variance index score (VIS) because when VI value for a particular result is less than 50 it contributes a nil score; this is to give encouragement to those laboratories whose results are closest to the mean. To avoid incorporating high VI values in the score, possibly due to a clerical error, VI values greater than 400 are treated as 400.

The mean VIS may be calculated for different determinations and several distributions, the resultant calculation is *the over-all variance index score*. In practice it has been found useful to calculate the *'running' over-all variance index score*. In this the over-all variance index score for the most recent forty analyses is calculated. Where the score for more recent results are added, the appropriate number of the earliest results are dropped out of the calculation.

The calculation of VI is illustrated graphically in Fig. 6.

Fig. 3 shows the results for all participants, the mean value is 7·72 m mol/l and the SD ±0·7 m mol/l. All values outside the mean ±2 SD, this is below 6·3 m mol/l and above 9·4 m mol/l, are ex-

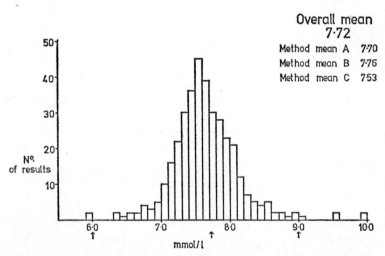

FIGURE 3. A histogram of all the results obtained from the determination of urea for one distribution. The over-all urea and the mean for these different methods are also given.

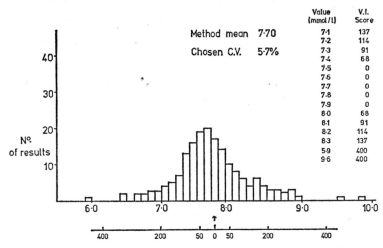

FIGURE 4. The results for a particular analytical method showing the values associated with the VIS.

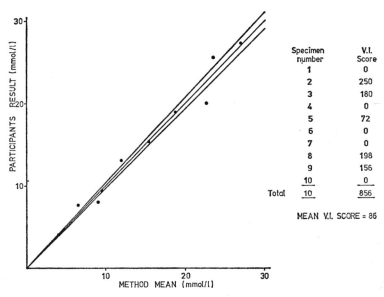

FIGURE 5. An example of a participants' results for several distributions of material. The calculation of the mean VIS is shown.

cluded from the method mean. The three methods each give slightly
different method means. The calculations of the VI for the laboratories using Method A with a chosen CV of 5·7 per cent is shown in
Fig. 4.

Fig. 5 illustrates the calculations of mean VI score for a number
of results (10) for an individual laboratory. Results which lie within
the 5·7 per cent CV limits (specimen nos. 1, 4, 6, 7, and 10) have a
nil score, others score according to their distance from the method
mean.

RUNNING VARIANCE INDEX SCORE

Figs. 6 to 9 illustrate the running VI score graphs which are drawn
on the computer graph plotter.

Each square represents a distribution of serum which was used for
calculation of running VI score. The graphs involve a period of two
years. A break in the graph indicates that a laboratory did not return
a result for that particular determination.

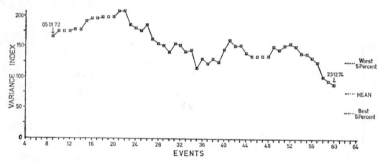

FIGURE 6. Example of the running variance index score computer print-
out.

The worst 5 per cent and best 5 per cent lines delineate the area in
which 90 per cent of laboratories have their VIS.

Fig. 6 illustrates the results from a laboratory where performance
was poor for the first six months of the period, gradually improved
in the next six months, remained static as regards performance in
the next six months, and then dramatically improved within the last
few weeks.

Fig. 7 shows the results from a laboratory with a very consistent
performance kept up over a period of two years.

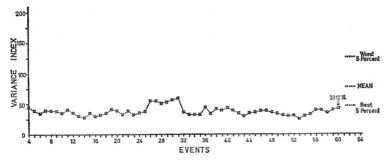

FIGURE 7. For comment, see text.

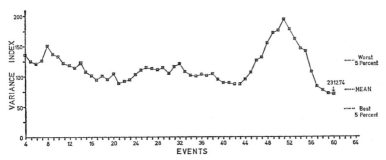

FIGURE 8. For comment, see text.

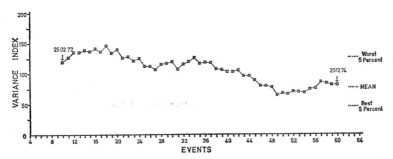

FIGURE 9. For comment, see text.

Fig. 8 shows the results from a laboratory which had an average performance which dramatically deteriorated over a period of a few weeks due to staff difficulties and then improved when these problems had been solved.

Fig. 9 is a typical running VIS graph.

Throughout the scheme it has been shown that the laboratories with the smallest workload have the highest VIS. The current mean values for various levels of workload are shown in Table 4. There is good evidence that those laboratories making extensive use of automatic methods of analysis have the lowest VIS. Smaller laboratories using more manual methods are less precise.

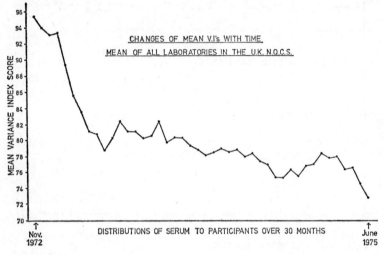

FIGURE 10

The mean VIS has significantly fallen during the last three years from a value of 93 to a current value of 73 (see Fig. 10). This has been associated with a decrease in the use of manual methods and an increase in the use of automatic methods of analysis. Tables 5 and 6 illustrate this point for the detection of cholesterol and uric acid.

TABLE 5. *The changes in the methods used. The determination of serum cholesterol, 1971–4*

Year	Auto-Analyser AAI	AII	Manual L. Burch	Manual ZAK	Others
1971	43 (16%)		93 (34%)	49 (18%)	86 (32%)
1972	48 (17%)		98 (35%)	52 (18%)	86 (30%)
1973	87 (30%)	32 (11%)	80 (27%)	25 (9%)	68 (23%)
1974	94 (32%)	37 (13%)	76 (26%)	19 (7%)	66 (23%)

TABLE 6. *The changes in the methods used for the determination of serum uric acid, 1971–4*

Year	Auto-Analyser AAI	AII	Manual cholesterol	Manual uricase	Others
1970	101 (41%)		109 (44%)	29 (12%)	7 (3%)
1971	112 (42%)		123 (46%)	26 (10%)	5 (2%)
1972	120 (44%)		120 (44%)	26 (10%)	5 (2%)
1973	137 (49%)	37 (13%)	83 (30%)	12 (4%)	8 (3%)
1974	142 (49%)	49 (17%)	76 (26%)	11 (4%)	9 (3%)

In the UKNQCS, at intervals, a table of the type illustrated in Table 7 is distributed to individual laboratories. It shows the VIS for the individual determinations and the mean VIS for each determination for all laboratories.

TABLE 7. *Example of results of a participating laboratory showing the VIS for individual determinations compared with the mean VIS for all participating laboratories*

Determination	No. of possible results	No. of results returned	Mean VIS	Mean VI for all laboratories
Sodium	34	34	46	86
Potassium	29	28	42	88
Chloride	20	11	61	80
Urea	34	34	21	79
Glucose	33	33	21	85
Calcium	34	34	45	78
Phosphate	34	32	33	75
Iron	20	19	90	77
Uric acid	33	33	28	79
Creatinine	32	32	51	98
Bilirubin	31	23	25	96
Total protein	33	31	47	75
Albumin	33	33	17	79
Alkaline phosphatase	28	26	38	79
Cholesterol	33	32	56	88

In this way participants can judge which determinations are making significant contributions to their over-all VI score.

FREQUENCY OF DISTRIBUTION

Running VIS graphs and other VI calculations are most useful when distributions are frequent. Table 8 shows for individual determinations the number of times distributions were made in 1974.

TABLE 8. *The number of distributions made by the United Kingdom National Quality Control Scheme in 1974*

Determination	No. of times material was distributed in 1974
Serum sodium	11
Potassium	11
Chloride	11
Urea	11
Glucose	11
Calcium	11
Phosphate	11
Iron	11
Uric acid	10
Creatinine	10
Bilirubin	10
Total protein	10
Albumin	10
Alkaline phosphatase	10
Cholesterol	10
Blood lead	8
Serum pH: P_{CO_2}	1
Standard bicarbonate	1
Serum asparate amino transferase	2
Buffer solution for pH measurement	1
Total	171

Discussion

A decision on acceptability of performance in the scheme has not been made. Many laboratories have shown that over a period of several years they can maintain an over-all running VIS of less than 40. This is not necessarily 'acceptable' but it does show what is possible. In contrast, there are laboratories which have had over-all running VIS of over 150 for several months.

With the help of a small Working Party of clinical chemists based upon the Standards and Quality Control Sub-Group of the Laboratory Development Advisory Group of the DHSS, the results of all laboratories in the scheme were considered in 1973. In the examination of running over-all VIS graphs for each laboratory, the Group identified several laboratories whose VIS was greater than 150 and who had been at such a level for a period of several months without any indication of improvement. The author wrote to twelve such laboratories. Anonymity was not affected as the letter was addressed to a laboratory number and labelled by the computer staff. The letter offered help in improving performance. The eleven laboratories which replied improved their performance by reconsidering their methods.

The reasons why certain laboratories have better performances than others whilst using the same analytical methods is still obscure and the Nuffield Provincial Hospitals Trust is financing a survey of clinical chemistry departments in various parts of the country to assess the factors which contribute to good performance in the UKNQCS.

In many countries the results of external quality control surveys are used for assessing laboratories for licensing. This is the usual situation in the USA. In the German Federal Republic the Medical Board has legally instituted quality control of clinical laboratory results and requires that laboratories have certain basic equipment, perform internal quality control checks, and also take part in four external quality control checks a year.

In the UK there are no such regulations. The approval of laboratories by the Royal College of Pathologists for training purposes includes an inspection procedure and the use of quality control methods by laboratories is usually scrutinized at such times.

The use of external quality control systems for licensing purposes has the following advantages:

It ensures that all clinical laboratories performing routine work on patients take part in the scheme. Voluntary schemes cannot ensure this.

It ensures that some action, for example, closure of a laboratory, can follow the demonstration of bad performance, in this it protects the patient against poorly performing laboratories.

It helps to ensure that laboratories employ properly qualified personnel.

It gives laboratories acceptability targets.

The disadvantages include the following.

It may tend to destroy any educational aspects of the schemes. Such activity by the organizers will be made more difficult by the official licensing action.

Meeting acceptability criteria may reduce a desire for further improvement in laboratory performance.

The operation of such schemes almost always involves a bureaucratic machinery and this is a poor weapon with which to control professional conduct. Many would argue that professional bodies should be responsible for the professional activities of their members.

In the UK we are now proposing that the professional bodies such as the Royal College of Pathologists and the Association of Clinical Biochemists should be involved in communicating with and helping the poorly performing laboratories. We do not plan to use legislation for licensing purposes. However, the vast majority of clinical laboratories are financed by the DHSS and, therefore, the situation is different from countries with large private sectors.

Anonymity in the scheme has been the subject of much discussion.

The strict anonymity of the UKNQCS was used in 1969 to encourage laboratories to take part. In retrospect it would have been better if the code had been held by a small committee of clinical chemists who could have taken direct action on evidence of poor performance. There is good reason to believe that all laboratories would now accept this, though completely open declaration of the performance of all laboratories would not be accepted.

This scheme has become an integral part of quality control in clinical chemistry laboratories in the UK and has been copied by many other countries. General expansion and particularly exploitation of the educational potential of the scheme is planned by the DHSS.

Such extension of the scheme would involve surveying a wider group of analytical substances and at varying levels in order to carry out the surveys at the levels found in routine practice. Extension of the educative role would involve more detailed analysis of results according to methods and instrumentation.

ACKNOWLEDGEMENTS

This work would not have been possible without the organizing ability of David Browning. Anne Gregory was responsible for the computer programmes. Margaret Peters, Drs Buttolph, Kenny, and Wilding, Mr Desmond Neale and Professor H. J. Wilkinson have given freely of their time to advise the Scheme. The work was made possible by a grant from the Department of Health and Social Security.

6

The role of the autopsy
in medical care

TONY WALDRON
BSc, MB, ChB, PhD
Lecturer in Social Medicine

LORNA VICKERSTAFF
BA
Research Associate
University of Birmingham

The role of the autopsy
in medical care

Introduction

Until comparatively recently the autopsy occupied a dominant role in both the teaching and the practice of medicine. Although it may be inferred that some of the ancient civilizations had a familiarity with anatomical and pathological structure, it was not until the seventeenth century that post-mortem examinations began to be performed with any regularity and then, mainly, for anatomical or medico-legal purposes (1). The forerunner of the clinico-pathological conference was instituted by Theophilus Bonet, who published his compendium of post-mortem investigations, *Sepulcretum anatomicum, seu anatome practica* in Geneva in 1679, but it was the great Morgagini who is generally considered as the founder of pathology. His book, *De sedibus et causis morborum*, published in 1761 in his eightieth year, provided the model for those who followed and developed the study of the subject. During the nineteenth century, first France, in the persons of Bichat, Laennec, and Louis and then Germany, through Frank, Rokitansky, and Virchow, made pathology the vehicle through which medical progress was made. The process whereby clinical signs and symptoms were later correlated with findings at autopsy was developed by the physicians of the first Paris school and copied as the epitome of sound medical practice. In the Vienna of the late nineteenth century, the fortunate patient was said to be the one who had had his diagnosis made by Skoda and confirmed, after death, by Rokitansky.

The decline in the importance which was formerly attached to the autopsy appears to be related in large measure to the rise in medical technology. Physicians now have at their disposal means for assessing pathological lesions *in vivo* and so, in many cases, are able to confirm their diagnosis before the need for an autopsy arises. Advances in microscopy and biochemistry have resulted in increasing attention being paid to cellular and sub-cellular aberrations, and to alterations in body chemistry as means of explaining disease states and causes of death and correspondingly less to gross anatomical change, the delineation of which is the forte of the autopsy. A number of authors has supposed that it is this change of emphasis which has led to the decline in the post-mortem rate and to the decline in the use of the autopsy as a teaching instrument (2).

The decline in the autopsy rate has not been allowed to go un-challenged, however, and there have been many voices raised in lament. The argument most often put forward for reversing the downward trend is summarized succinctly by Hasson and Gross (3) whose contention is that *post-mortem examination provides the ulti-mate control in the self appraisal of a doctor's diagnostic and therapeutic ability*. In this view, the autopsy still has a key role to play in the medical audit and it is a view which has much support mainly from physicians and pathologists in America (4–8). Others, for example Angrist (5) and Gall (9), have emphasized the importance of the post-mortem examination as a method for discovering previously unsuspected disease entities. Gall's short list of recent discoveries attributable to autopsy is shown as Table 1.

TABLE 1. *Partial list of recent discoveries attributable to necropsy**

The carotid artery syndrome in strokes
Rheumatoid disease of the aorta and aortic valve
Scleroderma kidney
Kwashiorkor
. Veno-occlusive disease
Protein-losing enteropathy
Protein loss from villous adenoma and carcinoma of the colon
Chloride loss with gastric mucosal hypertrophy (Menetrier's disease)
Aldosteronism
Gastric perforation from congenital muscular defects of the stomach
Zollinger-Ellison syndrome

---

*Taken from Gall (11).

The autopsy lobby may be vociferous but there is no evidence to suggest that it is having its desired effect, that is, to increase the number of autopsies which are being performed. Few people have spoken out in favour of the decline, although the prediction which

Paton (10) has made, that post-mortem examinations will disappear from hospital practice and come to be confined to the teaching of students and specialists, may represent the most realistic assessment of the situation if the decline is allowed to continue unabated.

The study with which we have been involved has as its basis an assessment of the value of the autopsy in patient care and falls into three more or less distinct phases. In the first we examined the trend in autopsy rates in the teaching hospitals in Birmingham and in the second we have analysed the attitude of the clinicians in the West Midlands and Trent regions to the autopsy. The third phase of the study is a prospective study to see what level of agreement there is between ante-mortem and post-mortem diagnoses. This study is on-going in both the West Midlands and Trent regions and a parallel investigation is being conducted by Dr Hector Cameron in Edin-burgh.

Autopsy rates in the United Birmingham Hospitals

We have been able to show (11) that there has been a considerable decline in the autopsy rate in the teaching hospitals in Birmingham. In 1958 the over-all rate was 74·4 per cent whereas by 1972 it had fallen to 46·0 per cent. Even so, these figures are substantially higher than the rate for the West Midlands region as a whole (which was 27·3 per cent in 1972) or the national rate (approximately equal to

TABLE 2. *Percentage of autopsies recorded in standard regions of England and Wales, 1967**

	M	F	Total
South-East	36·6	30·0	33·3
East Midlands	32·2	27·1	29·8
West Midlands	33·3	25·3	29·5
Yorks and Humberside	31·4	24·1	27·9
East Anglia	30·1	22·3	26·3
Wales 1 (South-East)	35·1	13·6	25·5
North-West	28·8	20·4	24·8
North	29·6	17·2	23·9
South-West	25·5	19·6	22·6
Wales 2 (remainder)	26·8	15·4	20·5

*Based on data in reference 12.

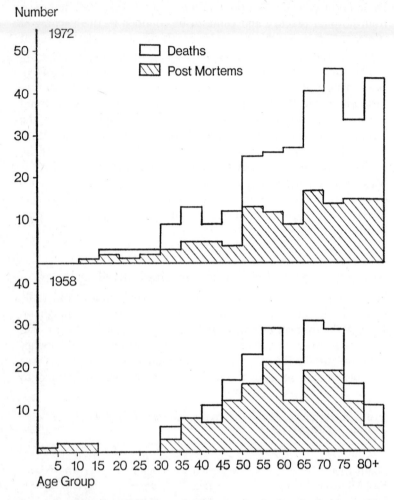

FIGURE I. Number of deaths and post-mortems in females by age-group, Queen Elizabeth Hospital, 1958 and 1972.

the West Midlands regional rate). The national rate, however, conceals within it a considerable variation as between different regions. In Table 2 we have summarized the findings of a special survey reported by the Registrar General (12). The over-all rates are arranged in descending order, but even within regions there is often

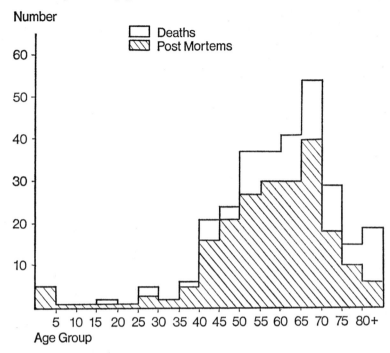

FIGURE 2. Number of deaths and post-mortems in males by age-group, Queen Elizabeth Hospital, 1958.

a marked difference between the rates for males and females. It is understandable that over-all regional rates will vary, since services and resources are not evenly spread throughout the country, but it is less easy to see why the rate should vary with sex. In the Birmingham teaching hospitals we also find that the autopsy rate in females is lower than in males, but by only a slight degree.

The decline in the autopsy rate may largely be explained by a reduction in post-mortem examinations performed in the older age-groups. In Figs. 1–3 we have compared the age-specific rates in males and females in the Queen Elizabeth Hospital in the years at the extreme ends of the period we studied, that is, 1958 and 1972, where the decline in the number of autopsies in the older age-groups is very marked. A similar pattern can be shown for the General Hospital.

Number

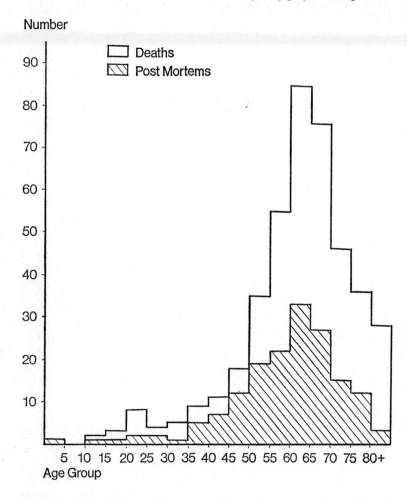

FIGURE 3. Number of deaths and post-mortems in males by age-group, Queen Elizabeth Hospital, 1972.

At the Birmingham Children's Hospital, the rate has dropped most noticeably in the 0–1 year age-group (Fig. 4), although, in this instance, there is now a higher rate in girls than in boys (55·7 per cent compared with 48·8 per cent in 1972).

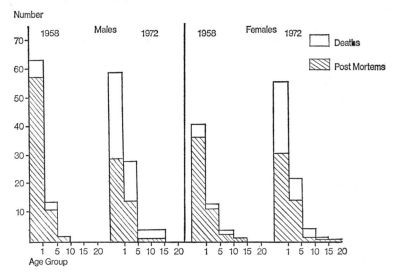

FIGURE 4. Number of deaths and post-mortems by age-group, Birmingham Children's Hospital.

Clinical attitude to the autopsy

The decision to perform an autopsy in hospital depends very largely upon the clinician in charge of the case making a request for the examination, the main exception to this rule being in those cases where the death is reported to the coroner. It is a reasonable *a priori* assumption that the decreased number of autopsies which are now being performed must be due in some way, and in some part at least, to the attitudes of clinicians to the autopsy and we have set out to examine this assumption by means of a questionnaire.

The questionnaire was sent to all the clinicians in the West Midlands Region and also in the Trent Region. A total of 528 questionnaires was sent out to clinicians in the West Midlands and 301 to those in the Trent Region. Of these 321 (60·8 per cent) and 167 (55·5 per cent) were respectively returned.

We attached particular importance to four of the sections in the questionnaire and the response to these is shown in Table 3. From the table it will be seen that about three-quarters of the clinicians still consider that the autopsy has an important part to play in their own practice. This percentage is constant in both regions, and in the

TABLE 3. *Percentage of consultants answering 'yes' to some key sections in the questionnaire*

	West Midlands			Trent		
	Medical	Surgical	Total	Medical	Surgical	Total
Do you think the post-mortem has an important part to play in your clinical practice?	76·4	73·9	75·2	84·5	69·5	76·6
Ideally would you like to see a post-mortem in every case?	60·1	55·9	57·9	57·1	52·4	54·5
Do you think it is a matter of concern that the post-mortem rate is declining?	76·7	68·3	71·5	79·8	64·6	71·8
Do you think the post-mortem has an important part to play in student teaching?	96·7	92·3	94·6	96·2	92·0	94·1

West Midlands is approximately the same for clinicians in both surgical and medical specialities. In the Trent Region, a higher proportion of clinicians in medical specialities answered in the affirmative than those in surgical specialities. In supplementary questions, it was possible to show that virtually all the clinicians in both regions found that autopsy findings caused them to change their ante-mortem diagnosis, 38 per cent saying that this happened in 5 per cent or more of cases. Fifty-nine per cent replied that the post-mortem revealed conditions unsuspected before death in 5 per cent or more cases. Many clinicians reported that post-mortem findings resulted in a modification of treatment in subsequent patients, 30 per cent stating that this was so with 5 per cent or more of their cases.

For the great majority of clinicians the post-mortem fulfils three purposes. To confirm the ante-mortem diagnosis, to supply a diagnosis where this is not known and to give information on the immediate cause of death. On the latter point, however, it is clear that other investigations are relied on to an equal or greater extent, those most favoured including a variety of biochemical tests, cardiography, radiography, and other clinical investigations.

Despite the importance which they obviously attach to the autopsy, only a slight majority of clinicians would wish to see a post-mortem examination conducted on each patient who dies in hospital (Table 3). Further questioning, however, revealed that only 40 per cent encourage their junior staff to ask for an autopsy in all cases. Reference to Table 3 shows that almost three-quarters of the clinicians view the declining rate as a matter for concern and so it is curious that a greater proportion do not encourage their junior staff to seek permission to conduct an autopsy on all their patients who die, since this might be expected to halt, or even reverse, the trend.

When asked why they consider the autopsy rate is declining, about a third of the clinicians gave as the reason, a greater confidence in the accuracy of the ante-mortem diagnosis, and a fifth that there has been a change in attitude amongst younger members of the profession. A third of the replies indicated that relatives were reluctant to give permission for the examination or became so distressed when the suggestion was made, that the clinician hesitated to press his request. Because of this alleged difficulty with relatives, one or two clinicians were in favour of a return to the system whereby it was not necessary to obtain permission to perform an autopsy. In Sweden this system pertains and the autopsy rate is high. The over-all rate is 44 per cent and in some cities much higher: in Stockholm, Gothenburg, and Malmo, 79, 77, and 88 per cent respectively in 1967. A study was undertaken (13) in Sweden to see whether relatives would refuse permission if they were asked, and it was found that only 6 per cent objected to the performance of an autopsy and hence the rate would be unlikely to decline if permission were to be required. Of course, it may be that the results of this relatively small trial, conducted for one year and involving 297 deaths, is an unsuitable sample for comparison with the general experiences in this country. One criticism of British practice, however, is that it is most often a junior member of the staff who actually has the task of seeking permission from relatives and he may often feel that he has too little experience to cope with the situation. An approach from the clinician in charge of the case might conceivably result in a more favourable reaction from relatives. One surgical consultant in the West Midlands commented that he personally sees the relatives of all the patients who die whilst in his care, and that none has ever refused his request for an autopsy. The results from a series of one are never conclusive, but, nevertheless, this example does point the moral for others.

A substantial minority of clinicians was inclined to lay the blame for the declining autopsy rate upon the shoulders of the pathologists and there were a variety of grievances expressed against the service provided by the departments of pathology. The most often voiced complaint was that post-mortems were held at times which were inconvenient for the clinicians and this was the reason they gave most often for their non-attendance at the autopsy of their patients. Some clinicians remarked that they would attend autopsies if they were informed of the time and date of the examination, but that liaison between themselves and the pathologists was not sufficiently well developed to permit for this to happen.

Other specific complaints were that the post-mortem examination was not of a sufficiently high quality always to allow for a final diagnosis of the cause of death to be made; that information was unreliable; that results of histological examination were long delayed or that the results of the autopsy were not made known to the clinician. Some clinicians found conditions in the post-mortem room poor; yet others felt that the effort and expense of the post-mortem could not be justified by the results which were obtained.

We are not able to present any rebuttal to these views on behalf of the pathologists since we have not involved them directly in the study. No doubt they would be able to lay counter arguments of their own and it is more than likely that if there really is a lack of communication, it is not due solely to the deficiencies of the pathologists. This is an area which might well profit from further investigations, because if there is a problem which can be defined, then its resolution should result in an improved service, assuming this to be the will of both parties.

Those clinicians who had teaching responsibilities were asked whether they considered that the post-mortem had an important part to play in the training of students and virtually all replied that it did (see Table 3), and most clinicians expected the students on

TABLE 4. *Percentage of consultants answering 'yes' to the four key questions, according to year of qualification*

	Year of qualification											
	1930-9			1940-9			1950-9			1960-9		
	WM	T	Total	WM	T	Total	WM	T	Total	WM	T	Total
Do you think the post-mortem has an important part to play in your clinical practice?	73·6	76·5	74·3	77·4	80·4	78·9	76·5	79·7	77·8	63·9	75·9	75·6
Ideally would you like to see a post-mortem in every case?	52·8	47·1	51·4	58·2	58·8	58·4	60·0	54·2	57·7	57·1	79·3	65·4
Do you think it is a matter of concern that the post-mortem rate is declining?	73·8	76·5	72·8	75·4	66·0	69·8	74·5	69·5	71·8	71·4	72·4	71·8
Do you think the post-mortem has an important part to play in student teaching?	93·0	77·8	89·5	93·4	96·8	94·7	95·5	93·1	94·9	95·8	95·8	95·8

their firms to attend all the post-mortems conducted on their cases.

One of the reasons which was given for the decline in the autopsy rate was that there had been a change in attitude towards the post-mortem on the part of the profession. Accordingly, we have looked to see whether the response to the key questions in the survey shows any variation with year of qualification (see Table 4).Generally clinicians seem to be consistent in their views regardless of when they qualified, with the exception that a higher proportion of the most recently qualified clinicians would prefer a post-mortem on all cases than those qualifying earlier. This difference is especially marked in the Trent Region.

The results on this part of our study indicate that despite whatever subjective impressions are current concerning the value attached to the autopsy, a substantial majority of clinicians consider it to be important to their practice and thus, one may infer, to the quality of medical care which their patients receive. Most also regret the decline in the autopsy rate.

This being so, it seems appropriate that clinicians should take positive steps to see how the trend could be reversed. This will, of necessity, require the active co-operation of the pathologists in some sort of evaluation of services and facilities: a high autopsy rate will not be achieved if there is no manpower available or if the mortuary and the post-mortem room are too small to cope with the demand. If services are to be improved, do the benefits which might be expected justify the expenditure of central funds for which there is already too great a demand?

Prospective study

In conducting our pilot study in the Birmingham teaching hospitals, we made an assessment of the degree to which the ante-mortem and

TABLE 5. *Percentage disagreement between ante-mortem and post-mortem diagnoses in two Birmingham teaching hospitals*

Year	Males	Females	Total
		Percentage disagreement	
1959	18	21	20
1964	19	29	23
1968	19	28	22
1972	20	25	22

post-mortem diagnoses were in disagreement. To do this we compared the clinical diagnosis given in the patient's notes with the post-mortem results as shown in the autopsy records. The study was confined to the Queen Elizabeth and General Hospitals and the results for four separate years are shown in Table 5. In about a fifth of all cases the ante-mortem and post-mortem diagnoses disagreed. There is nothing novel about this finding and, indeed, this is a lower rate of disagreement than has been found by some other authors (14). In most studies of this problem, however, no differentiation is made between those cases in which the correct diagnosis would have resulted in different (and perhaps successful) treatment and those in which the disagreement is of academic interest only. The study of Adler and de Morgan (15) did make such a distinction and in only 5 per cent of cases did they consider that the autopsy revealed a condition which, had it been diagnosed in life, would have changed the treatment which the patient received. On the other hand, Bauer and Robbins (16), considered that 15·6 per cent of patients dying from cancer died without the diagnosis having been made. Diagnostic errors of one kind or another were made in a third of all patients dying from cancer. It is implicit from their article, but not stated explicitly, that the treatment of some of these patients would have been different had the correct diagnosis been made.

Most of the reports concerning the difference between ante-mortem and post-mortem diagnoses have been retrospective. We have in hand a prospective study which is using as a model the method employed by Heasman and Lipworth (17). We have asked clinicians and pathologists in hospitals within the West Midlands and Trent regions and in Edinburgh to complete forms, similar to the standard death certificate, in the case of each patient who comes to autopsy. The clinician completes the first part of the form, giving primary and secondary causes of death before post-mortem information is to hand. The pathologist fills in the second part giving his causes of death, and then the forms are returned to us. We plan to run the study for one year. When analysing the results, we shall separate trivial from significant differences in diagnosis and we hope to arrive at some reasonable estimate of the percentage of deaths in which the autopsy reveals conditions which might have been amenable to treatment. If this should prove to be a substantial proportion, then this will strengthen the argument of those who see the autopsy as a major factor in medical audit.

ACKNOWLEDGEMENTS

We are most grateful to the clinicians who replied to our questionnaire and to those clinicians and pathologists who are so kindly participating in our prospective study.

References

1. SPIRO, R. K. (1971). *Int. Surgery*, 56, 27–40, 101–12.
2. *Br. med. J.* (1971), 2, 181–2.
3. HASSON, J., and GROSS, H. (1974). *Am. J. Med.* 56, 137–40.
4. PRUTTING, J. M. (1968). *Bull. N.Y. Acad. Med.* 44, 793–8.
5. ANGRIST, A. (1968). Ibid. 44, 830–42.
6. LUDWIG, J. (1972). *Current Methods of Autopsy Practice*, pp. 307–13 (Pennsylvania: W. B. Saunders).
7. STEHBENS, W. E. (1974). *N.Z. Med. J.* 79, 637–41.
8. EBERT, R. V., PORTERFIELD, J. D., TRUMP, B. F., ANGEVINE, D. M., BLOODWORTH, J. M. B., and FORAKER, A. G. (1974). *Hum. Path.* 5, 605–18.
9. GALL, E. A. (1968). *Bull. N.Y. Acad. Med.* 44, 808–29.
10. PATON, A. (1972). *Br. med. J.* 3, 287.
11. WALDRON, H. A., and VICKERSTAFF, L. (1975). Ibid. 2, 326–8.
12. REGISTRAR GENERAL (1971). *Statistical Review of England and Wales for the year 1967, Part III*, pp. 84–96 (London: HMSO).
13. BRITTON, M. (1972). *Acta Socio-medica Scand.* 1, 37–58.
14. PRUTTING, J. (1972). *J. Am. med. Assoc.* 222, 1556–7.
15. HOLLER, J. W., and DE MORGAN, N. P. (1970). *J. Med. Educ.* 45, 168–70.
16. BAUER, F. W., and ROBBINS, S. L. (1972). *J. Am. med. Assoc.* 221, 1471–4.
17. HEASMAN, M. A., and LIPWORTH, L. (1966). *Accuracy of Certification of Cause of Death* (London: HMSO).

*Administrative
means*

7

Questions of quality arising at regional medical officer's level

JOHN REVANS
CBE, LLD, FRCP, HonFRCGP
Regional Medical Officer
Wessex Regional Health Authority

Questions of quality arising at regional medical officer's level

Introduction

This paper sets out the development of the assessment of quality of care within the context of rationalization and development in one of the regions in England from the inception of the National Health Service in 1948. Situated in central southern England it started as an area of a metropolitan regional hospital board. A decade later it acquired regional status and ten years after that a medical school was established at the University of Southampton.

It considers medical staff, their educational requirements, their responsibilities, how quality control operates in the Region, in its many facets and how reorganization has affected medical care in the Region.

DESCRIPTION OF THE REGION

The Wessex Regional Health Authority brought into being in the reorganization in 1974 serves a population of 2,666,400 (estimated June 1974) in the administrative counties of Dorset, Hampshire, the Isle of Wight, and Wiltshire. The main concentration of population is in the coastal fringe which includes Portsmouth, Southampton, and Bournemouth. There are over one million people in these towns and their surrounding areas. Its industries include shipping, oil refining, chemicals, cables, rubber, railway works, and agriculture. The Region, with its headquarters at Winchester, is now divided into four areas: Hampshire which is a teaching area with four districts: Southampton and SW Hampshire, Winchester and Central Hampshire, Basingstoke and North Hampshire, and Portsmouth and SE Hampshire; Dorset with two districts: West and East Dorset; Wiltshire with three districts: Salisbury, Swindon, and Bath; and the Isle of Wight which is a single district area.

IMPROVEMENT OF QUALITY BY RATIONALIZATION
AND DEVELOPMENT: 1948–67

The precursors of the regional health authority were the Wessex
Regional Hospital Board, and before that body was inaugurated in
1959, the Western Area Committee of the SW Metropolitan Regional
Hospital Board.

The hospitals taken over by the Western Area Committee in 1948
consisted of the voluntary hospitals which were situated in the major
towns and the local authority hospitals which had been utilized by
the emergency medical services during the Second World War. In
the smaller towns cottage hospitals were also available. The medical
staffing at the time consisted of a number of specialists who were
working wholly within their specialty, while a larger number undertook specialty work but were also involved in general practice. In the
smaller towns, particularly those centred in agricultural areas, a
number of good group practices flourished.

In the early years it was relatively easy administratively with
simple statistical information to distinguish the structural gaps in
services. Thus, in order to provide a comprehensive service for the
population in the area it was deemed necessary to improve and aug-
ment the general medical and surgical services in each of the general
groups and also develop those highly specialized regional services
which elsewhere are usually associated with university medical
departments. Since it was an early hope that a medical school would
eventually be established the location of the University of Southampton was a key factor in the Board's decision to locate its regional
services at Southampton. Departments of audiology, cardiac and
thoracic surgery, medical physics, neurology and neurosurgery,
nuclear medicine, oncology, paediatric surgery, radiotherapy, and
the regional blood transfusion centre have now been established.
The regional plastic and oral surgical department had to be located
at Salisbury and the renal unit was developed at Portsmouth
where research into kidney function had been carried out for
many years. In fostering the development of these services the
Region made a positive acknowledgement that these units were to be
centres of excellence and had a considerable bearing on the quality
of care which would develop in the area. Before these units were
established it was necessary to transfer patients for specialized treatment to units in London, Oxford, or Bristol. In 1959, when the area
had become virtually independent of outside assistance, the Area

Committee were afforded regional status and the Wessex Regional Hospital Board was created. This Region was unique in that it had then no undergraduate teaching hospital within its boundaries. It retained links with St George's, St Thomas's, and the Westminster Hospitals in London, but distance made these links tenuous.

The Board, and indeed its predecessor the Western Area Committee, had long foreseen the necessity for close links with the University of Southampton for the following reasons which have a strong bearing on quality:

1. The high quality scientific support required by the regional services.

2. The academic contribution that should be given to medical research in the Region.

3. The requirements of postgraduate education.

4. The anticipation that a medical school would be established as part of the further development of the University.

The links between the Region and the University were forged in the co-operation both in service and research projects, particularly in radiotherapy, nuclear medicine, and in the Departments of Cardiac and Thoracic Surgery, with the University Department of Physiology and Biochemistry; between the University Department of Psychology and the Psychiatric Hospitals, and between the Audiology Research Unit and the Ear, Nose, and Throat Department of the Royal South Hants Hospital. The association was also begun between the Departments of Sociology and Social Administration at the University, and the Board itself to analyse manpower resources and examine existing employment practices.

If the quality of medical care is to be maintained then it is essential for medical staff to be kept up-to-date with developments in medicine. Not only must they participate both as teachers and students in medical education but it is for the management to ensure that adequate study leave both in this country and abroad is made available to them.

Normally the stimulus for postgraduate education in any region emanates from the regional medical school. In the absence of such a school in Wessex, the Board, with co-operation from the University of Southampton, and with the stimulus and financial assistance of the Nuffield Provincial Hospitals Trust immediately following the 1961 Christ Church conference laid a sound foundation for post-

graduate activities, the onset of which was marked by the opening
of the first new Postgraduate Medical Centre in this country in
Portsmouth in December 1962. By the middle of 1966 each and
every Group had its own postgraduate medical centre and flourishing
training programme. These covered general vocational training,
special vocational training (including the Basic Sciences Courses
covering the Primary FFA, the Primary FRCS, and the Primary
FDS), continuing education for established doctors, a special training
scheme for the psychiatric services, and finally the medical education
for the GP, both in refresher courses for established GPs and, with
the encouragement of the Nuffield Provincial Hospitals Trust, a
special GP training scheme known as the Wessex Nuffield Practitioner Scheme in which selected doctors on completion of their pre-
registration period undertook a further two years' training to equip
them for general practice.

ESTABLISHMENT OF THE MEDICAL SCHOOL

In 1967 the Royal Commission on Medical Education recommended the Government to set up a medical school in Southampton.
This medical school is only the second to be established since 1893.
Its first students were admitted in October 1971, and they will
graduate in July 1976. The development of the school comes at a
time when the administrators of a regional service are conscious
that a number of key elements are undergoing change. First, the
place of the medical practitioner in society is under examination,
secondly, the health services are in the process of being reorganized,
and thirdly, medical education itself, like all other forms of education, is the subject of discussion and review. These factors have made
it possible in planning a curriculum in Southampton which will
move from the existing pattern of traditional medical education to
one which has the ability to introduce new concepts and a more
flexible approach to undergraduate teaching.

When proposals were originally made by the University and the
Regional Hospital Board the concept was for the school to be based
on the Region rather than on a single teaching district. Although the
University and the Southampton General and the Royal South
Hants Hospitals will be the centre for formal teaching, the total
clinical resources of the Region both in the community and the
hospitals will be available for teaching clinical studies. In addition,
all district general hospitals in the Region will, by 1977, be taking

and teaching pre-registration house officers as well as fourth- and fifth-year students. From the Region's point of view the increased research and teaching facilities in Southampton will be widely available to the whole medical profession within the Region. Generally students will be educated in an environment similar to that in which they will work in the future and will be trained with an understanding of primary care. The value of the regional consultant/student relationship will inevitably produce benefit to both teacher and student and thus raise the quality of care in the district general hospitals.

FINANCE

The quality of medical care as far as basic structure is concerned depends to a large extent on a base of adequate finance to regions.

Capital. The development of the plan for the Region has been as a result of a continuous review of facilities and services. There have been major developments in Southampton where a new teaching hospital and medical school are in the process of being built, with new hospitals at the new town of Basingstoke, at Poole, and Swindon. Major developments have also taken place at Portsmouth, Dorchester, and Weymouth and in the Isle of Wight. Recent developments have included day-hospitals and centres and five-day bed units for the investigation and treatment of patients. It is possible by the selection of patients suitable for day or five-day treatment units to reduce waiting-times. As far as community care is concerned there is a development programme for health centres. These centres with attachment schemes for nurses, health visitors, and social workers, and with access to hospitals for diagnostic services, point a way for improving medical care in the community.

Revenue. The distribution of revenue funds to regions is made by the DHSS and is often influenced by political decisions. Over the years a variety of formulas have been used to distribute revenue funds. Recently revenue distribution has been examined by a Departmental Working Party who in September 1975, produced their first interim report (Resources Allocation Working Party). Proposals in this Report show a new method of distributing revenue monies. If the recommendations are implemented by the Department the regions which now have the greatest shortages (Trent, East Anglia,

Wessex, and the West Midlands) will be favoured over the next decade. The shortfall to be made good for the Wessex Region is 5·37 per cent. With the present revenue funding of £130·8 million for the Region the shortfall is £7,024,000 which by any standards is a significant amount. It reflects the shortage on establishment on the four regions named above. Certainly the medical staffing of the Teaching Hospital in Southampton is far below that obtained in hospitals in London. The extent of the difference is brought out even more starkly by a comparison of the teaching and research allowance (for London teaching hospitals is £10,000 per student, for South-ampton Hospital £5,500). This demonstrates quite clearly that the redistribution of junior medical *staff* from the metropolitan teaching hospitals to the provincial regions has not yet been effected.

MEDICAL STAFF

Concomitant with the development of the Region since 1948 is the increase in the number of medical staff. It will, therefore, be of interest to compare the medical staff for 1975 with that given for 1948. The Regional Health Authority covers a larger area than the Regional Hospital Board and to ensure comparability the figures for the Bath and Swindon Districts have been omitted. They reveal the great increase shown in Table 1.

TABLE I

	No. in post	
	1948	*1975*
Consultants	113	530
SHMOs	16	9
Medical assistants		74
Senior registrars	16	88
Registrars	27	161
SHOs	69	253
HOs		45
Totals	241	1,165

In sessional time the increase was from 880 sessions in 1948 to 6,295 sessions in 1975 for all medical staff other than the training grades (that is senior registrars, registrars, senior house officers, and house officers).

Yet above all the strength of any medical care system depends upon the quality of the staff who provide the care. Bishop Mervyn Stockwood in making an attack on the General Synod of the Church of England in June 1972, said this about his clergy:

I cannot speak about canon law with authority as I do not possess a copy and have never read it. I assume that my clergy behave in a sensible way and automatically do the sensible thing without any direction from me or a book. The handful—and it is only a handful—who are 'cracked' will continue to do the stupid thing no matter what I or canon law direct or suggest. So I cut my losses and leave them to get on with it, realizing that while there is death there is hope.

This opinion of the clergy could be applied equally to the medical profession.

It is unfortunately true that a small minority of consultants find themselves the subject of disciplinary inquiries. Various administrative procedures can be applied.

First, there is one to protect patients from harm which might arise from the incapacity of medical staff due to their physical or mental disability. The procedure is set out in Circular HM(60)45. Briefly, it postulates the 'Three wise men' Sub-Committee of senior medical staff, who if they were unable to exercise their influence to prevent the possibility of any harm to patients, reported to the senior administrative medical officer. The weakness of the system in practice is the reluctance sometimes of the 'Three wise men' Sub-Committee to take effective action when a potentially harmful situation is known to them. On occasions there has been reluctance to communicate with the senior administrative medical officer.

Secondly, if the evidence was so overwhelming that action to suspend or dismiss the practitioner was evident then an inquiry would be set up under the provisions of Circular HM(61)112. This offers a much greater opportunity to review professional standards.

Thirdly, serious complaints by patients regarding their treatment by consultants may result in litigation and can only be resolved in the courts.

Fortunately the number of incidents in which incompetence is caused by medical practitioners taking drugs, including alcohol and anaesthetic gases, are limited, but there is ample machinery for dealing with them.

Quality of service and care

GENERAL

The great advances in the quality of services in the Region which was a relatively backward area in 1948 with a paucity of staff and facilities has been due to a large number of people in a variety of roles, the extent and value of which are not always obvious.

Medical care, however, is based on medical practice. It is, therefore, a basic principle that the better quality of medical staff that can be recruited the better the quality of care. An early objective was the recruitment of high-quality medical staff. Although in the early days there was no teaching hospital in the Region its location and its nearness to the metropolis were certainly incentives for recruitment. After the first decade the introduction of postgraduate medical education offered a further inducement for young senior registrars to apply for consultant appointments within the Region. It was recognized that morale was all-important in difficult circumstances. It was realized that extensive capital investment was unlikely but at the time of recruitment the assurance was given that adequate equipment would be made available to enable them to carry out their work and their research. Morale has on the whole been excellent. There is no doubt that the majority of consultants within the Region undertook greater responsibilities and longer hours than indicated in their 'open' contracts and the relationship between the administration and the consultants was a happy and profitable one.

The National Health Service has always been compared with industry but what is seldom appreciated is the difference between the NHS and an industrial organization. In industry policy is made at the top in the board room. In the NHS the policymaker, the consultant, is on the floor or executive level. Any theory of management regarding the NHS needs to take into account this antithesis, and the problem of quality control presents special and complex difficulties.

QUALITY CONTROL

Quality control is undertaken in a number of ways.

First, there are the positive procedures. Examples of this are the National Quality Control Scheme for Pathological Service and the Confidential Enquiry into Maternal Mortality. Although all hospitals in the Region participate in the first scheme it must be pointed out that it is a voluntary one and is confidential. As a result no-one (apart from the participating laboratory and its own results) knows what standards appertain in other laboratories. Management which has the task of providing and developing the pathological service has no information on the results of their financial investment. The Confidential Enquiry into Maternal Mortality is, again, a confidential inquiry although mandatory; but, in fairness to the scheme, a report is issued every third year. This sets out maternal mortality rates and other relevant information of the previous triennium which certainly help in assessing the standards of obstetric care.

Secondly, there can be indirect means of affecting the quality of care. Amongst these can be listed:

1. *Peer review.* This has been used to a large extent in building up this Region. In the early days senior consultants from the teaching hospitals from outside the Region were invited to advise on the existing consultant services in the Region and on the developments they considered necessary. In undertaking these reviews it has always been the practice to invite the consultants responsible for the service in the Region to participate in the reviews. Distinction awards and their distribution are a form of 'Peer Review'; the consultants participating at local and regional level, while the higher awards are the subject of review by a central committee.

2. *Medical executive committees.* One of the most important developments in recent years has been the establishment of medical executive committees ('Cogwheel') with their divisional systems. The developments which have already taken place in certain districts have seen the start of medical audit, the examination of mortality and morbidity figures and the ability of consultants to discuss their own work and the gaps in the Service and the load distribution. Positive encouragement to those medical executive committees which have a policy of continuing and expanding these activities would be likely to lead to a national response.

3. *Postgraduate medical education.* It has already been indicated elsewhere in this paper that one of the greatest contributions that can be made to the quality of medical care is to ensure that medical staff have the facilities to keep up-to-date with recent advances in medicine. The continuous review of regional policies and practice in this area of interest is therefore a necessary activity to this end.

Thirdly, there is a number of administrative procedures which impinge on and affect (sometimes it is only marginally) quality of care.

1. *Monitoring.* The management and planning functions of Region *vis-à-vis* the areas, and the areas *vis-à-vis* the district, reveal gaps in the care system, and indicate service including manpower needs.

2. *Service and complaints.* Complaints by patients are, in effect, one of the important barometers of the standards of medical care. Circular HM(66)15 provides ample opportunity to review and monitor professional standards when dealing with complaints. Unfortunately the majority of complaints usually show that lack of communication and the failure to appreciate the special circumstances and changes in the clinical picture are factors in motivating patients to complain.

3. *Sources outside the NHS.* These include the Hospital Advisory Service, the ombudsman and consumer interests from the community health councils. All three can put pressure on the regional or area authorities as do court cases for malpractice.

REORGANIZATION

Although there was good co-operation before 1974 between the RHB and the local authorities with working parties on the care of the aged and the mentally handicapped, the reorganization of the NHS has brought with it benefits which can, indirectly, improve the quality of medical care. For example, the integration of health and local authority services in health care planning can now take cognisance of housing and education. The introduction of community medicine as a specialty promises to improve epidemiology and the management of health service facilities. These are areas for development.

A new major computer system has recently been installed in the Region and has allowed information services to develop in a number of ways.

First, it has been possible to develop Hospital Activity Analysis. Clearly, from the patient's viewpoint HAA does not make any immediate impact on his care since the patient has left hospital before the material is available. On the other hand the development of information generally and HAA in particular has the potential to influence future patterns of care in two ways: first, by contributing to the advance of medical knowledge; and secondly, by 'medical audit'. Both of these have largely rested on the initiative of individual doctors. Interest has occasionally been little better than lukewarm when individuals have been approached. There is now a 100 per cent return available for both the general medical services and psychiatry. The returns from the maternity services are at present limited to about 60 per cent of the units in the Region. A considerable amount of work has gone into ensuring a high quality of validity in the returns.

Secondly, an increasing number of individual consultants (now between 75 and 80) each year make demands upon HAA data. The requests include:
1. To aid a review of case material: listing patient data which may be preparatory to an attempt to publish.
2. For tabular material: particularly epidemiological.
3. To facilitate management or planning aspects.
4. With an educational motivation or seeking to throw light on an existing situation.

District diagnostic and operation indexes are now produced for each year's general HAA which may be used to trace the case-notes for particular sets of diagnoses or procedure. Apart from these involvements with doctors in the use of HAA, the Regional Medical Information Unit may have made a modest contribution to improve patient care by the involvement of their staff in clinical trials and similar special studies sometimes involving the use of HAA.

The absence of out-patient data is a major impediment. A start has been made in a pilot study regarding work in out-patient departments but a great deal more work has to be done before information can be utilized in the planning processes.

Thirdly, a 10 per cent sample of HAA, the Hospital In-Patient Enquiry (HIPE) is being used as a means of deciding the planning figures for in-patient beds for the future.

Fourthly, a regional mental handicapped register has been compiled. The association between the Medical Research Council and the Region enables an MRC team to evaluate the care of the mentally handicapped. As a result of this project decisions have already been made in providing special hostel units in the community which have produced better medical care for the mentally handicapped patient.

It is clear that the new computer system introduced this year will overcome many of the discouragements which have existed in the past when potential users have been dissuaded from making requests by a shortage of computer time or by delays in coding and computer input which results in recent material becoming available too late for topicality. The new information systems will not only relate to medical care but they will also improve the effectiveness of the management of medical manpower and other health resources.

THE FUTURE

The NHS has shown the ability to adapt to the changing pattern of disease and the advances in science, technology, and pharmacology which have taken place in the last twenty years. There is no doubt that the quality of medical care depends primarily upon the attitudes of the medical profession, and if any positive progress is to be made in the direction of a wider spread throughout the country of introducing systems of quality control it will have to be the medical staff who will be the disciples in such a movement. At present there is a confrontation between the Government and the medical profession and those of us who have been in the NHS since 1948 speculate whether a return to the halcyon days before 1974 will be possible. It will be a constant challenge to improve the quality of care in the next decade.

The important areas in which developments are likely to lead towards the improvement of the quality of medical care would seem to be these:

1. *Undergraduate medical training.* A major factor in the improvement of the quality of the medical care is a realistic undergraduate

curriculum. In Wessex the signs are promising because of the policy of the medical school. In Southampton where the student is introduced to clinical teaching in the first year and teaching is undertaken in the environment in which they will eventually work and practise.

2. *Postgraduate medical education* should be made more effective than it is now. There is no doubt that the standard of postgraduate medical education has been improved since 1961 but nationally the standard should be 'excellent' rather than 'good'.

3. The *information services* in the regions should be developed so that appropriate information can be made available to the medical executive committees.

4. Positive encouragement should be given to a small number of *medical executive committees* receptive to good ideas for improving quality so that they can become the leaders in the field. Development by example has been a feature in the NHS since its inception.

5. The *specialist in community medicine in information and research* at regional headquarters should be specially trained in the subject of quality assessment and assurance with a view to being able to advise the medical executive committees.

If the confrontation between the Government and the medical profession can be resolved then there is a chance to achieve progress in establishing a system which would lead to improved quality.

8

The Hospital Health Services Research Unit in the University Department of Medicine, Western Infirmary, Glasgow

Its relation to the quality of medical care

GRAHAM WILSON
MD, FRCP

*Regius Professor of Medicine, and
Honorary Director, Hospital Health
Services Research Unit, University
Department of Medicine, Western Infirmary,
Glasgow*

The Hospital Health Services Research Unit in the University Department of Medicine, Western Infirmary, Glasgow

Its relation to the quality of medical care

Introduction

Since the establishment of the National Health Service in 1948 several unexpected problems have come to light, in particular the rapid escalation in the demand for and cost of health services. This has meant that every request cannot be met and that some system of determining priorities and of making the best use of available resources is inevitable. Furthermore, despite advances in several fields such as the control of many infectious diseases, there have been setbacks elsewhere so that the life expectancy of a man of 45 has shown little improvement. Initially, when the NHS was started the medical profession was extremely resistant to any suggestion that their work, particularly in the clinical field, should be subjected to any critical scrutiny. However, in recent years there has been a considerable change in attitude and a scientific approach to medical problems is now welcomed as shown by the acceptance of many more whole-time academic and research units and the use of methods such as controlled therapeutic trials. Increasing attention is also now being given by doctors not only to the quantity but also to the quality of life that may follow certain forms of treatment. In these circumstances the proposal was made that a health services research unit should be established within a teaching hospital with a remit to investigate the functioning of the health service within the hospital and its related community and to encourage the scientific study of different methods of dealing with health problems. While such a unit would in the first instance concentrate on the local situation it would also be able to arrange and co-operate in investigations in other parts of Scotland and Britain so that appropriate comparisons of different methods could be made. There was little doubt that the unit would be more acceptable to the medical profession if it were located in a hospital so that the medical and scientific members frequently met and were in close contact with their clinical colleagues; it would be less likely to succeed if it were remote and based in an administrative headquarters. In addition to its research activities, a unit situated in a teaching hospital could be expected to have an important influence in the education of students and junior staff and so ensure a wider appreciation of the function and application of health service research.

The location and structure of the Unit

The Hospital Health Services Research Unit (HHSRU) was established in association with the University Department of Medicine at the Western Infirmary Glasgow by grants of £100,000 each from the Nuffield Provincial Hospitals Trust and the Scottish Home and Health Department to be paid over five years. The first appointments to the staff were made in August 1973 and the Unit was brought up to about full strength in January 1975.

The location of the Unit in the Western Infirmary brought certain advantages. A tradition of research of this nature was already partially established. Some studies of the relationship of the hospital to the community were already under way: for example the role of the Casualty Department in providing emergency medical consultation for minor complaints after 6 pm and at the weekends (18). The opening of the Clydebank Health Centre stimulated joint projects in relation to the provision of health care. There were many other links between the community and the Western Infirmary, for instance the epidemiological surveys being conducted by the MRC Blood Pressure Unit. There was an opportunity for close collaboration with the Alcohol Research Unit which had been established in the Department of Medicine and was engaged especially in studying the problem of abuse of alcohol in relation to the load on the hospital service. Computer and statistical help was particularly strong in the Western Infirmary. The records of the peptic ulcer and hypertension clinics were maintained by computer (SWITCH system) and the follow-up of thyroid patients was controlled by computer (SAFUR system). A link with the Health Services Operational Research Unit at Strathclyde University was also established.

The staff of the Unit is multidisciplinary. The Director of the Unit (Professor G. M. Wilson, Regius Professor of Medicine) and the Deputy Director (Dr W. D. Alexander, Reader in Medicine) are honorary appointments. There are four further medical members supported by the grants ranging in status from senior registrar to senior house officer; in addition to their research activities they all carry out hospital clinical duties in relation to their position in general professional or higher medical training programmes. Other members of the Unit comprise a statistician, a psychologist, and three science or arts graduates involved in data collection and analysis and a secretary: twelve in all at present.

While the core of the Unit is formed by the grant-supported staff it could not possibly hope to achieve its objectives if it was inward-looking and solely concerned with the activities of its own members. Considerable efforts have been made to involve other groups in research projects particularly junior medical staff in the hospital, medical students, pharmacy students, and nurses. Active participation is proving a most successful way of introducing them to health service research problems. In addition three seminars are held each term at which either a member of the Unit or an outside invited speaker gives a talk which has been followed by a lively discussion. These are open to all hospital staff and attendances have been large.

Research in relation to quality of medical care

The quality of medical care depends on many factors: the skill and attention of the clinical staff, the resources available to them and the co-operation of the patient to mention only a few. Assessment of many of these aspects is difficult as they cannot easily be measured and they interact in a complex fashion. The HHSRU has started some investigations which have a bearing on this topic and they will be briefly described.

EVALUATION OF CARE AFFORDED TO INDIVIDUAL HOSPITAL PATIENTS

The extent to which the care of patients is assessed must vary greatly in different hospitals and hospital units. In American hospitals the medical audit and peer review are well-established features now enshrined legally as the Professional Standards Review Organizations. In the Professorial Medical Unit at the Western

Infirmary in which the majority of the staff of the Hospital Health
Services Research Unit carry out their clinical duties we follow a
monitoring system similar to that described by Smart (1975). The
records of in-patients are regularly reviewed immediately after discharge. Our standard of practice is assessed by the criteria set out in
Fig. 1. In a teaching hospital with a mixture of University, NHS, and
research staff we are well placed to review our activities at our
departmental clinical meetings, teaching rounds and discussions. We

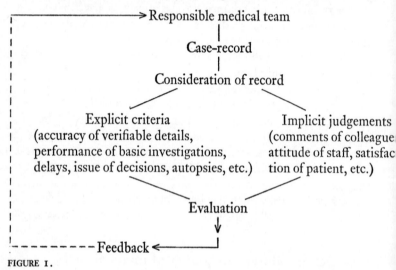

FIGURE 1.

have particularly concentrated since 1974 on the explicit criteria,
such as the accuracy of completion of the discharge document, the
delay in writing to the GP and the percentage of post-mortem
examinations in the case of death. The existence of four separate
clinical teams within the professorial unit permits comparisons of
activities and accuracy in recording verifiable data. The results are
published at our monthly meetings and with this induced element
of competition there has been a conspicuous improvement since
these measurements were started (25).

RECORDS AND COMMUNICATIONS ABOUT
HOSPITAL PATIENTS

The assessment of the quality of care received by a patient must to a
large extent depend on a scrutiny of his case-record though this is

certainly not the only approach. An inadequate record does not necessarily mean that he has received poor care; much may have been done for him that has not been written down and he may well have departed from hospital cured and well-satisfied. However, if the patient should return with a recurrence of his illness or be suffering from a chronic complaint and pass into the hands of another doctor there can be little doubt that his treatment may deteriorate if accurate information about his previous history is not available. Furthermore hospital statistics are compiled from these records and if such details as the diagnosis and the operations performed are not reliably recorded, the workload of the hospital cannot be properly assessed and appropriate provision for medical care will not be forthcoming. There can be little doubt that clear and accurate medical records can enhance the quality of care and failure to maintain a high standard in this respect can be associated with a deterioration in the service.

On surveying hospital case-notes a common finding is that on admission an adequate history has been taken and the physical findings have been described. Thereafter numerous laboratory and radiological investigations have been carried out all recorded on separate pieces of paper but notes on clinical progress and response to treatment are often deficient. Furthermore it is frequently far from clear what was in the mind of the doctor and why certain decisions were made in relation to the state of the patient. Again if only a single doctor is concerned this may not greatly affect the clinical care of the patient but nowadays in hospital several doctors are commonly involved. Some may have been called in consultation only at a late stage and may not have been present when some vital decisions were made. Hence if a high standard of care is to be maintained a clear narrative account of the patient's illness and progress must be available.

The introduction of the problem-orientated medical record (POMR) has done much to direct attention to the inadequacies of the present case-record and to point the way to improvement (24). The POMR method can be extended to assist communication between hospital and GP. In the Professorial Medical Unit the POMR system has been introduced into one general ward while in the other the conventional system has been continued. A film has been made in conjunction with the Television Service of the University of Glasgow to illustrate the POMR and to facilitate its introduction

(4). We have particularly concentrated on developing a form of letter on the POMR principle for conveying information on discharge from hospital or after attending a specialist out-patient clinic (5, 22). A survey of GPs receiving this new type of document indicated that it was well received and considered more useful than the conventional letter (6).

In the firm belief that the standard of the medical record is an indication of the quality of medical care that is being provided for the patient we are continuing our studies of this subject. It is difficult to assess objectively the value of different methods of record-keeping but an investigation of a random sample of discharge documents is being carried out to compare the two methods. The introduction of a new system into part of the Unit has created interest and discussion whatever method has been employed and has stimulated much closer monitoring of such matters as accuracy of entry of diagnosis in discharge documents and of delay in sending out discharge letters. A structured approach such as developed in the POMR can lead to clearer and more informative records which are the essential documents in any assessment of the standard of treatment that has been provided.

ACCURACY OF VERIFIABLE DATA REGARDING PATIENTS

Our attention initially was given to examining the accuracy of the data extracted from the in-patient case-record and entered on the form which constitutes the basis for the subsequent computer analysis of in-patient statistics (SCRIPS). Information regarding the number of patients discharged with a certain diagnosis is frequently required in relation to research on the quality of medical care. In the course of our investigations many grave errors and deficiencies have come to light. For example, in a study of the incidence of self-poisoning at the Western Infirmary (supported by an earlier grant from the Nuffield Provincial Hospitals Trust) it was found that in 1969 the diagnosis had been correctly entered in the record in only 77 per cent of cases; this improved to 89 per cent in 1971 after some publicity of our findings. A parallel investigation at another Glasgow hospital showed that the entry was correct in only 18 per cent and 64 per cent of cases for these two years. Similar large errors have come to light in relation to our research into head injuries and myocardial infarctions. The entries in relation to the consultant in charge of the patient were even more unreliable, one physician being credited with care of patients in the hospital for several years after he had retired. Unfortunately we have found that the information provided by SCRIPS is unreliable and misleading for scientific research in relation to evaluation of medical care and as a result we have had to rely entirely on collection of our own data which has considerably restricted our activities.

The inaccuracies in these official documents are extremely disturbing and must in the end affect adversely the function of the NHS in Scotland. Few would dispute that reliable information regarding the incidence of diseases which lead to admission to hospital and the work of the consultants is essential for improving medical care. Quite apart from the mistakes in future planning that may arise there is a most unfortunate effect on the medical staff. Readily detected gross elementary errors inevitably breed widespread distrust of the other results which cannot so readily be checked. Many doctors are not very amenable to having their performance compared with that of their colleagues and will quickly seize on these mistakes as a means of discrediting attempts at quality control. For this reason alone it is essential that a very high degree of accuracy should be attained in official statistics.

The source of these errors has been readily identified and described elsewhere (25). The entry of the diagnosis has not been made by the hospital doctor at the time of the patient's discharge and the blank has been filled in by someone ignorant of the case and without medical knowledge. We have found that this is being done in some 75 per cent of discharges. The system certainly needs changing and we are hoping that following our reports and suggestions high priority will be given to this task. If progress is to be made in the evaluation of hospital care much more attention must be paid to effective and accurate collection of primary data at ward level, and a system of quality control is required to keep this under regular surveillance.

HOSPITAL STATISTICAL RETURNS REGARDING PATIENTS

While the medical record is the source of much information for the planning of medical care in hospital there are other returns, the accuracy or otherwise of which can have a considerable influence on the quality of the attention which is provided. Accordingly an investigation into the reliability of some of the returns regarding bed state and the admission of patients has been carried out. Considerable inaccuracies were revealed. In the female acute medical receiving ward, one of the most important units in the hospital, the official bed complement in the return appears as nineteen. However, in this ward there are only spaces for sixteen beds but two extra beds can be put up in the middle of the ward though these do not provide any proper facilities for the unfortunate patients in them and create extra problems for the nursing staff. The hospital bed state return for this ward is made at midnight but in a detailed survey over 116 days with a four-hourly study of bed occupancy the maximum daily figure occurs at 8 am and the second highest at 4 am. Midnight comes only fourth in the survey. Furthermore the official return takes no account of 'boarding out' of patients from this ward, and if full merely indicates that every bed is occupied and gives no information as to the extent of any overflow. On many occasions patients had to be disturbed, often in the middle of the night, and moved to another ward; this certainly did not in their minds enhance the quality of care that they were receiving! In fact patients were boarded out on 64 out of the 116 days of the investigation. Furthermore, when the acute medical receiving ward is full and the nursing staff are reluctant to arrange further boarding out there is some evidence that the criteria for admission are changed and that patients who would otherwise have been admitted are sent home. Pressure of this sort can clearly influence the standard of medical care. Junior medical staff are called upon to make some of the most difficult clinical decisions during the night when it is only too easy to make a mistake. If the patient can be detained and reviewed in the clear light of day a more confident decision can be made.

The errors in the official information regarding the acute receiving ward led to a wider study of the whole hospital. In the twenty-eight wards of the Western Infirmary there are only nine in which the actual number of beds agrees with the official figures. There is a spread going from four actual beds more or less than the official figures. Further studies of the reliability of these returns are being carried out and we hope to be able to make suggestions for improvement of the situation.

These studies certainly confirmed the value of the presence of a statistician in the HHRSU based in the hospital and working in direct contact with the medical and nursing staff. The return of the bed state has often depended on a nurse, possibly only temporarily employed in the ward, attempting to count the patients at midnight while she is engaged on many other demanding tasks. She is only aware that the return is sent to a remote office and she certainly has no direct contact with those who analyse the figures. The personal visits from a statistician at midnight, 8 am, and at other times to record the figures and to ascertain how reliably they reflected bed use throughout the twenty-four hours at first caused surprise and subsequently generated much interest as the nursing staff were shown the results and the comparison with the official returns. The defects in this system for recording bed state and occupancy on which the future of hospital planning and the standard of medical care for the community depend raise the question of the allocation of resources for the collection of information. Our results may suggest that too much is going into the central analysis of data and too little attention is being paid to the process of initial recording at ward and clinic level. These investigations once again emphasize the absolute importance of ensuring accurate collection of primary data before quite unreliable information is fed into expensive computers and confirm the reality of the adage 'garbage in, garbage out'.

Communication between doctor and patient

The establishment of confidence between the doctor and his patient is essential for successful treatment. The difficulties in communication are commonly underestimated and often neglected. Medical education and professional examinations are to some extent responsible. Undue emphasis is placed on the elicitation of physical signs and especially on 'short cases' in examinations whereas in real life the majority of patients come to the doctor with symptoms but no signs and examiners never listen to a candidate taking a history from a patient. It is hardly surprising that a common complaint of patients about their health service is that 'I cannot talk to my doctor'.

The HHSRU is involved directly or indirectly with several projects in this field. The possibility that patients might be able to transmit certain basic information more readily through a computer has been explored in conjunction with the Gastrointestinal Unit at the Southern General Hospital (7). This approach has now been evaluated and the results incorporated in a successful PhD thesis (11, 12). Many patients seem to prefer an interview with an inanimate machine than with a doctor. In addition a more formalized system of history-taking may reduce errors and will eliminate omissions. If used as a preliminary move it may help a shy or hesitant patient, though of course it can never be a complete substitute for the personal interview with the doctor. Such an approach may also be valuable in getting certain important details that a patient might be reluctant to reveal truthfully in direct conversation, for example his alcohol consumption. Extension of this method of history-taking to patients with dyspepsia and with alcoholism and an investigation of the use of self-completed questionnaires in the out-patient department are being planned.

The application of an automated system has been fully justified in the follow-up of patients discharged from hospital but suffering from conditions liable to recur or to be followed by complications. One example is the follow-up register for thyroid disease in Scotland (Hedley *et al.*, 1970). In particular the insidious onset of hypothyroidism after treatment of thyrotoxicosis is easily overlooked and the apathy may lead to the patient failing to seek medical advice. There can be no doubt about the benefits of this method of after care. Originally introduced to cover an area of low density population it has proved equally successful in Glasgow (3).

The ability of a patient to comprehend common medical terms is often overestimated and this was brought out by one of our members while he was a medical student (2). This may often mean that he fails to understand what he is told by doctors and nurses about his medical condition and does not follow instructions about his treatment. Much more can be done to test a patient's capacity in this respect: for instance to ascertain that he can take his medication reliably while in hospital prior to discharge for if he is unable to do it there he will certainly fail at home. A particularly irritating and disturbing feature can be failure to keep a follow-up appointment at the out-patient clinic. It is often assumed that this is entirely the fault of the patient but there are several possible explanations that need to be explored such as failure to deliver the message, inadequate instructions, an appointment time manifestly difficult or impossible in view of distance or domestic circumstances, default of the ambulance service or loss of confidence in the medical service (for example through always seeing a different junior doctor at each attendance). These can reduce the quality of care and in conjunction with colleagues in the hospital an investigation into some of these factors in relation to failure to keep appointments is being started.

A particular group of patients who can experience considerable difficulty over communications in hospital are the deaf. Shortly after the formation of the HHSRU was announced in the press an excellent letter was received from a patient calling our attention to this problem. This prompted an investigation at the Western Infirmary (13). Five surveys carried out at monthly intervals have shown that 10 per cent of the in-patient population of 350 have some degree of hearing loss. This gives rise to problems in history-taking, the conduct of confidential interviews in the ward or clinics and in giving instructions against a background of noise. The hard of hearing patients mentioned feelings of bewilderment, isolation, and stupidity at not understanding the medical and nursing staff. Their difficulties were particularly great if they were placed in situations when they could not lip read, for example while undergoing a barium meal examination it was particularly difficult to follow instructions. Most of these patients did not have hearing aids when admitted: either they did not possess one, had omitted to bring it in or it was not functioning properly. This led to an approach to the Royal National Institute for the Deaf and an investigation of the ways in which the situation in hospital might be improved (14).

Guidelines for management

Recent developments in medicine have been characterized by the introduction of a multiplicity of tests and methods of treatment. In particular the annual requests for laboratory investigations have shown a steeply rising curve. As new methods and investigations are introduced they tend to be added to the battery rather than used selectively with a definite line of approach to a problem. This is nowhere more clearly seen than in the diagnosis of jaundice where there is available a vast number of biochemical, histological, and radiological examinations. Despite an increasing amount of available information about these patients, diagnosis was not becoming easier as might have been expected. Indeed the situation was even becoming more confused by the multiplicity of tests and some of the investigations used were expensive, possibly hazardous and of uncertain value. Knill-Jones (9), a member of the Unit, has shown how the use of statistical techniques and the computation of probabilities can greatly simplify the process and enhance the accuracy of the conclusion reached from standard tests alone. A prospective study was carried out on 219 patients and application of the method is now being extended to several centres in Britain. The implications of such a study are great. The method achieves similar or possibly greater accuracy than clinicians without extensive knowledge of liver disease, by the cheapest and most readily available tests. This stage can be accomplished in the out-patient clinic. It identifies a group of cases in which further investigation is necessary and can suggest the most appropriate investigations. It could lead to a considerable reduction in the use of hospital beds. Further work is being done in the development of simple decision trees based on four initial questions or investigations (23). No mathematical ability is required for their use and they may become useful aids to decision-making for less experienced members of a health care team. As the *Lancet* (10) succinctly summarized the position: 'If three simple questions and one well-chosen laboratory test lead to an unambiguous diagnosis, why harry the patient with more?'

The introduction of new methods of treatment has likewise brought problems of great medical and ethical complexity. Patients may now survive after severe illnesses or injury which previously were fatal but unfortunately the quality of their subsequent life is sometimes gravely impaired. This can apply particularly to survival after severe head injury. Admission to an intensive care ward immediately after an accident may ensure that the vital functions of heart and lungs continue but that the patient is condemned to a vegetable existence. The problem is to determine the ultimate prognosis at an early stage so that a decision can be made with confidence regarding further supportive measures. A study is in progress in the University Department of Neurosurgery at the Southern General Hospital, Glasgow, in co-operation with the HHSRU to assess the predictive power of different clinical features (8). The study has been extended to include hospitals in the Netherlands and USA. The importance of being able to forecast with reasonable confidence the outcome of a severe head injury needs no emphasis.

Thyrotoxicosis is a disorder for which there are three effective methods of treatment: antithyroid drugs which leave the gland intact and subtotal thyroidectomy and radio-iodine therapy which destroy part of the gland. In a proportion of the cases the thyrotoxicosis remits spontaneously after a variable period. While the disease is active the excessive production of thyroid hormones may be checked by drugs. There is much uncertainty regarding choice of treatment. Relapse may occur after drug therapy, surgery requires expensive hospitalization, and radio-iodine leads with the passage of time to a high incidence of hypothyroidism. It is clearly undesirable to submit to the hazards of surgery or the uncertainties of radio-iodine those patients who may ultimately achieve a long-lasting spontaneous remission of their illness after some months. The difficulty is to predict the outcome but here again a definite management plan with a sequential assessment of the probabilities of relapse of the disease on stopping antithyroid drugs can provide a rational basis for the choice of the most appropriate treatment with the most efficient use of hospital resources. This approach is being followed as a joint enterprise between our Endocrine Clinic and the HHSRU (1, Alexander *et al.*, 1975).

Selection and use of expensive equipment

The continuing introduction of increasingly sophisticated and hence expensive apparatus places a strain on the purchasing resources of the NHS and in these circumstances an assessment of the value of the new equipment in relation to the extent of improvement in patient care, the cost and the possible saving by eliminating other less satisfactory procedures is important. The HHSRU has been involved with other departments in exercises of this type.

The increasing load of work placed on Clinical Biochemistry Departments has been met by extensive automation of many analytical techniques. The introduction of machines which analyse serum for several substances simultaneously means that the laboratory rarely measures one constituent alone. The upsurge in information has led to a further refinement in automation; many machines now produce a print-out of the analyses which are sent directly to the clinicians who receive many results that they have not requested. In 1973 a Technicon SMA 18/60 auto-analyser was installed in the Clinical Biochemistry Department and a retrospective survey has been carried out in a medical and surgical unit to determine the reaction of the clinicians to this new mass of information (17). Usually less than 35 per cent of the abnormalities were acknowledged by being mentioned in the case-record or discharge letter or being ringed on the print-out by the clinician. A significant proportion (7·9 per cent) of the tests had not been specifically requested but were abnormal. Abnormalities in requested tests were always more often acknowledged than unrequested abnormal results. This preliminary study led to further discussions with the biochemists in relation to presentation of results and the grouping of the tests. Further prospective investigations are being carried out to assess the clinical usefulness of this innovation in hospital practice. Furthermore a Greiner auto-analyser is being installed in the hospital and the experience gained in these studies will greatly aid the planning of the assessment of this latest type of machine.

The introduction of the EMI scanner which carries out computerized transverse axial scanning of the brain afforded a further invitation to co-operate with other departments, this time at the Institute of Neurological Sciences. The machine costs about £120,000 but detailed study has shown that it possesses great advantages from the point of view of both doctor and patient. It is a truly non-invasive technique but at least as accurate as invasive methods, causes a minimum of discomfort and is entirely safe. Its diagnostic value is great both in showing up normal structures and intracranial lesions. It can also spare the patient more hazardous and unpleasant investigations such as angiography and air encephalography. Though the capital cost is high a considerable financial saving may be achieved by the elimination of other costly intracranial investigations (21).

Future plans

The development of research by the HHSRU will depend on two sources, the ideas of our own staff and the investigation of problems brought to us by other departments within the hospitals. We are aware of many areas in which research in relation to the quality of medical care might profitably be developed and have selected two for immediate further study.

Both general practices and the acute receiving areas of hospitals are haunted by patients who are unduly frequent attenders coming on their own initiative rather than at the request of a doctor. A preliminary survey of the problem at a health centre (15) showed that these patients consumed a substantial proportion of its resources. A diagnosis of the presenting physical illness gave a completely inadequate picture of the many problems responsible for attendances; they commonly included loneliness, unemployment, housing problems, and alcoholism. A survey of frequent attenders at the acute receiving area particularly outside normal working hours is being carried out and evidence so far suggests that similar factors are at work and that the care at present being given to these patients is not solving their difficulties.

A move into a newly built section (Phase 1) of the Western Infirmary will shortly take place and this affords a special opportunity to study how the new facilities affect the quality of the care that is being provided. We have particularly selected for investigation the arrangements that will be introduced in the Accident and Emergency Medicine Department. A detailed survey of the situation in the old part of the Western Infirmary is being completed before the move takes place so that a meaningful comparison will be possible.

As the function and activities of the HHSRU become more widely known we expect that there will be an increasing number of requests for help in the development of health service research projects. Indeed these are already coming forward and are most welcome. Wide collaboration in research is probably the best method of ensuring an adequate feedback to our colleagues of the results of our activities. The Unit will only really be a success if it can instil into the whole hospital an attitude of mind that leads to questioning of how we do our work and whether we are using our resources to ensure the best value and the highest quality of care for all our patients.

ACKNOWLEDGEMENTS

I am most grateful to the Nuffield Provincial Hospitals Trust and the Scottish Home and Health Department and our Advisory Committee for the assistance that they have given in starting the enterprise and to all members of the Hospital Health Services Research Unit for their help in compiling this report of our initial activities. I should also like to thank all who have collaborated with us in joint projects, particularly Professor W. I. Card, Professor B. Jennett, Dr J. T. Robson, and Dr A. Fleck.

References

1. ALEXANDER, W. D., McLARTY, D. G., HORTON, P., and PHARMAKIOTIS, A. D (1973). 'Sequential assessment during drug treatment of thyrotoxicosis', *Clin. Endocrinol.* 2, 43–05.

2. BOYLE, C. M. (1970). 'Difference between patients' and doctors' interpretation of some common medical terms', *Br. med. J.* 2, 286–9.

3. —— (1974). 'Scottish automated follow-up register for thyroid disease: four years' experience in Glasgow', ibid. 2, 490–2.

4. —— (1975). 'POMR—the logical step'. Film and accompanying booklet available from Television Service, University of Glasgow, Glasgow G12 8LB.

5. —— ALEXANDER, W. D., and STEVENSON, J. G. (1973). 'A new hospital letter for the specialist clinic, *Lancet*, i, 249–51.

6. —— YOUNG, R. E., and STEVENSON, J. G. (1974). 'General practitioners' opinions of a new hospital-discharge letter', ibid. ii, 466.

7. CARD, W. I., NICHOLSON, M., CREAN, G. P., WATKINSON, G., EVANS, C. R., WILSON, J., and RUSSELL, D. (1974). 'A comparison of doctor and computer interrogation of patients', *Internat. J. Bio-Medical Computing*, 5, 175–87.

8. JENNETT, B., TEASDALE, G. M. and KNILL-JONES, R. P. (1975). 'Predicting the outcome after head injury', *Jl R. Coll. Physicians*, 9, 231–7.

9. KNILL-JONES, R. P. (1975). 'The diagnosis of jaundice by the computation of probabilities', ibid. 9, 205–10.

10. LANCET (1975). 'Clinical decision (by numbers)', *Lancet*, i, 1077.

11. LUCAS, R. W. (1974). 'Computer interrogation: investigation of patients' response times', *IRCS (Research on: Biomedical Technology; Psychiatry and Clinical Psychology; Social and Occupational Medicine)*, 2, 1176.

12. —— (1975). 'The development of a computer-based system of patient interrogation', PhD Thesis (University of Glasgow).

13. McARDLE, C. (1974). 'Television in the ward', *Lancet*, ii, 1510.

14. —— (1975). 'Communicating with hard of hearing patients', *Age and Ageing*, 4, 116.

15. —— ALEXANDER, W. D., and BOYLE, C. M. (1974). 'Frequent attenders at a health centre', *Practitioner*, 213, 696–702.

16. McLARTY, D. G., and ALEXANDER, W. D. (1975). 'Assessment of thyroid function during and after treatment of thyrotoxicosis', *J. Clin. Pathol.* 28, 251–4.

17. ORMEROD, L., and BOYLE, C. M. (1974). 'Some clinical implications of a multi-channel biochemistry autoanalyser', *Health Bull.* 32, 1–5.

18. PATEL, A. R. (1971). 'Modes of admission to hospital: a survey of emergency admissions to a general medical unit', *Br. med. J.* 1, 281–3.

19. SMART, G. A. (1975). 'Monitoring in medicine', *Jl R. Coll. Physicians*, 9, 355–70.

20. STERN, R. B., KNILL-JONES, R. P., and WILLIAMS, R. (1975). 'The use of a computer program for the diagnosis of jaundice in district hospitals compared to a specialised liver unit', *Br. med. J.* 2, 659–662.

21. STEVEN, J. L., GROSSART, K. W., MACPHERSON, P., BLAIKLOCK, C. T., KNILL-JONES, R. P., and ROWAN, J. (1975). 'Diagnostic efficiency of C.T.: results of a preliminary study' (to be published).

22. STEVENSON, J. G., BOYLE, C. M., and ALEXANDER, W. D. (1973). 'A new hospital discharge letter', *Lancet*, i, 928–31.

23. TEATHER, D. and HILDER, W. (1975). 'The analysis of diagnostic data', *Jl R. Coll. Physicians*, 9, 219–225

24. WEED, L. L. (1971). *Medical Records, Medical Education and Patient Care*, Cleveland, Ohio.

25. WILSON, G. M. (1975). 'The Evaluation of Care' (in the press).

9

SCRIPS   Success or failure

A critical study of the Scottish Consultant Review of In-Patient Statistics

MICHAEL A. HEASMAN
MRCPE, MRCS, DPH, FSS
Director, Information Services Division,
Common Services Agency
Scotland

SCRIPS   Success or failure

A critical study of the Scottish Consultant Review
of In-Patient Statistics

Introduction

For some years now most Scottish consultants have received an annual statistical report of their work. This is known as the Scottish Consultant Review of In-Patient Statistics (SCRIPS). Its reception has been mixed, but with the majority of comments received being unfavourable. If SCRIPS is judged upon the correspondence received then it has been a failure. But is this necessarily true? This paper describes the system, and critically reviews some of its failings and its possible successes.

Background to SCRIPS

Dr Francis Clifton said in 1732 that

three or four persons should be employed in the hospitals (and that with out interfering with the gentlemen now concerned) to set down the cases of the patients from day to day candidly and judiciously, without any regard to private opinions and public systems, and at the year's end publish these facts just as they are, leaving everyone to make the best use he could for himself, . . . the benefit the public will receive will vastly more than balance the expense.

Other bodies and individuals from the eighteenth century to the present day have expressed similar sentiments. Notable among them was Florence Nightingale who wrote in 1860 that 'the relation of the duration of stay to the general utility of a hospital has never yet been demonstrated although it must be obvious that if by any sanitary improvements or improved treatment, the duration of stay could be reduced to one-half, the utility of the hospital would be doubled'.

These statements made more than two hundred and a hundred years ago respectively still epitomize some of the main purposes underlying the collection and publication of statistical data on hospital in-patient treatment. Progress in epidemiology and statistical interpretation has increased awareness of the difficulties of interpretation, and of the possibility of error, but the underlying objective remains to 'publish the facts just as they are' in order to 'increase the utility of the hospital' so that the 'benefit the public will receive from the statistics will vastly more than balance the expense'.

One suspects that Dr Clifton saw that it was up to the physician of the day to examine data on his own work and from the lessons learnt, to improve his practice. In 1967 the Joint Working Party on the Organization of Medical Work in the Hospital Service in Scotland (the Brotherston Report) reviewed American experience on medical audit. Many American hospitals had for some time been provided with data on their own performance by means of Professional Activity Study and related schemes but these had not been notably successful partly because of the bulkiness of the data. The Working Party decided that there were lessons for Scottish hospital doctors if it could be suitably adapted to the local environment. They therefore recommended that 'clinicians should be presented with readily intelligible statistical data concerning work done'.

It was this recommendation that led the Scottish Home and Health Department[1] to change the form in which they had been collecting statistical data on hospital in-patients, in order to identify the individual consultant in charge of the case. It then became possible to provide him annually with a brief résumé of his in-patient work, some national comparative data and a diagnostic index of his cases.

The diagnostic data provided has varied according to the specialty of the consultant but in general included such items as: number of cases treated; their age distribution; waiting time for admission; duration of stay prior to operation; total duration of stay; number of surgical operations; number of deaths.

Since 1969 data have been sent in confidence to each consultant. He has therefore received some crude material so that he can compare his own performance with that of the national average. No attempt has or indeed could have been made to provide any interpretation. To do so would have required extensive local knowledge.

---

1. Since health service reorganization this particular function of SHHD has been taken over by the Information Services Division (ISD) of the Scottish Health Service Common Services Agency.

Indeed it was not expected that the data themselves would do more than raise questions in the mind of individual consultants which might then set in train further study and discussion. In suitable circumstances practice might be altered, hypotheses set up and tested and, indirectly, both efficiency and effectiveness increased.

The Brotherston Report, as did its English counterpart, the Cogwheel Report, also recommended the establishment of divisional systems and it was suggested that a division could provide a forum in which the statistical data could be discussed. As formal or informal divisions were established, some requested grouped data for all consultants within a division. When this was provided it enabled local comparison of performance which might often be more meaningful than the national comparison hitherto available.

Analyses of some of the consultant data were undertaken in the Research and Intelligence Unit of the SHHD and described (4). The main purpose of that paper was to show the variation in aspects of hospital practice revealed. The basic unit of measurement was the consultant and some examples of the variations in practice are given below.

1. Mean duration of stay: The range in mean duration of stay was from eight to twenty-three days for consultants in general medicine treating patients with peptic ulcer. In teaching hospitals 65 per cent of consultants were at or below the Scottish median compared with a third of those in non-teaching hospitals.

2. Percentages of patients undergoing operation: While two-thirds of all patients discharged from the care of surgical consultants had an operation during their spell in hospital one consultant apparently operates on less than 50 per cent of his patients and another on 86 per cent. After admission for hernia some consultants were reported as operating on 100 per cent of their patients but a few operated on less than three-quarters.

3. Duration of stay prior to operation: One consultant was shown as keeping only 2 per cent of his patients in hospital for three days prior to extraction of lens of the eye. Others kept all their patients for this period or longer.

4. Post-operative stay: Some consultants were shown as keeping patients for two, and others for twelve days following operation for hernia and other equally wide variations of practice were shown for other common surgical operations.

That variations in practice existed was well known although such data had not been published on a national scale before. No judgement was made in the paper as to whether any particular practice was good or bad. The authors suggested that variations in length of stay should be assessed in terms of the end result for the patient and when longer stay apparently conferred no benefit on a patient then shorter stay would free resources for use by another.

In recent years there has been an increasing number of controlled clinical studies into various aspects of hospital stay. In general these show that shorter stay, or in suitable cases out-patient treatment, is in no way detrimental to the patient and is often preferred.

Thus evidence is accumulating that there is room for improvement in efficiency (in terms of resource use) and the implication is that consultants in general should find a use for data of this kind in this context. The reasoning behind the Brotherston Report and others before and since was sound enough but what has been the effect of circulating the data? This is discussed in the next section.

General reactions

It should be stated immediately that there is no way of objectively measuring the effect of circulating data to consultants. For example the average duration of stay in general surgery departments in 1969 was 10·7 days and in 1973 it was 9·4 days but there had been a continuing fall prior to 1969 (the first time the consultant data was circulated) and there was no sudden fall during that year or in 1970. The average duration of stay for hernia has decreased from eleven to ten days over the period but a similar fall has occurred in England where no similar form of data has been produced. Even if some noticeable changes of trend had occurred it would have been presumptuous to attribute them to SCRIPS for there are numerous pressures on consultants to increase efficiency, varying from increased awareness of both general and particular shortages of resources through attendances at management courses for clinicians, to the publication of the results of the clinical trials referred to in the previous section.

Thus any discussion of the effect of consultant feedback can be little more than anecdotal.

It is perhaps symptomatic of something that the first comment received by the author after the initial circulation of the data was related to distinction awards! After several similar comments had been received one was forced to conclude that an initial reaction was one of anxiety despite comment in the accompanying letter that the data was confidential to the consultant concerned. However, this reaction has not been heard by the author after these initial comments. Throughout the period of circulation of data there have been a few congratulatory comments and it is known that some consultants welcome the data provided and make considerable use of it. By far the greater part of the correspondence that has resulted has been critical, ranging from puzzlement over obscurity of the data to outright anger at the waste of public money involved. Although comments have always been welcomed the most common response has been a lack of reaction and there is thus no knowledge as to whether the data is used, filed, or simply thrown away in disgust or from lack of interest.

Soon after the initial circulation was undertaken a questionnaire was sent out. The response to this was not good (40 per cent) with favourable comment being slightly outweighed by unfavourable remarks. Critical comment was used to amend the form of the feedback for 1969 data but no further review has since been undertaken. It is now thought that the system has been in use long enough for it to have settled down, and a further review is now in progress (Summer 1975) in an attempt to make the data more generally acceptable and useful.

Types of criticism

In order to consider the role of routine data in self-audit it is necessary to consider each of the common criticisms made of the SCRIPS data in detail. Some will be seen to result from lack of understanding, some are more serious, few are easy to overcome.

Criticisms can be listed under the following headings: (*a*) errors; (*b*) irrelevancy; (*c*) lateness; (*d*) expense; (*e*) difficulty of interpretation including misinterpretation. Each of these will be considered in more detail.

THE ROLE OF ERROR IN NATIONAL DATA

In these modern times the existence of observer variation in medicine is readily admitted. The interpretation of clinical history, the existence of physical signs, the interpretation of laboratory results, are all topics on which the possibility is accepted of two views existing. The possibility not only of differences of opinion but of frank error is more acceptable than it was in the past. But error in statistics is apparently unforgivable. Unfortunately these errors exist and generally nobody is more aware of them than the statistician. However, because the data are produced electonically many feel that it must be right, until an error is spotted when the whole output immediately is considered to be all wrong. Comments such as 'the computer has made a nonsense' or 'lies, damned lies . . .' are all too frequently heard.

The present author has devoted a considerable time to the assessment of error in national data see, for example, Heasman, Liddell, and Reid (2), Heasman and Lipworth (3), and has been indirectly involved in other studies, for example by Lockwood (5). All these studies show that error exists in national mortality and morbidity data. Some of these types of errors are of importance to the interpretation of national data and are well understood by epidemiologists. For example, few will deny that part of the recorded increases in carcinoma of the bronchus or of ischaemic heart disease has resulted from increased accuracy of diagnosis. On the other hand many other errors are disguised to some extent by a certain amount of self-cancelling.

However this may be, the understanding of error in statistics is an important part of an epidemiologist's training. It is little different from the clinician's appreciation of the possibility that a patient may not always tell the truth which leads him to make allowances when interpreting a clinical history, or to the possibility that there may be differing interpretations of clinical signs or laboratory tests.

Error in health service statistics can be made in numerous ways. Occasionally systematic, it can also be of a random nature. Errors may be due to misunderstanding, inadequate training, plain clerical error, or sometimes to disinterest. The type of errors which may be found in one hospital may often be found to be specific to that one place. The stage at which error can occur is also important. It can occur during contact with the patient, through mistaken interpretation by the doctor, to errors in recording or coding usually accidental but occasionally deliberate (on confidentiality grounds). Errors can also occur in processing and tabulation. Error is also known to result from the difficulty that even skilled records officers can find in abstracting from unclear or confusing records.

Most computer systems have validity and feasibility checks built into them in order to attempt to obviate error. Validity checks permit the removal and correction of impossible error, for example code numbers for which there is no disease. Feasibility checks allow queries to be raised about unlikely events such as a case of leprosy in Scotland, or unlikely but not impossible combinations of events, such as breast disease in a male. By these checking procedures error rates are considerably reduced and 'impossible' errors are virtually eliminated. Unfortunately a technical procedure known as a 'by-pass' (since amended) has allowed some infeasible errors to enter the file but the amount of obvious[1] error contained in the data is very small.

The error level found in Scottish Hospital In-Patient Statistics by Lockwood was found to be quite low for individual items recorded with the exception that second and third diagnoses and second operations were frequently omitted.

Error is rather like sin. It is always with us but the wise man learns to live with it and recognizes that it exists. But while all admit to the existence of sin the shock of coming into one's home after it has been vandalized is none the less. Similarly when a consultant is presented with data which contains error it is often immediately obvious and the anger generated is instant and understandable. To press the analogy one stage further, as the vandalization may in part result from inadequate precautions so the error in the data may result from inadequate supervision of some part of the patient care or recording process; the anger is just as great. Unfortunately the analogy can be taken no further because while part of the anger is directed against 'authority' in both cases, another effect in the case of vandalization is to have one's house made more secure. In the case of statistical error the effect is often to ignore all the data even though most of it may be correct.

This discussion of error is important because it underlies much of the criticism which is directed at data which attempt to provide analyses of local situations. For national data, error is less easily spotted and is often of less importance. However error arises it must be considerably reduced if statistical data are to have relevance in local discussion. There is, of course, a vicious circle which has to be broken of irrelevant data, tardy production of results and error.

---

1. Obvious in the sense that it relates to an unlikely event when age, sex, diagnosis, and duration of stay are taken into account.

Probably what is needed most is to engender a feeling of personal involvement among consultants.

IRRELEVANCY OF DATA

A balance has to be struck in order to produce on a national scale data which purports to describe local situations and which is simple to understand. A standard output is desirable, the quantity of which must be severely restricted. At the same time diagnostic data must be of interest to members of a specialty. This means that individual interests of particular clinicians cannot be catered for in any systematic way, although an *ad hoc* service is available to meet some of these needs.

Limitations on the content of the data collected are a more serious problem. The content of the abstract is limited to such items as age and sex, duration of stay, waiting time and outcome. Nothing is included for example on laboratory tests, or post-operative infection. This inevitably means that unless the scope of the abstract is increased (and it would be costly to do this) there must be a limit on the relevance of the output to particular situations.

A common complaint is that as a measure of work, in-patient statistics are decreasingly important. This is obviously of more relevance to some specialties than others. This failing is readily admitted and collection of out-patient data is a high priority among future developments.

LATENESS

SCRIPS data are normally produced about nine months after the year to which they refer. Thus the data are on average fifteen months out of date. It is thus said that they are therefore too late to affect local management. This is true in so far as any immediate crisis situation is concerned. It is submitted, however, that clinical practice changes only slowly and therefore that the data are still relevant. This is not to deny the need for more rapid feedback. What is more problematical is whether annual data is necessary. Detailed analysis of a single diagnosis in the work of an individual consultant is almost impossible because numbers are so small. Would a three- or five-year run of data presented in greater detail be of greater value? This is one of the questions that needs to be answered in the current review of the system.

EXPENSE

The collection of data on hospital activity is now regarded as an essential part of the information required in any National Health Service. Ideally statistical data should be collected as a by-product of on-going work but this happens only in a few situations. As a result the collection of the data forms by far the largest element of the cost. SCRIPS itself only accounts for a very small part of the total cost of collection and processing of the data (probably less than 5 per cent). Even if the effect of SCRIPS on consultant practice is small it would more than pay for itself if it resulted in the reallocation of £10,000 worth of resources per year throughout the whole of Scotland. Thus the system is relatively cheap when considered against the total cost of hospital statistics, or what is much more important, the cost of the NHS itself. In these days of limited resources, increased efficiency in the use of these resources should be a high priority. There is little doubt that properly used these data could point the way to this increased efficiency in many local situations.

DIFFICULTY OF INTERPRETATION INCLUDING MISINTERPRETATION

Data sent to consultants are accompanied by an explanation of its content and of the statistical terms used and appropriate warnings on problems of interpretation are also included. The level at which to pitch such an explanation involves difficult decisions. If it is too simple the accusation can be made of 'talking down' or it may miss some of the points that should be made. If it is too complicated it confuses the statistically untrained or takes too long for the busy consultant to read.

The form of the print-out is probably too complex. It is certainly not an eye-catching production. For reasons of economy in programming the print-out has to be in a set of standard format, which means that some of the data may be of no interest (or relevance) to some clinicians because of the abnormal nature of their work when compared with that of their colleagues. In an attempt to keep down the bulk of the data as many factors as possible are included on one page. This makes the print-out difficult to read although considerable efforts have been made to render it intelligible.

There is thus no doubt that the non-statistical clinician is faced with some obstacles to be overcome before he can begin to use the data. If he gets past this difficulty he is then faced with questions of the interpretation of the data in the light of particular local circumstances. Both for strategic and tactical reasons the data is circulated without interpretation. Strategically because they are basically educational and any central interpretation will almost inevitably be seen as having punitive connotations or a risk of these. Tactically no interpretation can be included because nothing is known centrally about the local situation. Leaving aside questions of error in the data, local circumstances such as the availability of convalescent beds, closure of wards, outbreaks of infection may all have affected a consultant's activity during a period. These will not be known to those producing data. All this is quite apart from the time that would be required to produce a commentary thus inevitably increasing the delay.

Thus, the consultant is thrown upon his own resources to interpret the data. At a purely professional level he cannot be expected to have the epidemiological skill to spot some of the hazards in the way of interpretation. These may vary from abnormalities in the age/sex structure of his caseload to less obvious difficulties inherent in analysis, for example the selection of operation by severity according to predetermined rules. If some of these difficulties can delude even those skilled in epidemiology, how much more are they likely to confuse the unskilled.

There are thus formidable difficulties in the way of complete interpretation of data in a local situation. Nevertheless, having obtained the goodwill of consultants, the data should still be sufficient to arouse his interest and to obtain more skilled interpretation.

This catalogue of criticism can easily lead to an overwhelming desire to give up the whole project for the difficulties are easy to see. The successes are less easy to spot. Yet it is believed that it would be a mistake to condemn the SCRIPS scheme as a failure. There is much that is wrong, much that can and should be put right. The next section of this paper considers some of the possible remedies.

At the outset it was thought that there were two desiderata for self-evaluation of a consultant's performance. The availability of statistical data in a standard form and the existence of a professional forum in which to discuss the data. It is now appreciated that this is insufficient. Unfortunately although the divisional system was seen as the desirable professional forum its establishment has occurred considerably more slowly in Scotland than had been hoped. However even where it was successful it is doubtful if, on their own, the members of a division would generally be able or willing to make optimum use of the SCRIPS system. This is because of the general lack of statistical interest or expertise among clinical consultants. What is almost certainly required is an interpreter. This means somebody who can represent the data in a more meaningful way and who can suggest interpretations in the light of local situations. Such an interpreter must be considered as an integral member of a division with no particular axe to grind. The best person to fulfil this role is a community medicine specialist (CMS) who, whatever his other duties, needs to be regarded in this context as a neutral observer. Even here there are problems, for it must be admitted that many CMS are themselves not trained to play their full part in statistical analysis. In order to assist interpretation SHHD and later ISD have provided grouped data to divisions that have requested it. This enables individuals to be compared with the group or the group with larger national data. To date this offer of grouped data has been taken up by about a hundred formal or informal groupings of consultants.

In addition to an interpreter it is suggested that incentives are required to arouse interest in individual or group performance. Of course, incentives can involve either a carrot or a stick. It is obviously desirable to use a carrot wherever possible but the present NHS is not an organization which can readily provide carrots in a local, professional situation. It is unlikely that the distinction award, if the system is retained, could or would ever be used as a carrot. Personal financial inducement for efficiency is thus almost completely ruled out. More acceptable would be an inducement in the form of more resources, say freedom to purchase an extra piece of equipment, or perhaps the employment of an additional member of staff. Unfortunately increased efficiency either increases the level of activity so that more effort is required to maintain throughput, or alternatively resources saved are required elsewhere. Thus a carrot is difficult to find, a stick more so. No attempt would ever be successful in the British NHS to set up a true audit of consultants' work, with all the punitive connotations of the term. The reaction to such an attempt would be hostility sufficient to destroy not only SCRIPS but the NHS as well. Yet the fact remains that whatever else it does the SCRIPS system, crude though it is shows innumerable places where further investigation of efficiency is desirable.

Education undoubtedly remains the method by which efficiency should be improved. Peer group pressure is perhaps the most effective tool.

Thus interpretation of data in an educational setting remains the single method most likely to increase the intelligent use of statistical data by hospital consultants.

The particular format of that data remains an open matter, particularly in view of the review of the system now in progress. It might be that annual data should be very much simpler than the present form in which it is received and that more detailed analysis should be undertaken at intervals. Perhaps a single disease or the performance of a single speciality should be analysed with an appropriate report with statistical data included as part of a more general commentary, written with specialist participation. This would allow a much more flexible approach and thus would be more relevant to problems of the day. Scottish data relating to the mental and mental deficiency hospital in-patients (not included in SCRIPS) has been presented for the first time on a hospital rather than on a consultant basis and its initial reception has been very favourable. Development of obstetric data along similar lines is underway.

There are advantages as well as disadvantages in analysis at national rather than local level. The whole scene can be surveyed regardless of particular local problems. There is no immediate local involvement of the commentator who can thus approach his task from a completely neutral standpoint. The whole set of relevant data is available. But against this must be set the ignorance of a 'central' or 'national' author of local personalities and local problems.

It is clear that there is a place for both local and national analyses. There is probably a place for both general and special studies, for both routine and occasional reports. Above all there must be a flexibility of approach.

Up to the present virtually the whole effort in the production of SCRIPS has been devoted to standard national output. Indeed local initiative has to some extent been stifled by a fear of too close an involvement of local administration. This must be wrong, the fears must be shown to be ill-founded. In some instances a particular local problem may require a detailed local analysis. In others a chief administrative medical officer, for example, may wish to study the work of a specialty within the area of his health board. This should be encouraged although such a study should only be undertaken with the prior knowledge of the division concerned.

Even if the entire SCRIPS system were to be swept away it would not have been a wasted effort, but this is unlikely to occur for there has been success as well as failure.

SCRIPS has helped to make hospital consultants aware of the possibility of statistical analysis of their work. This has resulted in a large increase in the request for *ad hoc* analyses. The circulation of data has taken place during a period when the consultant has become increasingly aware that he is responsible for management of resources under his control. To fulfil this managerial function he needs data. But this data must be relevant, as up-to-date as possible, and it must be interpreted for him in such a way as to direct his attention to important findings. Finally it must be free from error. The latter part of this paper has been concerned with making the data relevant and meaningful for it is believed that this is the principal way to increase accuracy. Homilies on the responsibility for accuracy may have some part to play but the real pay-off will come when the relevance of the data can be seen in decision making at local level and for this help in interpretation provided locally is an essential prerequisite.

References

1. Cowan (1841). *Lancet*, i, 649.
2. Heasman, M. A., Liddell, F. D. K., and Reid, D. D. (1958). *Br. J. Occup. Med.* 15, 141.
3. —— and Lipworth, L. (1966). *Accuracy of Certification of Cause of Death*, Studies on Medical and Population Subjects no. 2 (London: HMSO).
4. —— and Carstairs, Vera (1971). *Br. med. J.* 1, 495.
5. Lockwood, E. (1971). *Br. J. prev. soc. Med.* 25, 2, 76.
6. Scottish Home and Health Department (1967). *Organisation of Medical Work in the Hospital Service in Scotland* (Edinburgh: HMSO).

10

The review of hospital resources and the implication for clinical practice

JOHN YATES
AHA
District Administrator,
East Birmingham Health District

The review of hospital resources and the implication for clinical practice

Summary

The first Cogwheel Report (1) suggested that divisions should review clinical practice in hospitals but there is little evidence of such review. The report also suggested that divisions should review use of hospital resources and this has been undertaken more enthusiastically. Examination of the use of resources can encourage clinicians to consider the implications for clinical practice. This method of encouraging clinical review is examined through the use of casestudies and the advantages and limitations of such a method are discussed.

Introduction

The desirability and practicability of involving clinicians in a review of the quality of the medical treatment they prescribe and administer has long been a subject of interest to those who study health care systems. In North America two of the motivating factors used to encourage the review of clinical practice are the setting up of an educational programme and the introduction of a type of financial and legal compulsion. In Britain the subject is less frequently discussed. Suggestions that the review of medical treatment or clinical practice should be made invariably produce no response or a defensive reaction from the medical profession. The attitudes expressed stem from a genuine belief that review is unnecessary, a concern that there is an implied criticism and a fear that clinical freedom is being infringed. In 1967 the first Cogwheel Report suggested that divisions had a role to play in the review of clinical practice, but the suggestion was not met with enthusiastic acceptance. In 1971 Forsyth and Sheikh (2) reporting on a survey of the reaction to 'Cogwheel' in fifteen hospital groups noted that reviews of variations in clinical practice were not being made.

The advice of the Cogwheel Report was not restricted to clinical practice and the need to review other hospital activity including the use of hospital resources was stressed. The third Cogwheel Report (3) commented on developments in this area and Goldsmith and Mason published the proceedings of a symposium (4) which illustrated examples of attempts to review hospital resources.

The separate identification of clinical practice and use of hospital resources can be a useful distinction to make and it frequently appears in Health Service literature. Cochrane (5) distinguishes 'effectiveness' from 'efficiency', Hunter (6) examines non-clinical reasons affecting the length of stay in hospital and an Office of Health Economics publication suggests that 'medical care can, broadly, be considered in two parts; firstly clinical or technical factors and secondly, organizational factors' (7). However, managerial and clinical issues cannot always be usefully separated. Virtually every clinical decision has some financial implication and unless clinicians are involved in the examination of the provision and deployment of finance or allow others to examine clinical decisions, they will be in a position 'to regulate the temperature without paying the fuel bills' (8). The clinician may rightly feel that his principal responsibility is for the treatment of an individual patient but he must also recognize the responsibility of finance of health care with a balanced provision for those who need that care. There are occasions when attempts to improve efficiency are frustrated by an ill-defined reference to the fact that the improvement can only be made at the loss of quality of clinical care. At this point, management is unable to distinguish between an over-cautious defence and a genuine constraint.

An artificial division between clinical and managerial issues may be obstructing our view of possible courses of action. If the NHS wishes the medical profession to examine clinical practice then perhaps one method is through the examination of the use of resources. The financial and legal motivation suggested in North America is not generally accepted in Britain but a properly conducted review of resources could encourage a clinical appraisal. This paper sets out to examine this possibility by examining case-studies and attempting to assess, admittedly subjectively, the clinical implications of some resource utilization issues.

Hesitant sparring

Case-study 1

The demand made by clinical divisions upon service divisions such as pathology and radiology is of concern to both clinical and service divisions. It was suggested to one service division by an administrator that the difficulties of controlling demand be the subject of discussion within the division. The discussion revealed that there was no precise knowledge of the sources of increasing demand and a study was mounted to collect data about the source of requests and determine what use could be made of such data. A method of linking HAA and X-ray in-patient data was devised and an analysis of three months' data undertaken. It was found that the regular linking of X-ray and HAA data was a practical possibility and there were also indications that source data could be of some value in three areas of activity: (*a*) in planning expansion or contraction of the department; (*b*) in the reallocation of resources within the department; and (*c*) for the control of workload. The findings revealed considerable variation in patterns between requesting departments. The data appeared to provide a sufficient basis for quantifying a discussion between the user departments and the service department. No such discussion took place.

COMMENT. This study revealed two areas of importance to the individual clinician. First, the data provided unexplained variations in requesting patterns and also unexpected growth areas. Members of the service division differed in their views towards the findings but the majority of members felt it was not the service division's prerogative to question the user's pattern of requesting and that such discussion might appear to infringe upon the individual clinician's right to request a particular type of investigation.

Secondly, the data could also be used to indicate positive or negative findings to provide some assessment of clinical practice but this possibility did not appear to be accepted or recognized by the majority of members of the division and certainly no further action was taken on the subject. This study also highlighted a lack of cross reference between divisions.

Case-study 2

In a period when divisions were being encouraged to undertake managerial activity, some members of a dental division had expressed concern about the collection and presentation of patient statistics to the division. The division set up a working party to review the data presented to the division and to attempt to produce information that could be used for divisional management. The working party, consisting of two dentists and two administrators, was advised by the division that the statistics presented in the past had been criticized on four counts:

1. Lack of relevance to the work of the division.

2. Incorrect or incomplete figures.

3. A large time-lag between the period under consideration and the presentation of figures relating to that period.

4. Too much time and effort was expended in studying and analysing figures.

The working party changed the method of presentation. Routine figures were only presented annually and an exception reporting system was introduced which required the division to predict activity in the forthcoming year. Estimates were made for activities upon which data were at that time being collected, for example, number of admissions, length of patient stay, out-patient attendances. Figures were estimated for individual departments with an acceptable range for each figure. Monthly and quarterly figures were calculated with due allowance being made for seasonal fluctuations. During the year reports were made to the division only when a figure appeared outside the accepted range. With the system operated on a quarterly basis during 1972 the division considered only five subjects. This compared with 164 items which would normally have been presented to the division. The exception reporting system reduced the 164 items to 44 before a dentist studied the figures. These 44 items were investigated by the working party and in 22 cases either the range predicted was found not to be a true reflection of the upper and lower limits of acceptability or alternatively, that insufficient allowance had been made for seasonal fluctuations. At the time it was considered that the number of such exceptions could be reduced when greater experience was gained in the selecting of the range. The remaining 22 items were discussed with the head of department or chairman of the division and only five of these were taken to the division for discussion.

The system did indicate that one particular department was accepting a very low number of new out-patients which according to the standards set by the division would create problems in that insufficient clinical material would be available for the teaching of undergraduate students. This was pointed out to the division on three occasions during the year but no action was taken. Some months later, when the head of the department concerned complained of the inadequate flow of patients, alterations were then made to the intake of out-patients to that department by altering the referral pattern from the 'Casualty Department'.

COMMENT. Had the exception reporting system been accepted, the flow of patients could have been modified at a much earlier period which would have averted the lack of teaching material and also possibly provided speedier treatment for patients who had been referred elsewhere. The exception reporting system that was implemented was experimental in nature and thus not unnaturally treated with some scepticism.

The results of the study indicated that the adoption of the proposed method of exception reporting might be of use to the division. The system was adopted for a short period but the work has not been continued. In this case-study the clinical implications of the managerial situation were relatively small. In these circumstances it is hardly surprising that a few members of the division saw the need to alter their activity

Inquiring curiosity

Case-study 3

The allocation of emergency admissions between wards is a subject of constant debate in hospitals. Attempts to provide an equitable distribution produce much heated discussion concerning the modifications to be made to numerical equality in order to obtain workload equality. The members of one clinical division were presented with a problem of this nature during one of their divisional meetings. The initiative to review the subject came mainly from the junior medical staff and nursing staff, with the purpose of suggesting a more even distribution of emergency admissions between wards. An opportunity for discussing the subject arose when the division asked for a report indicating changes in admission patterns for comparative periods before and after the participation in the City's Emergency Admissions Scheme. The admissions to the five wards concerned for

TABLE I. *Admissions to five wards, January to March quarters, 1971 and 1972*

Wards	1971 admissions			1972 admissions		
	Emergency	Planned	Total	Emergency	Planned	Total
1	57	87	144	58	79	137
2	57	55	112	65	60	125
3	52	81	133	58	69	127
4	97	62	159	124	79	203
5	52	90	142	89	100	189
Total	315	375	690	394	387	781

the first quarters of 1971 and 1972 were presented to the division (see Table 1).

The chairman of the division pointed out that the workload did not appear to be shared equitably amongst the various wards. He noticed that Ward 4's figures were considerably different from those of other wards and he described it as 'top of the league table'. He went on to explain that it was difficult to make any value judgements based on the figures as there might be several reasons for the higher number of admissions on the one ward, for example, a different case-mix or a different death-rate. The members of the division promptly agreed with his remarks and one of the consultants from Ward 4 explained that he personally saw very few planned admissions and obtained nearly all of his work through the Emergency Admissions Scheme. He wholeheartedly agreed that the difference in throughput reflected a different type of case-mix and went on to say that Ward 4 was not over-stretched. Although the figures presented to the division initially suggested the need for some alteration to the emergency admission pattern, the division decided not to take any action on the figures.

COMMENT. In this situation, it is difficult for an administrator to assess the clinical implications of the emergency distribution pattern between the wards. The senior medical staff in the division clearly expressed the view that, in this particular instance, the workload of the wards and the clinical practice taking place on the wards were not adversely affected by the different admission patterns. Their comments were not so readily accepted by the junior medical staff and the nursing staff of the wards in question. On many occasions, considerable dissatisfaction had been expressed about the differing workload on the wards, both before and after the meeting of the division. Concern was also expressed on a confidential basis by some of the consultants outside the divisional meetings that the difference between the workloads was significant and could be rectified. It was felt unwise to tackle such a difficult subject in open debate. Other consultants contended that the clinical interests of each consultant contributed towards the tendency for wards to receive a selected type of case-mix and thus one could anticipate considerable differences in throughput. This type of selection undoubtedly did occur to some extent but it should be recognized that each ward was responsible for admissions on a set day. Whilst a certain degree of selection can be achieved, there is nevertheless an obligation for individual wards to accept any patients presented on their emergency take days. If case-mix selection was not a significant determining factor, the issue would then revert to one of whether the ward is able or willing to take its allotted case-load and whether the staffing structure would demand a more equitable distribution of emergency admissions. Assuming that resources in terms of beds available and staff time are adequately provided on all wards, then any inequitable distribution is unlikely to affect clinical policy or standards. However, in a situation where resources are limited, it may well be that clinical practice is affected by the pressure of work put on the individual doctors. No adjustment of workload was observed immediately after the discussion, and over eighteen months later the same inequitable distribution in terms of numbers was still apparent.

Case-study 4

A number of clinical divisions had expressed concern that greater participation in the City's Emergency Admissions Scheme would adversely affect clinical practice. Few clinicians were able to suggest quantifiable measures which could be used to determine these alterations. The general discussion led two clinicians and one administrator to study in some depth the length of stay patterns in general medicine. One diagnosis, acute myocardial infarction, was the subject of a particular study. It was selected because it was one of the most frequently occurring medical diagnoses. The purpose of the study was to examine any variations which occurred and to detect non-clinical reasons affecting length of stay. HAA data was collected and following accuracy checks of the HAA print-out against the discharge diagnosis in the case-notes, the data was adjudged to be of a satisfactory standard for use. The data was collected for patients admitted to two general hospitals and the length of stay pattern for each consultant was obtained. Differences in the mean and median length of stay were observed between the two general hospitals concerned and between individual consultants. Preliminary findings indicated that the difference in length of stay patterns between the two hospitals might possibly be explained by the difference in pressure placed upon the two hospitals. Discussion with senior and junior medical and nursing staff indicated that it was their opinion that pressure was much greater in one hospital. In an attempt to define ward pressure, it was suggested that the occupancy of the ward and the number of admissions to the ward during the day of discharge of each patient in the study, should be examined. Initial indications were that higher pressure correlated with low length of stay but the study has not yet been concluded. The only conclusions drawn from the study were that much further work was required in this area if progress was to be made quantifying clinical and non-clinical aspects of length of stay.

COMMENT. This study revealed an apparent close interaction between clinical and managerial issues as reflected in length of stay. The question which remained unanswered was whether the managerial action of reviewing the intake of emergency cases directly forced a change in clinical practice by shortening the length of stay considered desirable by individual clinicians, or whether the change simply decreased the patient's length of stay by reducing the number of days on which that patient stayed in hospital for non-clinical reasons (for example, social—no one able to look after the patient at home; organizational discharge normally taking place on the consultant's ward round but having to be brought forward). The clinicians concerned in the study both felt that the increased pressure at least enforced a review of clinical policy, if not a change in clinical policy. It is perhaps interesting to note that following the examination of the figures the length of stay pattern of one of the two consultants appeared to change considerably, the mean length of stay being reduced by seven days. There are many factors influencing length of stay, and it would be difficult to draw any conclusion from such an apparent change in policy. The change first occurred in the year that provided the hospital with much greater pressure and the decreasing length of stay could be entirely attributed to that factor alone. The consultant concerned has expressed the view that he did not mindfully change his clinical policy in 1972 and it may well have been that the increased pressure upon his ward enforced the shorter length of stay. Table 2 indicated that the length of stay pattern for the colleagues of the consultant concerned (Consultant 1) did not change as markedly.

TABLE 2. *Length of stay for patients with acute myocardial infarction (excluding deaths and cases with an additional complication)*

	Arithmetic mean for six consultants					
	1	2	3	4	5	6
1968	27·3(6)	20·8(5)	28·5(4)	24·6(10)	24·1(16)	24·5(4)
1969	20·4(6)	27·7(3)	19·2(6)	23·1(19)	24·0(10)	25·8(11)
1970	24·2(6)	27·0(10)	24·0(4)	25·1(21)	31·0(11)	28·9(15)
1971	21·7(13)	13·2(5)	19·5(13)	25·7(25)	26·4(14)	26·6(9)
1972	14·6(10)	19·8(16)	18·8(12)	22·6(36)	20·4(20)	26·3(15)
1973	15·0(22)	17·6(18)	14·8(16)	21·9(22)	17·2(17)	—
1974	16·4(15)	16·2(13)	18·3(11)	22·3(24)	20·0(11)	—

The figure in brackets is the number of cases.

Participation

Case-study 5

The difficulties expressed in achieving an equitable distribution of emergency admissions between wards can be mirrored in the problems of distribution of emergency admissions between hospitals. A clinical division faced with problems of apparent inequitable distribution of junior medical staff in relation to the distribution of emergencies made comparisons between the two hospitals over a period of two years. It was apparent that the number of emergency admissions at each hospital had increased in the second year but that one hospital was admitting many more patients per bed. The division discussed the emergency arrangements for the whole of the city and in particular, the arrangements between the two hospitals. During a long debate on the subject of junior medical staffing at the hospitals, it was initially recommended by a majority vote that a medical staff post be immediately moved from one hospital to the other. The debate was very wide-ranging and many reasons for proposing the move were put forward. Amongst the reasons for moving the post was the readily accepted point that one hospital was undertaking twice as many emergency admissions per day as the other. Although it was not unanimously agreed, it was accepted by the division that the increased admission rate would cause increased workload for both nursing and junior medical staff. Ultimately, it was agreed unanimously that the post be transferred at a future date and some months later, this transfer took place.

COMMENT. This division recognized and accepted in this case that matters of resource use and allocation were likely to have clinical implications. One member of the division, after the meeting, stated that he had previously felt that the examination of statistics on bed-use would be a waste of time, but his opinion had now changed. He suggested that the information presented had played a vital part in influencing the decision of the division. Others attending the meeting felt that the information presented was one of only a number of factors which swayed the decision and may not have been the principle factor.

It would appear that this division was prepared to accept that inter-hospital variations in emergency admission patterns were likely to affect staffing workload whilst in Case-study 3 the division was not prepared to accept that inter-ward variations would have a significant effect. There may well be good reasons for the different conclusions but they would be difficult to prove since not only were the two opinions reached by the same division, they were also reached at the same meeting.

Case-study 6
A clinical division was faced with the problem of coping with the temporary closure of a small single specialty hospital in order to allow urgent maintenance work to take place. The division needed in-patient accommodation in order to cope with the emergency workload. Without any formal study of bed utilization new admissions were transferred to wards of the same specialty in other hospitals. During the period of the closure the bed utilization as measured by length of stay patterns, turnover interval, throughput and bed occupancy altered considerably. A study of one ward indicated that length of stay patterns changed considerably for patients admitted with similar diagnoses and that occupancy levels and turnover intervals not normally supported by the clinicians were achieved. Upon the reopening of the small hospital the levels of workload returned to the original pattern. Three months later a consultant who had not

previously worked on the ward joined the ward team. From the time of his arrival, not only did the over-all length of stay patterns alter but the occupancy levels and turnover intervals moved to the levels achieved during the hospital closure.

COMMENT. Marked alterations in the management of the ward were mirrored by changes in length of stay patterns. Whilst some of the change could be explained by variations in case-mix, there was evidence that either clinical policy altered or a considerable reduction of clinically unjustifiable in-patient days occurred.

Discussion

The case-studies were selected to illustrate clinicians participating in some aspects of hospital management. It would have been unrepresentative and unhelpful to merely examine enthusiastic problem-solving by clinicians. The grouping of the studies into three pairs was made in an attempt to emphasize that the enthusiasm of clinicians in reviewing the use of resources varies considerably. The 'hesitant sparring' in the first two case-studies demonstrated a mild acceptance of the view that some advantage could be gained by examining resource use, but the chances of affecting useful change were seen as remote. Problems were raised concerning the accuracy and timeliness of information, the need for additional information and the need to overhaul and review existing data collection systems. It must be added that the scepticism shown was often justified and problems remained unsolved because of lack of data, inaccurate data, and unwilling or inflexible management. With 'inquiring curiosity' there was a desire to explain variations but in so doing problems were found in obtaining appropriate information. Nevertheless, there was an improved understanding of the managerial problems being tackled. 'Participation' occurred in response to internal and external pressures. External pressures, such as a sudden acute shortage of facilities which happened because of circumstances outside the control of the division, were seen to encourage or force participation. Participation was also 'self-imposed' by clinicians examining variations in practice and in so doing setting a new standard to which they became committed.

This retrospective analysis of a few case-studies does not provide conclusive evidence that well-conducted reviews of hospital resources by clinicians will encourage review of clinical practice. In these studies only a handful of clinicians demonstrated an active interest in the review of clinical practice although many others recognized the implications for clinical practice in the review of resources. The examples indicate a spasmodic and relatively shallow approach to review of clinical practice compared with the more active participation claimed for work undertaken through an educational programme. It may well be that those clinicians who demonstrate an active interest in this subject through the medium of resource review are those who would express such interest through any available channel.

A serious impediment in mounting studies at divisional level into clinical practice lies in the problems of sample size. In the fourth case-study consideration was given to one diagnosis in general medicine. Although one of the most common causes of admission is general medicine only 470 cases suffering from acute myocardial infarction were admitted to the two general hospitals (with over 200 beds allocated to general medicine) in one year. When cases dying in hospital and those having a second or complicating diagnoses are excluded, then only 273 are left in the sample. In the two hospitals thirteen consultants admitted patients with the diagnoses studied but the number under the care of each consultant varied from 7 to 92 or when making the exclusions mentioned above from 2 to 62. Such small numbers make detailed review of clinical practice difficult and the problem can not be easily resolved by extending the time period because of the possibility of changes in clinical practice or other factors during that period.

Whilst the limitations of this approach to the review of clinical practice are apparent two important advantages must be considered. Firstly, whatever criticisms are made, it can be considered a relatively inexpensive method of broadening the understanding of the connection between clinical and managerial issues. When any change in activity is required two factors are an appreciation of the problem and a commitment to action. It is advantageous if these can be encouraged at the level where the responsibility for the quality of care and treatment, for operational management and for the control of budgets exists. Such advantages may not be so easily gained at national or regional levels even if sample sizes are more appropriate. The second possible advantage that arises from the case-studies concerns establishment of review mechanisms or special studies. The fact that a subject is under review has been shown to alter performance.

Brown (9) described how, in an industrial situation, performance changed because of the interest taken in the individuals and the subject. The study he described illustrated that although it was possible to vary the factors which influenced activity, such as physical working conditions, the most significant changes in activity related to the interest taken in the individuals during the study. This situation also occurs in hospital activities. In one group of hospitals each hospital was under an obligation to complete diagnostic summaries for every patient discharged and forward the summary to a central office. The responsibility for the completion of these forms rested with the junior medical staff and the medical records staff. The accuracy and completion rate varied from hospital to hospital and from period to period but one hospital was consistently the worst on both counts. The hospital was a single specialty hospital and the division responsible agreed that a senior registrar and an administrator should review the problem. At no time were staff instructed to change their activity and no changes in system were introduced. Within three months the hospital had the highest level of completion and the accuracy of the forms also improved dramatically. The high level of performance lasted during the employment of the two staff concerned with the review but has since tailed off. It may be that the clinical situation can be similarly influenced and there may be occasions when the establishment of a review mechanism will in itself alter clinical practice.

ACKNOWLEDGEMENTS

This paper results from work undertaken by the author during the period of a research grant provided by the Nuffield Provincial Hospitals Trust, to analyse the information requirements of a divisional structure. The majority of the case-studies emanated from work in the hospitals of the Central Birmingham Health District of the Birmingham Area Health Authority (Teaching). My particular thanks go to Dr Denys Blainey for his critical examination of my paper.

References

1. MINISTRY OF HEALTH (1967). *First Report of the Joint Working Party on the Organisation of Medical Work in Hospitals* ('Cogwheel' Report) (London: HMSO).
2. FORSYTH, G., and SHEIKH, J. M. (1971). *In Low Gear? An Examination of 'Cogwheels'*. Occasional Hundreds 2 (Oxford University Press for the Nuffield Provincial Hospitals Trust).

3. DEPARTMENT OF HEALTH AND SOCIAL SECURITY (1974). *Third Report of the Joint Working Party on the Organisation of Medical Work in Hospitals* (London: HMSO).

4. —— (1974). *Joint Working Party on the Organisation of Medical Work in Hospitals—Information for Action* (London: HMSO).

5. COCHRANE, A. L. (1971). *Effectiveness and Efficiency. Random Reflections on Health Services.* Rock Carling Monograph (London: Nuffield Provincial Hospitals Trust).

6. HUNTER, B. (1972). *The Administration of Hospital Wards. Factors Influencing Length of Stay in Hospital* (Manchester University Press).

7. OFFICE OF HEALTH ECONOMICS (1967). *Efficiency in the Hospital Service* (Leagrave Ross Ltd).

8. FORSYTH, G. (1973). *Doctors and State Medicine* (2nd edn) (Sir Isaac Pitman and Sons Ltd).

9. BROWN, J. A. C. (1954). *The Social Psychology of Industry* (Harmondsworth: Penguin).

11

The Hospital Advisory Service

ALEX BAKER
CBE, MD, MRCP, FRCPsych
Consultant Psychiatrist,
Gloucester Clinical Area,
Formerly Director, Hospital Advisory Service

The Hospital Advisory Service

The Hospital Advisory Service was set up in 1969 following a series of scandals and investigations in psychiatric hospitals. The appointment of Director was made in November of that year and the first team began visiting in February 1970.

The initial plan of operation of the hospital advisory service was as follows:

Functions

1. The functions of the Hospital Advisory Service are:
   (i) by constructive criticism and by propagating good practices and new ideas, to help to improve the management of patient care in individual hospitals (excluding matters of individual clinical judgement) and in the hospital service as a whole; and
   (ii) to advise the Secretary of State for Social Services about conditions in hospitals in England and the Secretary of State for Wales about conditions in hospitals in Wales.
2. The Hospital Advisory Service will operate independently of the Department of Health and Social Security and the Welsh Office. In relation to England, the Director will report to the Secretary of State for Social Services, and in relation to Wales, he will report to the Secretary of State for Wales. The Advisory Service will draw on information available to the Departments about the hospital service and associated community services. It will be free to comment on the aspects of the organization of the hospital service from the Departments down to ward level.

It should be noted that the proposals to improve the management of patient care were given priority with reporting to the Secretary of State as a second main function.

At the time, Richard Crossman said that he was tired of sending round memoranda nobody read, and he would prefer people to visit so that there could be a dialogue. It should also be noted that the

Hospital Advisory Service was not limited to the long-stay services only. It was agreed that visiting should begin with mental illness, mental handicap, and geriatric services, and would not be extended until there had been further discussion with the professions.

The Hospital Advisory Service provided a unique opportunity to try new techniques, in disseminating information, in assessing hospital function and in the propagation of good practices. The use of visits by a multidisciplinary team where the professions involved worked as equals set a particular example of relationships for the hospital being visited. The team members were expected to function as peers and equals of equivalent staff in the hospital concerned. It was considered important that they should not be looked on as superior beings, bearing new wisdom, but as fellow professionals working in similar hospitals with similar difficulties, anxious to discuss common problems, learn from mutual experience, and suggest possible new solutions. Although the visiting teams would assess and report on the facts and figures and physical state of the hospitals visited, it was recognized from the beginning of the Service that the way the hospital functioned was of much greater importance than its physical status. It was also recognized that it was much easier to assess the physical state than to assess the way of life, the relationships, and the policies which would underlie the hospital's functioning. It was expected that individual team members would try to assess the personality and attitudes of their opposite numbers in the hospital and also try to find out the policies which staff were implementing. In some hospitals this was relatively easy, and a few would have clearly understood agreed policies. Many hospitals, however, seem to live from day to day, year to year by carrying on old methods of working and adapting as best they could to fresh stress and difficulties without ever reviewing their basic policies. Although individual team members could often form a shrewd assessment of the total organization, sometimes such assessments were significantly erroneous. It was very rare, however, to find that the team as a whole had made serious errors of judgement.

The Hospital Advisory Service

THE VISITING TEAMS

The team usually consisted of a consultant with experience in the speciality concerned, a senior administrative nurse at the level of matron or chief male nurse, or chief nursing officer, a senior administrator, a social worker, and a ward nurse, usually ward sister or charge nurse, also with experience in the speciality. In the case of psychiatric hospitals, an occupational therapist was also a member of the team; in the case of the geriatric hospitals then it would be a physiotherapist. Additionally, at times, a general practitioner or other staff with particular skills would be added to a team. In general, however, every effort was made to keep the size of team down to five or six, as both in theory and in practice once a team gets above this size, effective debate on the many issues that are necessary becomes more and more difficult, and decision-making unduly prolonged.

Before visiting the hospital letters were written individually to the senior staff of the main professions, asking for their comments on the good points and on the difficulties within the hospital. Letters were also sent to the local medical committee, the local dental committee, and notices provided to be placed on the notice-boards throughout the hospitals. Some fifty letters were also sent to the most recently discharged patients of the hospital, asking them for their comments on the satisfactory or unsatisfactory aspects of the service they had received. This meant that before the team visited the hospital, they would have the basic statistics provided by the regional board and management committee, the comments from the senior staff in the hospital, additional points of view provided by the patients, and also by the GPs and others working in the community.

In general, a visit would last two weeks in the larger hospitals or occasionally three. For the smaller units of one or two wards, the visit might be as short as a day. As would be expected, there were often differences of opinion on many aspects of hospital life dependent upon the point of view of those replying to questions. The form of reply was also relevant. In some hospitals there would be a very wide response from a variety of staff at all levels, often with good ideas and imaginative suggestions. In other hospitals, there would be but the one reply, perhaps from a senior doctor or administrator, saying that he was writing on behalf of other staff, in his opinion, 'such and such' were the relevant factors. This occasionally occurred in spite of the letters emphasizing that individual opinions were requested from all the professions involved. The visit usually commenced with a relatively brief meeting with senior staff, primarily to make the initial introductions and to arrange the work of the team for the week. It also provided an opportunity for the staff concerned to raise questions about the method of visiting or details of the final report. These meetings too could be very revealing of relationships within the hospital, but their general intention was not to explore problem areas, so much as to set an informal scene and arrange the early introductions. During the course of the visit, the individual team members would visit all parts of the hospital and talk to as many staff as possible. Inevitably, however, the nurse would tend to make contact with the nursing organization, the doctor with the medical staff, and so on. In the evenings the team would meet over a meal and discuss the findings of the day and to pool their information. At the end of a visit there would be a final meeting which was regarded as very important. The staff who met the team were invited to the final meeting again, but also as a rule additional staff including particularly representatives of ward level staff. At the final meeting, each member of the team was expected to present in five or ten minutes his own conclusions on the hospital, its assets and problems, and possible solutions. The staff of the hospital were then invited to state whether they agreed with these opinions or disagreed or felt that other matters should be raised. Many of these meetings were welcomed, and proved very valuable with a brisk discussion on problem areas, methods of solution, and possible lines of improvement. Some hospitals, however, found it very difficult to accept criticism. Again, at some meetings there would be a very free expression of opinion from a wide variety of people on the hospital staff, in others one or two key figures would speak and in effect, inhibit any expression of opinion by others. It is sometimes very difficult for senior people who are often very efficient and competent in their own roles to accept that other people also need to develop their roles and leadership potential. A highly efficient departmental head could leave the Service in considerable disarray when he retires if he has not taken active steps to develop the competence of others around him and to encourage their initiative and skills. A modern hospital with its complex organization cannot afford to have a lot of 'yes' men around a few key figures. For the same reason, one must suspect the effectiveness of any hospital where there are never any difficulties or conflicts. A hospital that claims that there are never any differences of opinion or conflicts between the professions is either covering up problems or, alternatively, one or other profession has learnt simply to give in to the others, to their own detriment.

At the final meeting it was made clear that the report would in some measure be determined by the response of the staff to the comments made at the final meeting. They were therefore in a position to influence the final report, either by proposing an alternative emphasis on many matters, or indeed, by rebutting specific criticisms or problems. In general, however, it was notable that the vast majority of hospitals accepted the assessment made. There was greater difficulty, however, in accepting the necessity for change as this was often a much more painful process involving the lifestyle of key individuals. After the final meeting, and usually within a matter of two or three weeks, the team would have a week at headquarters to write their report, which was then edited by the Director. The first copy of the report went direct to the Secretary of State and further copies, within twenty-four hours, to the Department of Health and Social Security. Regrettably, delays at the DHSS often held up the arrival of the report at hospital level, not uncommonly for months at a time. There is no doubt that the report was more likely to be effective and to lead to discussion and progress, if it was received as soon as possible after the visit. With the resources at its disposal, the Hospital Advisory Service was not able to initiate follow-up visits even to known problem areas, with one or two very rare exceptions.

The process of visiting is obviously more complex than the simple matter of collecting facts and assessing personalities. Visiting is a dynamic process, which begins before the team arrives. At all levels the very fact that a visit would take place led to changes in attitude and the allocation of time and resources. During the visit the sort of questions that were asked, the response during discussion, and the contents of meetings, would all tend to emphasize particular aspects of the hospital, and show which aspects were regarded as important by the visiting team. It is not possible to have a visiting system which will simply assess the local situation. Some changes are inevitable, and it is obviously preferable to use the opportunity to initiate helpful change in the organization. In particular, the Advisory Service stimulated development of the multidisciplinary approach to hospital life.

Planning and decision-making

The effectiveness of any modern psychiatric or geriatric service is dependent upon the very close co-operation of the different professions involved at all levels. This means there should be very close co-operation and agreement on policies for the hospital as a whole, and at area and regional level on agreement on major planning, allocation of resources, new building, or other major matters. It was striking, perhaps, that when the Hospital Advisory Service started visiting services for the mentally handicapped, very few regional boards had any comprehensive plan whatever for the development of these services. Within a year of the visits commencing, however, all regional boards had plans, some of them in very good detail. Similarly, at hospital management committee level, it was rare to find a management committee with clear and positive proposals for the development of their services. They often seemed to assume that the medical staff would be responsible for planning, yet had rarely asked even for the basic facts on admission and discharge rates, population served and matters of such kind, which would have enabled them to manage their own resources more effectively. One of the more serious gaps in the management of resources which was found in hospital after hospital by the Advisory Service, was the absence of anyone with clear responsibility for deciding on the development of local services. If there was an active doctor interested in planning in post, considerable progress might be made in one hospital, but in another with exactly similar problems there might well be a static service, where the doctors accepted the situation they found on their arrival, and apparently, would have been content to leave it unchanged on their departure. It is often forgotten that doctors have been given very little training in management, alloca-tion of resources, or indeed, their own responsibilities to a popula-tion in their training at teaching hospital level. It is only when they become consultants and have a particular population to look after that some, at least, begin to consider how best to allocate their time, or how best to advise on the allocation of those resources they see available. One of the more valuable aspects of the Hospital Advisory Service was the encouragement it gave to those who did have ideas about planning and the use of resources, to develop their interests and skills. The opportunity of the Advisory Service to see how different services were developing and pass on ideas to other hospitals was often invaluable to the recipients.

The very fact that the Advisory Service was a multidisciplinary organization had considerable impact on many hospitals. The team were expected to demonstrate, particularly at the final meeting, how professional staff could maintain their own standards, and yet in the process of discussion and debate, help to develop the skills and potential of others. It was often demonstrated that the multi-disciplinary approach was more valuable than an assessment made by any one profession. The fact that a multidisciplinary approach had been made by the team usually meant that the hospital, too, had to develop its multidisciplinary system if they were to make an effective response to the visit and the subsequent report. In particular, the Hospital Advisory Service would emphasize the need for multidisciplinary assessment and decision-making at ward level, and also at hospital level. In general, there was a ready acceptance of the need for multidisciplinary involvement at the level of the individual patient, but more difficulty in accepting the need for a similar in-volvement when management of hospital resources as a whole were concerned. There had often been a tendency for the medical staff or the group secretary, but usually the former, to take major decisions, and the concept of discussion and consensus agreement involving all the professions was not always welcome. On the other hand, it was often striking that in hospitals where the doctors had insisted on keeping all the decision-making authority to themselves, they were well aware of the difficulties this caused and the unsatisfactory nursing and other response they were obtaining. Sometimes, the initial response to suggestions that there should be a multi-disciplinary approach was to agree that a nurse and administrator should attend medical staff meetings, thus ensuring that medical dominance would continue with a massive voting majority. On the other hand, some hospitals readily accepted that the concept of a multidisciplinary team of administrator, medical, nursing, remedial and social work staff was more likely to commit all the professions involved to any real change or progress, and having once committed themselves to this system, found there were significant benefits.

The problems and disadvantages of the Advisory Service are fairly obvious. The DHSS has always had anxiety at the idea that another organization could report directly to the Secretary of State and, perhaps, give contrary advice to that given by Department officials, or contrary advice to DHSS policy. On the other hand, in view of the rapidly changing scene in many fields of medicine, it is probably a mistake for the DHSS to consider that one particular policy can always apply, and equally, the Department should welcome sugges-tions and alternatives which may be more appropriate in local areas.

There is no doubt that the Advisory Service does make extra work for the administrative tiers, whether they were the old regional boards or the present regional and area health authorities. Again, it could be argued that the extra work was in many cases necessary, and if it led to more effective planning and a concentration on neglected areas, it was essential. At hospital level, again, some hospital staff resented the implication that there could be anything wrong with their service, and found a joint discussion on problem areas traumatic. It is particularly unfortunate, of course, that the hospitals in the greatest need of help, often overburdened and with low morale, found it most difficult to use the services and assistance offered by the Advisory Service. It was not unknown, however, for hospitals to reject advice totally during the course of the visit, but then to discreetly implement the advice given when the team had gone away.

Facts and figures

Some basic facts should give a rough idea of the likely standard of the service being provided. Unfortunately, acquiring accurate facts is not as easy as it might seem at first sight. Even the crudest figures need careful interpretation. Teams found it extremely difficult to get agreed figures on the population being served, differing figures often being given by regional boards, local authorities, and the local management committee. These might differ by tens of thousands in some cases. Again, the size of the hospital, one might have thought, would not be in dispute. It was not uncommon to find that even the number of wards, let alone the number of beds, was in dispute. Sometimes this was because a ward had been converted into another type of accommodation, and at one hospital, such accommodation might still be called a ward, and in another hospital, a hostel. Buildings at a distance from the main hospital often seem to have different titles. In one, a hostel would be called a long-stay ward, in another, an after-care hostel, and in a third, a minimum care unit. The number of consultant psychiatrists to a given population ought to determine the number of consultant hours available, and in theory, the number of patients likely to be seen. However, teams found striking variations in the way a consultant would allocate his time, one consultant perhaps involved with psychotherapy, seeing relatively few patients, and another, limiting himself largely to advice on physical treatments, seeing twenty times as many. The standard of nursing care between hospitals might vary enormously, even when the nurse/patient ratio was exactly the same. In one hospital, nurses would be doing a wide variety of non-nursing duties, including some domestic work, or running an occupational therapy department. In another hospital, where there was an adequate supply of domestics and occupational therapists, the amount of nursing time actually available to patients, might be very considerably increased. It was not uncommon to find hospitals who were largely oblivious both of the way their service differed from that of other hospitals, and also of the effects of their own policies. One of the commonest examples of this were the hospitals for the mentally ill, where all the consultants serving a population of say, half a million, admitted their patients to one or two admission wards. Inevitably, with current admission rates, the admission ward was quite unable to deal with the intake, which meant the patients were passed on very rapidly to back-up wards before their treatment was completed. Some hospitals seemed to be largely unaware of the trouble this caused for everybody and the waste of human relationships. Others might be well aware of it, but had taken no effective steps to alter it. Surprisingly few hospitals had undertaken the logical step of analysing their admissions per consultant, working out the number of admission beds needed and deliberately providing the necessary wards. In my opinion, one of the most valuable aspects of the Hospital Advisory Service lay in the ability of teams to bring to the attention of hospital staff the results of their own activities. Familiarity undoubtedly breeds contempt, and may also produce a situation where highly unsatisfactory practices are tolerated by all involved over long periods of time.

In the same situation, a common problem was found where several consultants shared a ward. There might be an obvious need to change the policy of the ward, but this required the consent of all the consultants. For a variety of reasons this may be difficult to obtain, and the situation, however unsatisfactory, may persist over long periods of time for lack of any person with authority to alter it, or the necessary goodwill and give and take between those involved. Sometimes a visit by an outside and uncommitted person may enable a change of policy without loss of face for those who have to continue with the day-to-day situation. The quality of relationship between consultants can be the key to a developing or static service, even where the relationships cannot be improved, outside visitors may assist significantly in the solution of well-known problems.

Rotation of staff

The Hospital Advisory Service teams were formed by the secondment of staff from their usual post in the National Health Service, such secondment usually lasting about a year. In the formation of a team, attempts were made to choose staff who would complement each other both in skills and, as far as possible, personality. For example, there was an obvious need on every team for at least one member to be relatively senior with a great deal of experience. Equally, there was a need to have someone who would be likely to have new ideas and be an innovator. If one member of a team had experience which was almost entirely in large hospitals, this had to be counterbalanced by staff who had experience of smaller units. The teams, therefore, often tended to reflect the very problems in terms of relationships which are commonly met with in hospitals. These problems consist of the understandable conservatism of older members of staff, who have been brought up within one particular system of management. They will have some areas of conflict with the younger and more progressive staff, who wish to develop new ideas, sometimes at a pace which the older organization cannot tolerate. Within the team there would inevitably be some measure of conflict between those members of staff who were largely hospital-orientated, and those, such as the social workers, who would be more community-based. The individual team members undoubtedly acquired skills and understanding of interpersonal relationships and relationships between the professions, and were then able to use their added skills when visiting hospitals. There can be little doubt that a year's experience in the Hospital Advisory Service was a very valuable form of postgraduate education for many of those who joined the service. Since there was a constant renewal of staff, there was no opportunity for the Hospital Advisory Service to form set patterns or standards of its own. The constant interchange of ideas between people from different hospitals also helped to spread the knowledge of good practices and solution of common problems.

Visiting teams were, therefore, able to compare the relationships they had been able to form within the team, with the relationships they found in hospitals. Obviously, there would be some differences in the relationship formed in a team only working together for a few months with that of teams perhaps which have been working together for ten or twenty years. The areas of conflict and the influence of personality on these various conflicts, however, tended to be very similar, and it was notable that where some follow-up had been done, or more than one team visited a hospital, their assessments of the relationships and problems were very similar indeed. The most effective organizations are those where there is a balance between the personalities of the senior staff in the varying professions. In the emerging professions, such as nursing and social work, it was often apparent that the equality of status given to the nursing and social work members of the Hospital Advisory Service team encouraged their opposite numbers within the hospital and gave them fresh confidence in developing their own status and roles within their hospital. For some hospitals the example of a multidisciplinary team in action was a stimulating one, in others it was a painful reminder to them of the problems within their own organization, and some of these hospitals rejected the concept of multidisciplinary equality. This, understandably perhaps, was most common in those hospitals which had had a very strong medical or other hierarchy, which was finding it difficult to share authority with the emerging independent professions.

The future

It has been shown that the visiting system can be organized, which is economical, uses existing staff's skills, and can be generally acceptable to the staff involved at hospital and administrative level. There is no doubt that the system could be extended to cover the whole of the hospital service, and indeed, the links between the hospital service, general practitioner and local authority services. The style and details might well be different, when visiting casualty departments, maternity departments, or surgical departments, but the principle of visiting by a team of fellow professionals, to join in a mutual examination of the service, seems basically sound.

From the point of view of logistics, it would be possible, for example, for two teams visiting mental illness hospitals to visit every hospital in the country on a rota basis, every three to five years.

This system, however, should be backed with the ability to call on specialist teams to follow-up visits to help deal with particular problem areas. I feel it is essential that such an Advisory Service should remain independent of the DHSS, and should not be associated with official policies.

The US scene

12

Quality assurance mechanisms in the United States : from there to where ?

ROBERT H. BROOK
MD, ScD

*Senior Health Services Research Staff Member,
RAND Corporation, Santa Monica, California;
Director of the UCLA Clinical Scholars
Program, School of Medicine, University of
California, and Assistant Professor of
Medicine and Public Health at UCLA*

ALLYSON DAVIES AVERY
MPH

*Health Services Research Staff Member,
RAND Corporation,
Santa Monica, California*

Quality assurance mechanisms in the United States: from there to where?

The American medical care system has been described as an amorphous 'non-system', employing organizational techniques of a century ago that are unsuited to an industry that consumes more than $100 billion annually. Critics have attacked the system for a variety of faults: no evident over-all objective; lack of planning; lack of a national financing mechanism; lack of a national delivery system; and inequity in the use of medical care resources by different segments of the population. Whether any of these criticisms are justified is debatable; what is not debatable is that many other countries have been able to deal directly with these same criticisms by organizing fundamentally new or even radical (by United States standards) medical care delivery systems.

Yet none of the countries that have instituted innovative arrangements to deliver care have mounted programmes to measure, and then if necessary change, the level of quality of care being provided to individuals or groups of patients. The need for such a programme is obvious, given the radical shift in the function of the medical care system over the past century. One hundred years ago, the primary function of the medical care system was the compassionate caring for patients. Today, due to advances in the biomedical sciences, another function must be added: efficient delivery to the entire population of efficacious medical services that result in cure or control of disease and in maintenance or improvement of health. Some type of quality assurance system appears necessary in order to measure the performance of this second function.

The United States finds itself pushed to the fore in development of a quality assurance system. Three forces are chiefly responsible for this development: (*a*) escalating costs in the federally funded Medicare and Medicaid programmes led to passage of PL 92–603, which contains provisions for establishing Professional Standards

Review Organizations (1); (*b*) disenchantment with the efficiency of the prevailing fee-for-service delivery system led to passage of the Health Maintenance Organization Act of 1973, which requires quality assurance systems in each organization (2); and (*c*) rapidly increasing premiums for malpractice insurance coverage led to the 'malpractice crisis of 1974–5' (3), which has resulted in considering the replacement of physician liability with relicensure or mandatory continuing education.

The purpose of this paper is threefold: to place recent developments in quality assurance in the United States in a historical perspective; to describe ongoing quality assurance programmes and analyse their potential for actually improving quality of medical care and thereby the health of the American people; and to indicate those areas in which continuing research on both the methods of quality assessment and on the actual level of care rendered must proceed. Hopefully policymakers in other countries can benefit from a review of the United States' experience and will not repeat our mistakes.

I
BRIEF HISTORY OF QUALITY ASSESSMENT

It would be unnecessarily pedantic to begin this review of efforts to assure quality of care with examples taken from the ancient Greeks or Egyptians, or from the Bible. This historical review must, however, place in proper perspective several ideas, supposedly developed during the last two decades in the United States, that actually originated over a century ago in the United Kingdom.

By 1858, Florence Nightingale (4) had conducted a series of studies describing the quality of hospital care available to the British Army during the Crimean War. She used data such as the number of hospital deaths per diagnostic category to describe the unsafe conditions prevailing in army hospitals. Nightingale argued that changes in sanitary conditions could produce dramatic changes in these case-fatality rates.

A few years later, Nightingale (5) proposed what today would be considered a uniform hospital discharge abstract system. The objective of this system was to relate the use of hospital beds to indicators of health in order to encourage the most efficient and effective use of beds. Examples of items to be collected were: (*a*) the number of patients admitted to the hospital during the year; (*b*) the number of patients who died in the hospital and/or who recovered and were discharged during the year; and (*c*) the numbers of patients discharged as incurable or unrelieved, or who left the hospital at their own request.

Nightingale recognized that the analysis of such data, after controlling for demographic variables, would provide the following information: (*a*) specific medical and surgical treatments could be correlated with diagnostic categories; (*b*) mortality rates could be calculated for each diagnostic category; and (*c*) the proportion of hospital beds used for restoration of function as opposed to providing a place to die could be determined. Thus, Nightingale appreciated the need to examine both what was done to patients and what happened to patients: both the process and the outcome of care. It is ironic that while the importance of such analyses is now recognized, debate continues in the United States over how the system necessary to support these analyses should be established (6).

A half century later, in 1908, Groves (7) issued a plea for the uniform registration of the results of operations. The basis for his plea was succinctly stated:

If . . . a surgeon makes a specialty of some disease or operation and tabulates all his own results, or another by chance has some notable successes and records them, or the author of a textbook collects published records of various writers and summarizes them, is it not obvious that such collection of figures will represent the best and not the average results?

In order to obtain information about 'average results', Groves conducted a survey of the 50 hospitals in Great Britain with over 200 beds. Data from the 27 hospitals responding showed a 44 per cent operative mortality from radical operations for malignant diseases of the stomach, a 24 per cent mortality from prostatectomy, and a 9 per cent mortality from an operation to cure appendicitis. Groves's proposal for implementation of such a system raised two generic points: (*a*) the need to develop an acceptable standard classification for diseases and operations that would permit comparisons of data from different hospitals; and (*b*) the need to establish a follow-up system for particular categories of disease, such as malignancies, that would allow assessment of long-term results, such as mortality, level of disability, or extent of symptoms.

Only a few years later (1914), Codman (8), a surgeon at the Massachusetts General Hospital, lamented the lack of outcome assessment in the United States.

One might say that the instruction of the students is irrespective of the results to the patients, but let us suppose, in surgery, for example, that all the operations which have been watched by these students have been misdirected efforts at the cure of disease, and the students have learned to do something which is not worthwhile and does not really improve the patient. The product of the hospital in this case, even as regards student instruction, would be nil—even worse than nil. We are, therefore, referred again to the classification of disease and the results to the patients, because a student would naturally wish to receive his instruction at a hospital where the treatment was shown to be of benefit to the patient. We may then say that the product of the hospital in medical education, like the product in the number of cases treated, depends on whether or not the cases are well treated . . .

In an effort to determine whether patients were well treated, Codman attempted to institute a follow-up system at the Massachusetts General Hospital. The objective of this system was to raise his own level of performance by examining one year later all the patients on whom he had operated. From information to be gathered at this examination, Codman hoped to determine whether the operation had been indicated, and if it had improved the patient's symptoms.

After being thoroughly frustrated in his initial effort, he resigned his position at Massachusetts General and started his own hospital in which he instituted a follow-up system. Each surgical patient was recalled a year later for assessment of health status in terms of the original objectives of the operation. From this assessment, Codman was able to determine whether his original diagnosis was correct, the operation was a technical success, the patient had benefited from the operation, and whether the operation had produced some untoward or iatrogenic effect.

After considering the significant contributions that Nightingale, Groves, and Codman had made by 1914, it is disappointing to observe that little substantive work in the field of quality assurance was done during the next three decades. Perhaps the Flexner report (9), which prompted major improvements in the structure and content of medical education in the United States, had an untoward result as well. Since the process of medical education was assumed to be adequate after Flexnerian reforms, the need to measure the results of care delivered by physicians trained in the new schools may have been considered unnecessary.

When interest in assessing the quality of care began again in the late 1940s and 1950s, the focus of these efforts had undergone a striking metamorphosis. No longer was assessment of quality of care based on end-results of care. Instead, emphasis was placed on examining the adequacy of diagnostic investigations and therapeutic interventions: the process of medical care.

Three landmark studies of this period were Morehead's study (10) of the quality of ambulatory care provided in the Health Insurance Plan (a prepaid group practice) of New York City; Payne's study (11) of the quality of care rendered in a select group of short-term general hospitals in Michigan; and Peterson's 1953-4 study (12) of the quality of care delivered by GPs in North Carolina. Morehead's assessment relied on physicians' judgements of the process of care, arrived at both by reviewing medical records and by talking to physicians who gave the care. Payne judged adequacy of the process of care by comparing the information contained in the medical record against a set of explicit, disease-specific criteria established by a group of physicians. Peterson observed the GPs while they were providing care, scoring their practice on the basis of the adequacy of the history, physical examination, therapy, and type and amount of follow-up care. All three studies concluded that there were major deficiencies in the care provided.

Other attempts to assess quality of care during this period focused on structural variables: innate characteristics of physicians such as age or length of training, and of facilities, such as structural soundness or staffing patterns. The best-known proponent of this type of assessment was the Joint Commission on the Accreditation of Hospitals (JCAH), which sent expert teams to hospitals to evaluate their quality against a checklist of minimum standards.

The shift away from outcome assessment as an indicator of quality care during the forties and fifties may have been motivated in part by concerns for practicality and feasibility. Information about what a physician did for the patient could be obtained from the medical record. Information about the end-results of care could only be obtained from follow-up patient interviews, which required increased expenditures and extensive co-operation by physicians and patients. At the same time, emphasis was being placed on new procedures which used sophisticated instrumentation to probe the inner recesses of the body. A non-critical fascination with the technology of modern scientific medicine prevailed, one which did not encourage questioning the value of these procedures. This changing view of medicine, emphasizing use of technology rather than the 'laying on of hands', may also have contributed to the focus on medical process rather than patient end-results in quality assessment.

Regardless of the focus, however, the results of these studies were similar. Serious deficiencies in care were found, which suggested that many practising physicians had trouble taking basic histories and performing adequate physical examinations.

Since 1965, a combination of circumstances has prompted renewed efforts to assess the quality of care by measuring patient end-results. Costs of personal medical care services have risen rapidly in all countries, in the face of increased demands by all social systems (such as education) on scarce resources. In the United States, the contribution of the federal government to financing medical care has tripled in the past decade. This increased financial involvement has brought with it increased governmental regulation of both costs and the quality of the services purchased. Finally, there is growing public concern that improved financing and delivery of medical care services may be less effective in maintaining or improving health than would improvement of other social conditions, such as housing or employment.

The need to control costs and the increased questioning of the effectiveness of medical care services spearheaded a variety of efforts to evaluate the effectiveness and efficacy of expensive yet commonly accepted medical procedures. The majority of these have been undertaken by researchers in the United Kingdom. For example, Mather (13) examined the relative efficacy of the coronary care unit versus home care in treating individuals following acute heart attacks. Analysis of the results of his experiment demonstrated that for the group of patients that was assigned randomly to home or hospital care, hospitalization in the coronary care unit did not decrease the risk of dying. In another experimental study, Weddell and his colleagues found that out-patient treatment of patients with varicose veins using an injection procedure produced an equally satisfactory cosmetic result and less morbidity than did the generally accepted and more costly in-patient operation (14, 15). Finally, an experiment performed in the United States showed that hypoglycemic agents, the usual treatment for patients with adult-onset asymptomatic diabetes, may increase mortality instead of decreasing it (16).

The results of investigations such as these have produced an environment which permits the value of technical medicine as practised in the average community to be questioned. Many powerful new therapies (antibiotics, intensive care units, radical surgical procedures, antineoplastic drugs) have been shown to produce serious iatrogenic disease as well as to save lives. The effectiveness of these therapies is dictated by the preciseness or quality with which they are applied, intensifying the need for implementation of a valid quality assurance system. The old adage that it did not make any difference what type of doctor one saw since his armamentarium contained only placebos is no longer operative in an era of space-age technology and potent medication. Given this realization, establishment of a quality assurance mechanism for the personal medical care system is by no means an irrational wish, but a practical necessity.

This review supports several conclusions about the state-of-the-art of quality assessment that are directly relevant to a description of present-day attempts to regulate the quality of medical care. Interest in evaluating quality is common to medical care systems world-wide, regardless of their particular form of financing or organization; it is not solely a concern of fee-for-service systems. Rather than being a product of recent forces, efforts to evaluate quality have gone on for over a century. During that time, research has documented major deficiencies in quality of care, and great variation in the level of quality provided in several countries. Even more serious, little of this information has been used to actually improve the quality of care provided.

It is apparent that new conceptual frameworks for assessing quality have not been developed in the last two decades. Although three time-honoured approaches stand out (assessment of quality using structural, process, and outcome variables), there is no consensus as to which produces the most valid judgements. In each approach, judgements of quality have been based on either implicit or explicit criteria. Here again, no consensus exists regarding which type of judgement provides the most valid result. Data on quality of care have been obtained from a variety of sources, ranging from claims for payment of services rendered to medical records to direct observation of medical practice. The extent to which the validity and reliability of the quality assessment depends on each of these data sources is not known.

II
ONGOING QUALITY ASSURANCE SYSTEMS

After reviewing the history of research in quality assessment, it is appropriate to consider current policies and programmes to assure quality in the United States before exploring the contribution further research can make to increased effectiveness of these programmes. Each of these policies and programmes has contributed a new acronym—PSRO, EMCRO, PEP, MAP, TAP, QAP—to the already bewildering array of shorthand in the medical care field. The 'attack of the alphabet' can be made light of, but deserves more serious consideration. The variety of names given to quality assurance programmes is indicative of the many different approaches taken to quality assurance. These, in turn, indicate that any attempt to institute quality assurance systems in the United States must take account of the complexity and pluralistic nature of American medical care. The success of these attempts may to a very real degree depend as much on this as on their ability to improve quality.

Professional Standards Review Organizations

The largest and most controversial of the quality assurance systems, the Professional Standards Review Organization (PSRO) programme was established in 1972. The federal government is required to take action to assure that its financial resources are used efficiently and that services are of high quality. (These two objectives—cost containment and quality assurance—may be mutually exclusive, and it is debatable as to which will emerge as the primary focus of the programme.)

The law (1) provides that: (*a*) payment for services covered under certain sections of the Social Security Act will be made only when and to the extent services are judged medically necessary; (*b*) payment will be made for services provided by a hospital on an in-patient basis only when such services cannot be provided effectively on an out-patient basis, or more economically in an in-patient health care facility of a different type; (*c*) Professional Standards Review Organizations are responsible for determining that: (i) services and items are medically necessary; and (ii) the quality of such services meets professionally recognized standards of health care. As a quality assurance system, PSRO's scope is limited in two important ways. Only the care delivered to persons enrolled in federally financed programmes (chiefly Medicare and Medicaid) will be reviewed, and only services rendered in an institutional setting—the hospital and nursing home component of medical care—are subject to review. (Although the law does provide for eventual review of ambulatory services delivered to enrollees, such an expansion is not likely soon.) Medicare provides coverage for part of the medical care received by the elderly; Medicaid covers most of the medical care provided to low-income persons. Thus, the PSRO programme will monitor costs and quality of care delivered to approximately one-fourth of the United States population, which consumes about one-third of its medical care services.

It is interesting to consider why a law was passed that regulates only one part of the medical care industry. The Medicare and Medicaid programmes began operation in the mid-1960s. By the early 1970s, costs, particularly for hospital services, had far exceeded budgetary expectations, so much so that attempts at cost control were inevitable. Narrowing the scope of benefits was politically unattractive at the federal level, where responsibility lies for virtually all Medicare financing; such changes were made by several states in their Medicaid programmes, which are jointly funded by state and federal governments. Changes in cost-sharing to Medicare enrollees were made at a federal level, chiefly by increasing deductibles, but these too were politically unattractive measures. Utilization review committees were set up in participating hospitals and charged with reviewing the necessity for hospitalization, but they were ineffective in stemming the rising utilization of services.

While these federal efforts were proving ineffective, peer review activities were developing within the profession. The 'medical care foundation' movement, which traces its roots to California in the mid-1950s, gained considerably in numbers during the early 1970s. These foundations are not-for-profit organizations of a hundred to a few thousand physician members. While the functions of individual foundations vary considerably, the 'foundation' is best known for its review of care delivered by participating physicians to determine appropriateness and quality of services before authorizing payment for such services by fiscal intermediaries.

This interest in peer review resulted in the participation of several foundations in the Experimental Medical Care Review Organization (EMCRO) programme (17, 18, 19). The dual purposes of this federally funded programme were to determine if medical foundations, organized as they were on an area-wide basis, could both improve the quality of care delivered and increase the efficiency with which scarce resources were used. Some leaders of these organizations quickly argued that the review activities led to stabilization of costs and to improvement in the quality of care. Objective evidence to support that rhetoric is limited. This lack of data is due chiefly to the fact that these programmes, particularly the EMCROs, were not funded in a manner which facilitated rigorous programme evaluation. A few articles suggest that these programmes did contain costs by decreasing hospital utilization by about 2 to 5 per cent (20, 21). However, due to weak evaluative techniques and the relatively small differences found, the conclusions are extremely controversial and may in fact be erroneous. Furthermore, a recent study of the New Mexico EMCRO could find no impact of the programme's pre-admission hospital certification programme, which determined medical necessity for services, on utilization of such services (22). This organization, however, has had a marked effect on one aspect of quality, the inappropriate use of injectables. Education of physicians and denial of payment for claims submitted for inappropriate injections decreased the number of injections given from 37 per 100 ambulatory visits to 19 per 100 visits, a 50 per cent reduction, over a two-year period. Since half of these injections were antibiotics, of which 75 per cent were judged by local peer review as medically unnecessary, iatrogenic complications of medical therapy were obviously prevented.

Despite the lack of solid, objective evidence of worth, modelling PSROs on the medical foundation and EMCRO experience seemed reasonable from a political point of view. Many physicians supported these organizations, some information documented their efficacy, and rhetoric suggested that cost containment and quality improvement were both possible. The needs of government and at least some of the profession were to be met.

IMPLEMENTATION

Implementation of the programme began in earnest after January 1974, by which time the country had been divided into 203 PSRO areas with populations of approximately one million each. Since there are about 7,000 non-federal short-term hospitals in the United States, each area contains about 35 hospitals.

The promise of $50,000 in planning funds, and the implied threat that the Secretary of Health, Education, and Welfare could designate any group, including a non-physician group, as the PSRO if local physicians did not organize a PSRO before July 1976, prompted physicians to begin forming local groups. Each area-wide PSRO is a not-for-profit corporation. All licensed physicians (and only physicians), including medical doctors and osteopaths, are eligible for membership in the local PSRO. Membership is voluntary, and the PSRO can not charge membership dues. If more than 10 per cent of the physicians in a PSRO area object to the particular group organized, a vote of all physicians practising in that area is required by law to accept or reject the PSRO. Once such an organization is founded, it competes through a grant process for federal planning funds. After successful completion of the planning stage (usually one or two years), the PSRO obtains conditional status and another year or two later becomes fully operational. At present, some 30 per cent of the areas are in the planning stage, and another 30 per cent have a conditional organization ; there are no fully operational PSROs.

PSRO QUALITY OF CARE ASSURANCE

In order to adequately carry out its legal mandate, each PSRO will be responsible for seeing that studies directed at utilization review and quality of care assurance are performed in each of the area hospitals. The authority to perform these studies may be delegated to each hospital's utilization review committee rather than being retained by the PSRO, but responsibility for fulfilling legal requirements remains with the PSRO. The utilization review activities of the PSRO are described elsewhere (23, 24). The quality of care assurance activities are described here in more detail.

To fulfil the quality assurance function, each hospital in a PSRO area must do four diagnosis-specific medical care evaluations (MCEs) annually. Selection of diagnoses could be made independently by each hospital, which could produce up to 28,000 different

MCEs each year. In selecting diagnoses for study, hospital committees must consider the frequency of each diagnosis and the ability of medical care to alter the natural history of the diagnosed problem, and must have some reason to believe that the quality of care for the diagnosis is currently inadequate. Again at the individual hospital's discretion, information used in the MCE may be drawn from either the medical record or patient interviews, and either process or outcome criteria may form the basis for the quality judgement. Demonstrated deficiencies in care must be corrected, and a second MCE is required to document improvements.

Sample size will prove a major problem in using MCE results to improve quality of care. In 1973, there were 32·1 million discharges from non-federal short-stay hospitals in the United States (25). If one-fourth of the discharges in each of some 200 PSRO areas were due to Medicare and Medicaid patients, then approximately 40,000 discharges in each PSRO area would have been subject to review. If a diagnosis accounts for 2 per cent of all discharges (a high estimate), a typical PSRO will have about 800 cases per year in that diagnostic category. Each hospital within the PSRO will have 800 ÷ 35 or 23 cases to review for each MCE. Thus, the ability to document improvements in quality of care resulting from the MCEs performed by individual hospitals will be in most cases a statistical impossibility.

In summary, the PSRO programme is a government-mandated cost control and quality assurance system, organized and operated by physicians and hospitals at a local level. Local control and local establishment of criteria and standards for peer review will make it difficult, if not impossible, to compare findings of MCEs across PSRO areas. Results from the planned nationwide evaluation of the PSRO programme, if it is ever performed, may be the only solution to this problem (26). The evaluation design requires detailed examination of the care delivered to patients in 20 to 30 disease-specific categories. For each disease category, the impact of the PSRO system on cost of care, quality of care, and utilization of services will be evaluated. Since a standardized set of criteria and data instruments will be used, this evaluation should permit the comparison of regional differences in cost and quality of care. However, like the EMCRO programme before it, the PSRO programme was not implemented in a manner that permits the development of a strong evaluation design, and the results of the programme evaluation will very likely be controversial. Finally, since MCEs review services delivered only to that portion of the population that is elderly and/or low-income, it will be impossible to use these findings to describe the quality of care received by the entire United States population.

Performance Evaluation Procedure

The second major ongoing quality assurance programme in the United States is also focused on hospital care, and was developed by a voluntary non-governmental agency, the Joint Commission on Accreditation of Hospitals (JCAH). In the United States, hospitals are licensed by state governments, rather than by the federal government. In addition, hospitals can also become accredited by the JCAH. While most US hospitals are accredited, it is strictly a voluntary procedure. The main incentives to accreditation are an increase in prestige, and automatic certification by the federal government for reimbursement of services delivered under the Medicare and Medicaid programmes. Until recently, JCAH accreditation was based largely on whether the hospital met certain structural criteria, such as posting a poison chart in the emergency room or following minimum personnel standards.

A few years ago, the JCAH devised an aggressive quality assurance programme known as the Performance Evaluation Procedure (PEP) for Auditing and Improving Patient Care. Eventually, in order to keep its accreditation, each hospital will be required to do from 4 to 22 PEPs annually. Currently, the JCAH is conducting a series of seminars—TAP (Trustees-Administrator-Physician Institutes) (27) and MAP (Medical Audit Programmes)—to describe the use of PEP and train appropriate personnel to carry out its functions. The method of performing a PEP has been described in great detail elsewhere (28), and will be discussed only briefly here.

Before performing a PEP, criteria and standards are established for a selected disease or procedure. Selection of the topic for evaluation is done locally by each hospital. The criteria established must provide answers to the following three questions: (*a*) Did the physician make the appropriate diagnostic and major intervention decisions? (*b*) Was the patient's outcome (especially mortality) what it should have been? (*c*) Do other clues (such as length of stay or complications during hospitalization) indicate that the patient received optimum care? Once the criteria and standards have been established, a trained auditor employed by the hospital reviews medical records to determine compliance with the standards. When the audit indicates that standards have not been met, the records are sent to a physician review committee for re-audit. If this committee confirms deficiencies in care, follow-up efforts to solve the problem are undertaken.

In summary, the major features of PEP are: (*a*) local determination by hospital personnel of the diagnostic categories for audit and of the criteria and standards against which care will be audited; (*b*) emphasis on the outcomes of care as well as on iatrogenic complications of care; (*c*) reliance on the medical record for data on which to base judgements about quality; (*d*) detailed examination of each and every case that fails to meet either standards set for management of the problem or standards set for the end-results of care; (*e*) re-audit to determine if deficiencies have been corrected; and (*f*) reporting of results to the JCAH rather than a governmental regulatory body.

While a PEP may qualify under PSRO guidelines as an MCE, there is a major difference in the approach taken by each programme to quality assurance. The responsibility for PSRO review activities is delegated solely to physicians; the JCAH programme encourages the assumption of responsibility by administrators and trustees as well as by physicians. Given these different inputs, PSRO review activities will be focused chiefly on physician care; PEP audits, on the other hand, are more likely to be patient-centred, reviewing all the care given to each patient. One can imagine the development of individual PSRO-like organizations to assure the quality of nursing care or the care given by physical therapists. To prevent proliferation of quality assurance programmes that examine only certain aspects of patient care, participation of all relevant providers in a single patient-centred audit system is required. Patients themselves should also be included in this process, since decisions about the quality of medical care reflect value judgements that are clearly in the public domain.

Quality Assurance Programme

A third quality assurance system directed at hospital care is currently being tested. Like the PEP system, the Quality Assurance Programme (QAP) (29) was also developed by a voluntary organization in the hospital field, the American Hospital Association. The approach taken in QAP is similar to that of the PEP programme, with two major differences: (*a*) emphasis is placed on examining compliance with process criteria rather than outcome criteria (as in the PSRO approach); and (*b*) the review process focuses on deviation from standards in care given to groups of patients rather than individual patients. A relatively new programme, QAP is being field-tested in some ten hospitals across the country.

HMO quality assurance

The second federally mandated quality assurance system was a result of the Health Maintenance Organization Act (HMO) of 1973 (2). Briefly, an HMO is a prepaid group practice which delivers ambulatory and hospital care to an enrolled population. As a delivery system, the prepaid group practice stands in competition with the fee-for-service system. To qualify for federal funding, HMOs must display certain characteristics as defined in the 1973 legislation, which also made available limited funds for developmental activities.

Expressing concern that the prepaid group practice might cut corners to stay within its budget by controlling delivery of expensive services and by fostering under-utilization, the law requires installation of a quality assurance system in each HMO. The quality assurance system will focus largely on outcomes of care for a defined population, and unlike those described above, will review quality of both ambulatory and hospital services.

Regulations for implementation of the HMO quality assurance systems were published only recently, so there is no experience with their operation. However, a potential model exists in John Williamson's health accounting system (30). In this system, local providers first identify the health problem that is associated with the greatest amount of preventable impairment in the relevant population (hypertension is frequently selected). Providers then establish outcome criteria against which to measure the extent of impairment reduced by medical care. (For hypertension, this standard might be that 90 per cent of patients with a diastolic pressure of >105 should have a diastolic of ≤ 90 measured one year later.) Standards by which to judge the adequacy of treatment are established. Outcomes are judged by patient follow-up for physiological testing (in this example, a blood pressure), or completion of a questionnaire (in this example, to establish whether the patient has suffered a morbid event, such as a stroke). Follow-up data are then compared to the outcome standards, and if quality is found wanting the process of care is audited through the medical record to determine the reason for poor outcome. At this stage, corrective action is taken and the problem re-audited to determine improvement. The practicality of implementing this system, particularly in HMOs serving low-income populations, has recently been questioned (31) and the costs of operation may be too expensive when compared to the benefits it produces.

A rider to the HMO bill may prove even more important to quality assurance efforts than inclusion of such systems in HMOs. This rider authorizes the Secretary of Health, Education, and Welfare to

contract . . . for the conduct of a study to: (1) analyze past and present mechanisms . . . to assure the quality of health care; (2) provide a set of basic principles to be followed by any effective health care quality assurance system, including . . . specifications for the development of criteria and standards which relate to desired outcomes of care, and means for assessing the responsiveness of such care to the needs and perceptions of the consumers of such care; (3) provide an assessment of programs for improving the performance of health practitioners and institutions in providing high-quality health care, including a study of the effectiveness of sanctions and educational programs; (4) define the specific needs for a program of research and evaluation in health care quality assurance methods; and (5) provide methods for assessing the quality of health care from the point of view of consumers of such care [2].

Little has been done to implement this section of the law other than to assign responsibility for it to the Institute of Medicine of the National Academy of Sciences, and exactly what form its implementation will take is uncertain, but the scope of the study gives it great potential for affecting quality assurance in the United States.

Other efforts

Several state medical associations and many medical foundations not involved in EMCRO (32–35) have also participated in quality assurance activities. Under federal sponsorship, the American Medical Association (36) co-ordinated the efforts of medical specialty organizations to develop criteria that can be used as guidelines by local PSROs in their efforts to develop criteria. Fiscal intermediaries (insurance carriers) have also become involved in these endeavours.

Most of these organizations have been involved in setting explicit criteria for review of the process of care. Most of these criteria relate to controlling excessive utilization of services, an approach more germane to cost control than to quality improvement. An example of one such criterion is a limit of two visits for treatment of a common cold. Criteria directed at uncovering under-utilization of services, which are more relevant to quality improvement, are few in number.

The malpractice crisis

Recent developments in malpractice litigation and malpractice insurance have done as much to further the issue of quality assurance as have the numerous regulatory and voluntary efforts described above. During the last several years, premiums for malpractice insurance coverage have increased by as much as 500 per cent for some specialties. In southern California, as of 1 January 1976, paediatricians can expect to pay $4,300 annually for malpractice coverage. A GP who does not do surgery will pay $7,700 while one who does will pay $21,000. A neurosurgeon or orthopaedic surgeon can expect to pay $36,000.

This rapid rise in premiums provoked the 'malpractice crisis of 1974–1975'. Physicians went on strike in several areas and they mounted major lobbying efforts to encourage state governments to pass laws that would regulate the medical care system directly, rather than continuing to rely on the ancient tort procedure to correct deficiencies. This effort represented a major reversal in form for many of the physicians involved.

However, some state governments have been reluctant to accommodate the physicians, since to some degree they view the threat of malpractice suits as a quality assurance system. (The relationship between malpractice and quality is unknown, but few if any physicians [less than 0·001 per cent per year] have ever been removed from the practice of medicine after losing a malpractice suit [3].) Other states have passed bills that partially alleviate the malpractice crisis and that require physicians to undergo relicensure, recertification by specialty boards, and/or mandatory continuing education.

This approach may be effective if its underlying assumption, ie, that inadequate knowledge is what produces poor quality care, is true. Unfortunately, there is little evidence to support such a view. As Peterson (12) found in his classic study of the quality of care provided by GPs, there was no relationship between physician performance and receiving and/or reading medical journals. Furthermore, the formal continuing education programmes make little effort to determine the relevance of the topics they select to the problems faced by the practising physician (37). Continuing education conducted in this vacuum may be both costly and ineffective. If the problem is more one of physician behaviour and habits, a quality assurance mechanism that requires re-audit to demonstrate that documented deficiencies have been corrected will be more effective in promoting quality than will mandatory relicensure or continuing education.

It is interesting to contemplate the effect on delivery of care if the increased malpractice rates are permitted to stand. The new rates would very likely be an incentive to part-time physicians, particularly surgeons, to quit the practice of medicine. Certainly, they would discourage primary care physicians from performing surgery. In so far as non-surgeons and part-time surgeons produce poorer results than full-time surgeons, the level of quality will rise. However, the increased rates could also have an adverse effect on quality by prompting physicians to increase the number of unnecessary procedures performed to cover increased premiums, or to withhold certain procedures with too great a risk of adverse effects. Only time will determine which result predominates.

Following this description of the voluntary and compulsory quality assurance systems that now exist (ignoring for the moment the malpractice crisis), it is possible to draw some conclusions about the approaches taken to quality assessment. These conclusions, which have definite implications for further research in the quality assessment and assurance area, are discussed at greater length in the following section. (*a*) Virtually all quality assurance activities review hospital care and not ambulatory care. (*b*) All quality assurance programmes emphasize local selection of problems for review and local development of criteria and standards. (*c*) All review efforts concentrate on only a few disease conditions for quality assurance. (*d*) Virtually all programmes propose to audit both process and outcome of care, but the emphasis (particularly in the

PSRO programme) is on process. (*e*) The medical record usually provides much of the data for the quality assessment, as opposed to other written sources or direct observation. (*f*) All quality assessment methods propose to use explicit criteria and standards against which to review care. (*g*) When the process of care is assessed, attention is focused on its technical aspects; the 'art-of-care' is virtually ignored. (*h*) Data to evaluate the effectiveness of any method, in terms of changes in provider behaviour or in the health of the patients whose care is reviewed, are sparse or nonexistent. (*i*) There is a distinct possibility that there will be in the United States, at least for the next several years, duplication of expensive quality assurance activities.

III
IMPLICATIONS FOR CONTINUING RESEARCH IN QUALITY ASSURANCE

Hospital versus ambulatory care review

Virtually all operational quality assurance programmes emphasize the hospital component of medical care and ignore the ambulatory care sector. This focus is a natural outgrowth of research in quality assessment, since most studies have been performed in hospital settings. However, the question must be raised as to the validity of this approach. Will quality assurance activities conducted in the hospital increase the health of people more than would similar activities in the ambulatory component of medical care? The answer to this question is unknown. Intuitively, since the drugs and procedures used in the hospital are more dangerous (their safe therapeutic range is narrower and side-effects are more severe), quality assurance activities in hospitals should produce larger changes in health than similar activities in ambulatory care.

However, a recent study performed by Payne and Lyons (38, 39) questions this intuitive judgement. They assessed the quality of care given by physicians in Hawaii to patients in both hospital and office settings. Adequacy of the quality of the care rendered to patients with one of twenty diagnoses was judged by comparison of data contained in the medical record with a list of disease-specific process criteria generated by members of the Hawaii Medical Society.

These criteria were weighted and combined into an over-all physician performance index. The index was scaled so that compliance with all criteria would be given a score of 100; a zero score indicated that none of the criteria were met. Across all diagnoses, the average performance index for the hospital component of care was 77; the average score for office practice was 44. Hospital care was thus judged to be far superior and less in need of improvement than office-based care. A literature review of several hundred studies supports this conclusion (40). What are needed, however, are studies that address the question of the marginal increase in health obtained for the same investment when hospital care is improved as opposed to ambulatory care.

The decision to assess only hospital care in the PSRO programme was probably based on practical considerations. It is far easier to perform an audit in a hospital than in the office of a solo practitioner, and costs of hospital care represent the greatest proportion of Medicare and Medicaid budgets. Nevertheless, this decision may partially invalidate the audit judgements. For instance, suppose a PSRO establishes process criteria for the treatment of patients with pneumonia. These criteria certainly would require performance of a sputum culture and a chest X-ray. If two doctors each complied with these criteria, one in his office before the patient was admitted and the other in the hospital, and if only data in the hospital record were used in the quality of care judgement, it would appear that these physicians had provided different levels of care. These erroneous conclusions could lead to practices that would result in higher (ie, worse) cost/effectiveness ratios for the medical care system. The physician who correctly performed these tests on an out-patient basis may feel compelled, because of the quality of care assessment system, to repeat them on an in-patient basis. This course of action may be least expensive in terms of physician time, since reviewing the case with the hospital audit committee would be more time-consuming than redoing the tests. The potential duplication of services and consequent increase in costs as the result of a hospital-only quality assessment system needs to be confirmed or denied by proper research. Eventually, quality of care assessment must integrate the review of both ambulatory and hospital care.

Local control

The quality assurance programmes now operating in the United States emphasize local selection of problems and local establishment of criteria and standards. The reasons given for this emphasis are three: (*a*) local physicians are more familiar with the medical care needs and problems of the populations they serve; (*b*) physicians would be more likely to change their behaviour to meet local criteria than nationally mandated criteria; and (*c*) physicians display a built-in antipathy toward use of national or 'federal' criteria.

There is no evidence to support either of the first two reasons, and the third is not amenable to rational discussion. Problems in the delivery of medical care may be so generic that complete freedom in the selection of problems may be unnecessary and very time-consuming. For instance, every community study which has examined the adequacy of blood pressure control for hypertensive patients has demonstrated gross deficiencies in care (40). Knowledge of socio-economic and environmental conditions in a medical care area (which is readily available) should permit 'outsiders' to identify important medical care problems. Local physicians may lack the epidemiologic data base necessary to make these predictions in an equally valid manner.

There is no evidence that physicians will change their behaviour more readily if it proves wanting when local standards are used as opposed to national standards. Since this is such a crucial point, this belief should be tested rigorously through controlled experimentation. Furthermore, the establishment of local criteria and standards raises ethical and moral questions. Should a physician in a rural area who prescribes chloramphenicol for a cold be permitted to practise as usual, while such an action by a physician in an urban area is treated with harsh sanctions? Criteria will vary according to local social and economic conditions; for instance, a patient with pneumonia who has an unheated home may require a longer hospital stay than the patient who can be discharged to a home with central heating. However, is it justifiable to reject valid criteria and standards for the delivery of good quality of care based only on local physician acceptance of such criteria as indicative of good care? Sooner or later ethics will require that those process criteria shown to be related to health are uniformly applied throughout the country; likewise, those criteria that do not meet this level of validity should not be used to judge care, regardless of local physician opinion.

Scope of review activities

All operational quality assurance systems select only a few conditions or procedures for intensive study. The vast majority of conditions or procedures go unstudied. However, there is a strong tendency to generalize findings based on the quality of care given to patients with one or two conditions to all the care given throughout an institution or region. The validity of such a generalization must be tested rigorously. Only a few research studies have reviewed the quality of care given to patients in a defined population with one of several diagnoses. When such studies have been performed, such as those by Brook (41) and Payne and Lyons (38, 39), they have demonstrated that substantial variation in the level of care provided can occur even when comparisons are made among patients with similar conditions who are treated by the same set of providers. For instance, in Brook's study, the medical house-staff at a large city hospital provided a significantly lower level of care to patients with urinary tract infection than they did to patients with an ulcerated lesion in the stomach or duodenum. Yet both of these conditions are common chronic medical problems, and are often chosen as indicator conditions for quality review.

Type and source of data

Virtually all quality assurance systems propose to use some combination of process and outcome data to assess quality of care, and to abstract those data from the medical record. Most systems, PSRO in particular, emphasize the use of process data. The question that must be addressed is how the validity of the results of the quality assessment varies as a function both of the type of data used and the source from which they are obtained. For instance, the process of ambulatory care has been assessed on the basis of data contained in insurance claims forms. The same process of care could be measured by examining the medical record; the correlation between the quality of care assessment based on examining claims data with that based on reviewing the medical record is unknown.

Findings of a recent study underscore the importance of these issues. The Joint Commission on Quality Assurance for Children and Youth (42) reviewed the care given by board-certified paediatricians to children with one of six conditions, such as well-child examination or asthma. The level of quality of care was ascertained by comparing the practitioners' medical records with explicit process criteria agreed to by the members of this Commission.

The results of the study showed that care given by supposedly excellent practitioners was seriously inadequate. The Commission concluded, however, not that care was deficient, but that the recording process was deficient. A study that would have confirmed this finding by comparing compliance as determined by observing physician practice with compliance as determined by examining the medical record, was not done. An answer to this question is vital since without it, the rejection of findings of deficient care based on data obtained from the medical record will be easy. Lyons and Payne (43) partially answered this question by demonstrating in a record review that physicians who complied with criteria that required both doing and recording, such as examining the fundi in a hypertensive patient, also had higher scores on those criteria that required doing but were recorded by office personnel, such as ordering measurement of a potassium level on a hypertensive patient. The correlation found was only weakly positive. Unless medical recordkeeping is upgraded, it may not be desirable to push assessment of the quality of ambulatory care too far. Whether such recording is beneficial and should be paid for by increasing the cost of an ambulatory visit is also debatable. For instance, if the patient presents with a cut on the hand and the physician tests for sensation, mobility, and strength and does not record this information, should he be penalized by a quality assurance system which derives its data from the medical record and mandates the testing for these attributes before suturing the lesion? Such a quality assurance system may do more harm than good if it results in the physician spending less time with the patient and more time with his record.

Despite the common focus of quality assurance systems on process assessment, the issue of which type of data—structure, process, or outcome—produces the most valid result has not yet been resolved. The results of the quality assessment are clearly dependent upon the type of data used. For instance, Fessel and Van Brunt (44) studied the quality of care given to patients who suffered from symptoms of appendicitis and were treated in one of three hospitals. They judged the process of care given to these patients by comparing the level of

TABLE 1. *Process and outcome assessments of the quality of care given to patients with acute appendicitis who were treated at one of three hospitals*

Part 1. Recorded data on the process of care

Datum	Hospital A (%)	B (%)	C (%)	Probability difference due to chance
Referred rebound	82	26	36	<0·001
Guarding	96	52	88	<0·001
Psoas sign	48	14	6	<0·001
Obturator sign	32	8	2	<0·001
Bowel sounds	98	94	80	<0·001
Organ enlargement	30	26	36	<0·001
Rectum:				
Tender on right	68	50	28 ⎫	
Other tenderness	12	6	8 ⎬ <0·001	
Normal	20	36	34 ⎭	

Part 2. Diagnostic outcomes

Hospital	No. of patients	Pathologically proved acute appendicitis (%)	No pathological findings (%)	Diagnosis other than appendicitis (%)
A	466	82·2	13·6	4·1
B	167	83·1	13·7	4·2
C	104	89·4	10·6	0

Modified from Fessel and Van Brunt (44).

care as recorded in the medical record with an explicit set of process criteria. They then judged the outcome of care by examining the proportion of patients operated on who actually had acute appendicitis (Table 1). The hospital scoring lowest on the process assessment (Hospital C) had the best score when judged by the outcome assessment. Clearly, treatment at the hospital in which fewer inappropriate operations were performed is preferable to treatment at the hospital in which the most data were recorded in the medical record.

Brook (40) studied the quality of care given to 296 patients who had either hypertension, a urinary tract infection, or an ulcerated lesion in the stomach or duodenum. The quality of care given to

TABLE 2. *Summary of the assessment of quality of care as measured by each of the five methods studied for 296 patients with either hypertension, urinary tract infection, or ulcerated lesion of the stomach or duodenum*

	Results: acceptable quality of care	
	No. of	
Quality assessment method	patients	%
1. Implicit process judgement	69	23
2. Implicit outcome judgement	187	63
3. Implicit process and outcome judgement	80	27
4. Explicit process judgement	6	2
5. Explicit outcome judgement:		
(*a*) For urinary infection	42	40
(*b*) For hypertension	50	44

Modified from Brook (40).

these patients was assessed independently by five different methods: (*a*) process information judged by implicit criteria; (*b*) outcome information judged by implicit criteria; (*c*) process and outcome information judged by implicit criteria; (*d*) process information judged by explicit criteria; and (*e*) outcome information judged by explicit criteria (Table 2).

The judgement of the level of quality of care provided varied considerably as a function of the method used. Only 2 per cent of the patients were judged to have received adequate care by the explicit process method, while the implicit outcome method indicated that 63 per cent received adequate care.

The American Society of Internal Medicine (45) completed a study in which practising internists in six areas of the United States established process criteria for six common conditions. Subsequently, the care given to patients with these conditions by the practitioners who had established the criteria was assessed. An inverse correlation was found between the weight given to a criterion and the compliance with it. To say the least, what the physicians stated they should do was not what they did.

The results of the work by Brook, Fessel, the Joint Commission, and the American Society of Internal Medicine illustrate the strong dependence of the resulting quality of care assessment on the method used to make the assessment. First, large discrepancies will be found as a function of whether process or outcome information is used in

TABLE 3. *Process criteria for pneumonia: Hawaii Medical Association*

Indications for admission: Presence of proven or suspected pneumonia	
Services recommended:	*Weights*
1. HISTORY: Specific reference to:	
(*a*) Character of sputum	2·0
(*b*) Pain in chest	2·0
(*c*) Duration and degree of fever	2·0
(*d*) Onset of illness	1·0
(*e*) Previous episodes and social history	1·0
(*f*) Contact history	1·0
2. PHYSICAL EXAMINATION: Specific reference to:	
(*a*) Breath sounds, character, presence or absence of	2·0
(*b*) Friction rub	1·0
(*c*) Rales	1·0
(*d*) Chest movements	1·0
(*e*) Percussion	1·0
(*f*) Cyanosis	2·0
(*g*) Vital signs: temperature, pulse, respiration, blood pressure	2·0
(*h*) Character of respiration	2·0
3. LABORATORY:	
(*a*) CBC	2·0
(*b*) Blood culture in seriously ill patient (temperature of or over 104°, cyanotic, needs oxygen)	3·0
(*c*) Sputum or throat culture with sensitivities	3·0
4. ROENTGENOLOGY:	
(*a*) PA and lateral of chest on admission	3·0
(*b*) Follow-up chest X-ray in 7 days or before discharge	2·0
5. THERAPY: Appropriate antibiotics (not sulfa drug or chloramphenical)	3·0

Adapted from Appendix C, p. 38, in Payne and Lyons (38).

the assessment. It is not clear which type of information produces the more valid judgement of care. Clearly, however, process assessment will produce a much harsher judgement of the quality of care rendered than will an outcome assessment. The reason for this is obvious once the probabilistic nature of medicine is considered. If a hundred patients with bacterial pneumonia were incorrectly diagnosed and not treated with antibiotics, most of them would recover. An outcome assessment based on recovery from the pneumonia would indicate that most of the patients received good care while a process assessment, based largely on whether an antibiotic was prescribed, would indicate that poor care was given to all. The 'truth' would be more on the side of the process assessment, except for the fact that many of the process criteria that are selected by physicians are invalid. Does every patient with pneumonia actually require all the treatment procedures indicated by the process criteria in Table 3? If lists such as this one are used to assess quality of care, then the number of 'things' to be done to patients in order to meet these criteria would increase by two to three-fold in the ambulatory care area and by one and one-half in the hospital area. This increased activity would probably raise the percentage of the GNP spent on health to over 15 per cent yet would improve health very little, since the quality of care assessment included invalid process criteria.

Why do practising physicians accept on paper invalid process criteria? The American Society of Internal Medicine's study certainly suggests that physicians do not follow these criteria in their daily practice. Perhaps it is the 'academic' approach of the techniques used to produce these criteria that causes this behaviour. This issue is another in need of more research.

Finally, the artificiality of the weighting scheme used to derive an over-all quality score represents a serious methods deficiency. If all of the criteria in Table 3 were met except that of giving an antibiotic, the physician could achieve a near perfect score and yet the patient could easily die. Clearly the weighting scheme does not replicate the decision-making process of the clinician. The artificiality of this weighting scheme may explain why implicit judgements of the process of care, whereby the care is examined in a gestalt manner, produce different and probably more valid results than does the explicit review (Table 2). At least the implicit process judgement is closer to the physician's decision-making process than is the explicit process judgement. The UCLA EMCRO (46) has used several decision-making principles in developing process criteria and is advancing the state of the art. Their explicit process criteria are branched so that an action indicated by one criterion is often dependent upon the results of a previous action. In many cases, a physician can use one of multiple pathways in reaching a decision during the process of care. The feasibility of applying this complex system to the average medical record still is in need of further testing.

Technique versus art of medical care

All of the approaches described above concentrate on measuring the technical aspect of the process of care; the art-of-care is ignored completely. Ware (47) has recently developed and tested the reliability of a health care perception questionnaire that contains a measure of the patient's perceived quality of care. It is time to validate this measure of the art-of-care against variables such as: (*a*) patient compliance; (*b*) willingness of the patient to discuss sensitive problems; (*c*) willingness of the patient to change health behaviours associated with increased morbidity and mortality; and (*d*) utilization of medical services in an appropriate and timely manner. As these measures become more sophisticated, they should be incorporated into an operational quality assurance system so that at least some emphasis is given to improving the art as well as the technical component of care.

Evaluation of quality assurance systems

Unfortunately, virtually all these systems for assessing and assuring quality have been implemented in a manner that inhibits their evaluation. Thus, the impact of these systems on changing physician behaviour or improving the health of people will remain largely unknown. Only a few studies have documented any changes at all (22), and others question whether the documented changes are temporary or permanent. Furthermore, little is known about the most effective way to change either system or provider behaviour to produce higher levels of quality. How should quality assessment information be reported? Should the assessment be done on a group or individual basis? Should data be aggregated by specialty, by region, by hospital, or by community? What should be done about the 'bad doctors': should they be removed from the practice of medicine or should continuing education be mandated? Efficient and effective mechanisms for changing unnecessary or inadequate provider behaviour must be found, since a quality assurance system is likely to consume 2 to 5 per cent of available medical care dollars. If change could be accomplished by data aggregated to the community level rather than disaggregated at the individual provider level, sampling could be done and operational expenses decreased. Research along these lines is clearly necessary.

Duplication of systems

Finally, it is apparent that duplicate or overlapping quality assurance systems are being established in the United States. Because of economic considerations, federal regulatory systems will likely come to the fore, and the role of voluntary agencies such as the JCAH may disappear. With the coming of national health insurance, the PSRO programme will likely expand to review the care provided to the entire population. As the PSRO review activities expand to include ambulatory care, which eventually they must, they will duplicate those activities mandated by the HMO act. The decision as how best to eliminate this costly duplication of activities will be partly political, but should also be made at least partially on the basis of information. That information must answer the question: does area-wide review (PSRO) work better than does review that is co-extensive with the agency providing the care (HMO), or that is performed under the auspices of a voluntary agency?

IV
SUMMARY

The United States is engaged in implementing a series of quality assurance activities. In the short run, the success of these programmes depends on rigorous programme evaluation and feedback of results so that deficiencies can be corrected and improvements made. Without such feedback, these programmes may be extremely costly yet produce no demonstrable improvements in health. In the long run, their success will depend on the development of more valid and reliable methods of assessing quality of care and of more efficient and effective ways to modify provider and patient behaviours.

The knowledge to accomplish this will come only with completion of carefully performed research. This search for newer and better methods must be interdisciplinary, and should not be confined to a single country or system of medical care. The issue of measuring and improving quality of care is one of continuing international importance, regardless of whether care is provided on a fee-for-service basis, is partially subsidized, or is nationally organized.

While further research is without a doubt necessary, this discussion should not be taken as advocating a pause in quality assurance activities until the perfect answer is found. Implementation of quality assurance does not necessarily require waiting for a perfect quality assessment method. Present-day quality assessment methods are clearly capable of detecting major deficiencies in quality of care, as the results of the large number of studies done here and abroad will attest. Until these gross deficiencies are fully identified and corrected, more sophisticated quality assessment techniques are not necessary.

The biggest threat to the success of quality assurance programmes, whether or not they benefit from advances in methods, lies with the failure to use the results of quality assessment studies to correct and improve medical care. Most studies have described deficiencies in care but have done little else with the information. This luxury can no longer be afforded.

References

1. *Public Law 92-603*, 92nd Congress of the United States of America, HR 1, 30 October 1972, pp. 101–14 (Washington, DC: US Government Printing Office).
2. *Public Law 93-222, Health Maintenance Organization Act of 1973*. Laws of the 93rd Congress, 1st Session, pp. 1015–42 (Washington, DC: US Government Printing Office).
3. BROOK, R. H., BRUTOCO, R. L., and WILLIAMS, K. N. (1976). 'The relationship between medical malpractice and quality of care', *Duke Law J.* (in press).
4. NIGHTINGALE, F. (1858). 'Mortality of the British Army at Home and Abroad and During the Russian War as Compared with the Mortality of the Civil Population in England', reprinted from: *Report of the Commission Appointed to Inquire into the Regulations Affecting the Sanitary State of the Army* (London: Harrison and Sons).
5. —— (1863). *Proposal for Improved Statistics of Surgical Operations* (London: Savill and Edwards).
6. MURNAGHAN, J. H., and WHITE, K. L. (eds) (1970). 'Hospital Discharge Data: Report of the Conference on Hospital Discharge Abstracts Systems', *Med. Care*, 8 (4): Supplement.
7. GROVES, E. W. (1908). 'A plea for a uniform registration of operation results', *Br. J. Med.* 2, 1008–9.
8. CODMAN, E. A. (1914). 'The product of a hospital', *Surg. Gynaec. Obstet.* (April) pp. 491–4.
9. FLEXNER, A. (1910). *Medical Education in the United States and Canada: A Report to the Carnegie Foundation for the Advancement of Teaching* (Bulletin no. 4) (Boston: D. B. Updike, The Merrymount Press).
10. MOREHEAD, M. A. (1958). 'Quality of medical care provided by family physicians as related to their education, training and methods of practice' (New York: Health Insurance Plan of Greater New York) (mimeo).
11. FITZPATRICK, T. B., REIDEL, D. C., and PAYNE, B. C. (1962). 'Character and effectiveness of hospital use', in McNERNEY, W. J. (ed.), *Project 2, Hospital and*

Medical Economics, pp. 361–592 (Chicago: Hospital Research and Educational Trust).

12. PETERSON, O. L., ANDREWS, L. P., SPAIN, R. S., *et al*. (1956). 'An analytical study of North Carolina general practice, 1953–1954', *J. med. Educ.* **31** (part 2), 1–165.
13. MATHER, N. G., PEARSON, H. G., REED, K. L. O., *et al*. (1971). 'Acute myocardial infarction: Home and hospital treatment', *Br. med. J.* **3**, 334–8.
14. CHANT, A. D. B., JONES, H. O., and WEDDELL, J. M. (1972). 'Varicose veins: A comparison of surgery and injection/compression sclerotherapy', *Lancet*, ii, 1188–91.
15. PIACHAUD, D., and WEDDELL, J. M. (1972). 'Cost of treating varicose veins', ibid. ii, 1191–2.
16. UNIVERSITY GROUP DIABETES PROGRAM (1970). 'A study of the effects of hypo-glycemic agents on vascular complications in patients with adult onset diabetes', *J. Am. Med. Assoc.* **19** (Supplement 2).
17. NATIONAL CENTER FOR HEALTH SERVICES RESEARCH (1973). *EMCRO Program* (DHEW Publication No. [HSM] 73–3017) (Rockville, Md: Department of Health, Education, and Welfare).
18. SANAZARO, P. J., GOLDSTEIN, R. L., ROBERTS, J. S., MAGLOTT, D. B., and McALLISTER, J. W. (1972). 'Research and development in quality assurance: The Experimental Medical Care Review Organization program', *N. Engl. J Med.* **287**, 1125–31.
19. GOLDSTEIN, R. L., ROBERTS, J. S., STANTON, B. A., MAGLOTT, D. B., and GORAN, M. J. (1975). 'Data for peer review: Acquisition and use', *Ann. Int. Med.* **82**, 262–7.
20. BRIAN, E. (1973). 'Foundation for medical care control of hospital utilization: CHAP—A PSRO prototype', *N. Engl. J. Med.* **288**, 878–82.
21. ARTHUR D. LITTLE, INC. (1972). *An Evaluation of the Effectiveness of Utilization Review Activities in Hospitals and Extended Care Facilities* (Final Report on Contract HSM 110–71–192) (Cambridge, Mass.: Arthur D. Little, Inc.).
22. BROOK, R. H., and WILLIAMS, K. N. (to be published). *Effect of the New Mexico Peer Review System on Cost and Quality of Medical Care: A review of the impact of the New Mexico Experimental Medical Care Review Organization on medical care delivered to the Medicaid population, 1971–1973* (Santa Monica, Calif.: The Rand Corporation).
23. OFFICE OF PROFESSIONAL STANDARDS REVIEW (1974). *PSRO Program Manual* (Rockville, Md: Department of Health, Education, and Welfare).
24. GORAN, M. J., ROBERTS, J. S., KELLOGG, M., FIELDING, J., and JESSEE, W. (1975). 'The PSRO hospital review system', *Med. Care*, **13** (Supplement).
25. 'Utilization of short-stay hospitals—Summary of nonmedical statistics: United States, 1973', *Monthly Vital Statistics Report*, **24** (Supplement 2), 1–7 (19 August 1975).
26. OFFICE OF RESEARCH EVALUATION AND PLANNING, OFFICE OF PROFESSIONAL STANDARDS REVIEW (1975). *PSRO Program Evaluation Plan* (draft) (Rockville, Md: Department of Health, Education, and Welfare).
27. *TAP Institutes* (Chicago: Joint Commission on Accreditation of Hospitals, 1973).
28. JACOBS, C. M., and JACOBS, N. D. (1974). *The PEP Primer: The JCAH Performance Evaluation Procedure for Auditing and Improving Physician Care* (Chicago: Quality Review Center, Joint Commission on Accreditation of Hospitals).
29. *The Quality Assurance Program for Medical Care in the Hospital* (Chicago: American Hospital Association, 197[ ]).
30. WILLIAMSON, J. W., ARONOVITCH, S., SIMONSON, L., RAMIREZ, C., and KELLY, D. (1975). 'Health accounting: An outcome-based system of quality assurance—Illustrative application to hypertension', *Bull. N.Y. Acad. Med.* (2nd series), **51**, 727–38.

31. SCHROEDER, S. A., and DONALDSON, M. (in press). 'The feasibility of an outcome approach to quality assurance: A report from one HMO', *Med. Care.*

32. *Metropolitan Health Care Foundation*. Available from Metropolitan Health Care Foundation, 1535 Medical Arts Building, Minneapolis, Minnesota 55402.

33. BUCK, C. R., JR (1972). 'Peer review: The impact of a system based on billing claims', DSc thesis submitted to the School of Hygiene and Public Health, Johns Hopkins University, Baltimore, Md.

34. —— and WHITE, K. L. (1974). 'Peer review: Impact of a system based on billing claims', *N. Engl. J. Med.* **291**, 877–83.

35. FLASHNER, B. A., REED, S., COBURN, R. W., et al. (1973). 'Professional Standards Review Organizations: Analysis of their development and implementation based on a preliminary review of the Hospital Association and Surveillance Program in Illinois', *J. Am. Med. Assoc.* **223**, 1473–84.

36. AMA CRITERIA DEVELOPMENT PROJECT, AMERICAN MEDICAL ASSOCIATION (1975). *Model Screening Criteria to Assist Professional Standards Review Organizations* (draft) (Chicago: American Medical Association).

37. BROWN, C. R., and UHL, H. S. M. (1970). 'Mandatory continuing education: Sense or nonsense?', *J. Am. Med. Assoc.* **213**, 1660–8.

38. PAYNE, B. C., and LYONS, T. F. (1973). *Method of Evaluating and Improving Personal Medical Care Quality: Episode of Illness Study* (Chicago: American Hospital Association).

39. —— —— (1973). *Method of Evaluating and Improving Personal Medical Care Quality: Office Care Study* (Chicago: American Hospital Association).

40. BROOK, R. H. (1974). *Quality of Care Assessment: A Comparison of Five Methods of Peer Review* (DHEW Publication No. HRA–74–3100) (Rockville, Md: Department of Health, Education, and Welfare).

41. —— (1973). 'Quality of care assessment: Choosing a method for peer review', *N. Engl. J. Med.* **288**, 1323–9.

42. OSBORNE, C. E. (1975). *Criteria for Evaluation of Ambulatory Child Health Care by Chart Audit: Development and Testing of a Methodology* (Final Report on Contract No. HSM 110–71–184) (Evanston, Ill.: American Academy of Pediatrics).

43. LYONS, T. F., and PAYNE, B. C. (1974). 'The relationship of physicians' medical recording performance to their medical care performance', *Med. Care*, **12**, 463.

44. FESSEL, W. J., and VAN BRUNT, E. E. (1972). 'Assessing quality of care from the medical record', *N. Engl. J. Med.* **286**, 134–8.

45. HARE, R. L., and BARNOON, S. (1973). *Medical Care Appraisal and Quality Assurance in the Office Practice of Internal Medicine* (Sacramento, Calif.: American Society of Internal Medicine).

46. GREENFIELD, S., LEWIS, C. E., KAPLAN, S. H., and DAVIDSON, M. (1975). 'Peer review by *Criteria Mapping*: Criteria for diabetes mellitus', *Ann. Inter. Med.* **83**, 761–70.

47. WARE, J. E., and SNYDER, M. K. (1975). 'Dimensions of patient attitudes regarding doctors and medical care services', *Med. Care*, **13**, 669–82.

Retrospect

13

Some reflections

ARCHIE COCHRANE
CBE, MD, FRCP, FFCM
Formerly Director,
MRC Epidemiology Unit,
Cardiff

Some reflections

The invitation to write a Rock Carling prize essay about the Health Service came by telephone. I was talking to Dr R. H. L. Cohen at the time and, as usual in his company, was slightly euphoric. As a result I accepted. In cold blood I would almost certainly have refused—and quite rightly. I knew far too little about health services; I had too little experience of clinical work and medical administration and above all I was, as Professor, Director, and chronic Committee member, far too busy. But owing to Dick Cohen's persuasive powers I accepted. It led to some unseemly delays, a lot of writing between 11 pm and 3 am and an increased consumption of whisky.

The title deserves a note. Neither Nuffield nor I liked it, but we couldn't think of anything else. In retrospect it should have been called 'So much goes in . . .'. (The comparison between the NHS and the crematorium was the most popular passage in the book.) The title also caused real trouble in certain countries. When lecturing in Brussels to a large WHO audience, with multilingual translation, a section of the interpreters went on strike and held up the meeting for about two hours because I used the word 'efficiency'. The interpreters involved with the French language argued that there was only one word in French for 'effectiveness' and 'efficiency': 'efficacité'; that French was a perfect language and therefore I must be talking nonsense (although they admitted they understood my definitions perfectly). I offered 'efficience' as a word widely used in French engineering, but it was turned down as 'Franglais' as opposed to 'Français'. The same difficulty appears in other languages, such as Danish: and even the Americans have let me down by using 'efficacity' instead of 'effectiveness'. Oddly enough, I was allowed to use 'efficience' in French Canada.

Turning now to criticism, may I thank the critics for, in general, being so kind, and the minority for being so irrelevant. I am not ashamed of my ignorance of sociological theory. I am not ashamed of trying to improve a small part of the world, although the world as a whole is imperfect. Some other criticism was certainly true. The book could certainly have been written ten years before—on the basis of my own remarks. But no-one had done it or asked me to do it. There were also serious omissions; although I never claimed to be comprehensive. One is my lack of reference to 'monitoring'. Fortunately the gap has been most comprehensively filled by Sir Richard Doll in his lectures. I have nothing to add to his words, except to underline the problem of the effectiveness of monitoring. Monitoring can be very expensive and it should be validated in the usual way, if it is possible. In general it is hoped that monitoring will be effective in improving clinical and administrative decisions and in stimulating research. Can we be sure that all monitoring really has one of these effects? To take an example: Hospital Activity Analysis is generally believed to be more accurate and efficient in Scotland than elsewhere. Is 'length of stay' decreasing more rapidly in Scotland than in other parts of the UK? And if so, is this desirable in the absence of detailed knowledge of optimum length of stay from the patients' point of view? It is possible that the recent spate of randomized controlled trials on length of stay on IHD cases were stimulated by the publication of the extraordinary between-clinician variation in length of stay for this condition, but even if this were true, do we need continuous HAA? I must repeat that I do not want to decry the idea of monitoring. I merely want a more critical attitude towards the effectiveness of each type of monitoring, less we drift into the situation of monitoring for the sake of monitoring.

Another valid criticism was my neglect of any discussion of quality. The explanation is simple. I find the subject so complex and it has such strong emotional associations for me, that the section on quality was not finished in time. One of the incidents in my own life which helped to delay the writing of that section, occurred when I was a POW. I was faced by a ghastly medical problem. I had a young Soviet POW patient dying in great pain. He was making a fearful noise in a large ward. I had no drugs or side ward. No-one could talk Russian. In despair, and purely instinctively, I sat on his bed and took him in my arms. The effect was almost magical; he quietened at once and died peacefully a few hours later. I was still with him, half asleep and very stiff. I believe that by personal intervention I improved the quality of care dramatically in this case, and I know it was based on instinct and not on reason. I feel therefore rather diffident about a rational discussion about quality. We all recognize quality when we see it and particularly when we receive it. In 'cure' outcome plays an important part in determining quality, but it is certainly not the whole story. The really important factors are kindliness and ability to communicate on the part of all members of the medical team. In 'care' of course the latter two become very much more important. But what can we do about it? We attempt to teach medical students psychology and sociology, but will we really make them kindlier? We desperately need a test which we could apply to aspirant medical students which would tell us whether they would remain kindly in middle age; but I am advised that the development of such a test is very improbable.

The book has been far more popular than I ever dreamed. Though not approaching the world-wide success of Sir Richard Doll's book in the same series, it has been translated into Polish, Spanish, and Italian and has been widely 'xeroxed' in the US! I found the book's popularity in the US hard to understand. It is possibly explained by a remark made by an American when introduced to me: 'So you're Archie Cochrane. I bought 50 copies of your book as Xmas cards last year.'

The effect on myself is hard to judge; so much else was changing at the same time. I became, unexpectedly, President of the Faculty of Community Medicine in the same week as the book was published. I was also slowly organizing my retirement. But the success of the book undoubtedly gave me great pleasure, and an opportunity through lecturing and travel to 'sell' views that I think are important.

There were two side-effects. Through a feeling of having got away with murder, I became a serious student of health services literature, all the way from Donabedian to Ivan Illich. (I can't say I enjoyed it, but I no longer feel I'm skating on thin ice.) The other effect depressed me. After the publication of the book, the medical world forgot my work on pneumoconiosis and common diseases in the Rhondda Fach. I believe I did my best work there and I'm sorry to see it forgotten, but I suppose one can't have it both ways.

Two great, and I fear somewhat undeserved, honours came to me almost directly through the book: the 'Dunham' lectures at Harvard and an honorary degree at York. My debt to Nuffield is very great indeed.

The effect, if any, of the book is hard to judge as it was published during a period of rapid change. The extent of this change was brought home to me by lectures I gave in Cardiff, one in 1968 and the other this year. They were both concerned with cervical cytology. In the first one I concluded that there was no hard evidence as yet that cervical cytology screening had lowered the death-rate from cancer of the cervix. This produced an uproar with banner headlines attacking me in South Wales newspapers, abusive letters (some anonymous), and no colleague in Cardiff could be found to defend this 'dangerous heretic'. This year I concluded a similar lecture in Cardiff by arguing that we would never know whether cervical smears were effective or not. This was followed by a very un-emotional discussion as to whether our present position, in en-couraging such screening, was ethically justifiable, and even the practicalities of a randomized controlled trial (which would be very difficult) were calmly discussed.

There are of course many other signs of this change. The im-proved status of community physicians, the increased acceptability by clinicians of the randomized controlled trial technique and the acceptance in the US of the idea of PSRO. If one looks at individual fields, although there have been great advances there could have been so much more. For instance, in the cardiovascular world there has been the striking (though much delayed) recognition of the need for RCTs in the treatment of slightly raised blood pressure. This is of great importance but it is to be hoped that in this prospect of chemically prolonged life with all its side effects the interesting paper describing an RCT of the effect of relaxation will not be forgotten.

The cardiovascular world also deserves credit for the series of papers randomizing the length of time before mobilization and dis-charge after IHD attacks. These are outstanding and an example to all other branches of medicine, but how does one relate this activity to the conspiracy of silence which greeted Mather's first paper com-paring treatment at home for IHD cases with that in coronary care units? There has really been no reply. Surely, if one feels such trials are unethical, there was scope for a carefully controlled observational study? It is particularly interesting that the main criticism of Mather's trial is that his population was selected in the sense that only 31 per cent of the incident cases were randomized. No one, as far as I know, has succeeded in randomizing all the incident cases falling within the medical definition. Mather is unique in telling us what happened to the cases that were not randomized. The same criticism would apply, to a greater extent, to the American Veterans' blood pressure trials, whose results have been widely accepted. There is a touch of schizophrenia in the cardiovascular world at present. Their reaction to Mather's second paper should be carefully studied by the psychiatrists!

Again there is evidence of the orthopaedic surgeon's lack of reaction to an RCT which established the value of oral anticoagulants for patients with fractures of the femoral neck. Professor J. R. A. Mitchell of Nottingham, in a note attached as an addendum to this chapter, has drawn the group's attention to a situation in which, although the beneficial effect of prophylactic treatment was clearly demonstrated sixteen years ago, a recent survey showed that only 3 per cent of surgeons routinely prescribed anticoagulants.

The responsibility for establishing the causes of this seeming disregard of trials of treatment for IHD cases and for fractures of the femoral neck can hardly be willingly surrendered by the profession to others. Discussion could well, in view of the significance of such trials for the quality of patient care, extend to the question whether it is sufficient that they should depend upon sporadic initiatives.

Space forbids a detailed examination of each medical area but in general I would suggest that priorities for research in the general applied area should be aimed:

1. To prevent the introduction of new drugs and therapeutic procedures unless they are more effective (or equally effective and cheaper) than existing therapies.

2. To evaluate all existing therapies (accepting present constraints), slowly excluding those shown to be ineffective or too dangerous.

3. To determine the optimum place of treatment for those therapies about which there is any doubt.

4. To determine optimum lengths of stay where hospital admission is necessary.

As regards diagnosis, which is costing us so much with so little evidence of effect, the problem is more difficult, because of the efficiency of relating the value of tests to outcome. This, of course, has led to the widespread belief that diagnosis is an end in itself.

Several ingenious statistical solutions have been proposed as to how the general problem could be solved—in time. Some progress has been made in reducing the number of tests required to reach the 'correct' diagnosis (although there is usually little evidence that this improves outcome), but the problem is urgent (and our present economic situation so depressing) that I would like to suggest a more rapid crude approach.

The basic idea is that a crude value of a clinical test can be measured by the product of two probabilities:

1. The probability that the result of the test will alter the clinician's therapy.

2. The probability that the alteration in the therapy initiated by the clinician as a result of the test will alter the natural history of the disease for the better.

The interesting point about this approach is that the first probability can be measured reasonably accurately from retrospective data. We may need to do some trials to measure the second probability, but some data may be already available. I admit however that I am relying heavily on the astronomical probabilities revealed by the first one to control the present inflationary diagnostic situation. (I admit this approach excludes the value of excluding other treatable disease, the limited value of diagnosing untreatable disease and the value of excluding legal reprisals.)

In conclusion, as regards 'prospect' I think there has been some improvement (which is almost certainly unassociated with anything I have said or published), but it certainly isn't fast enough. In spite of the Rothschild reorganization, the shift in medical research from 'pure' to 'applied' and from 'process' to 'outcome' has not really happened. Possibly our present economic difficulties will supply the necessary stimulus. I remain, illogically, vaguely optimistic. We have the most cost-effective health service in the world and we have all the skills needed to improve it, so (in Masefield's words):

> I have seen good deeds done—by men with
> ugly faces,
> and flowers grow in stoney places,
> So I trust too.

I hasten to add that I do not wish to suggest that my medical and statistical colleagues are less well favoured facially than the average of the population.

Addendum

PROFESSOR J. R. A. MITCHELL

The University of Nottingham Medical School

Sixteen years ago Sevitt and Gallagher established the value of oral anticoagulants in the prevention of venous thrombo-embolism in patients who sustain fractures of the femoral neck. Three hundred patients were equally divided into treated and control groups. The treated patients were given phenindione to prolong the prothrombin time to between two and three times normal and the control patients received no prophylactic treatment. The frequency of clinically diagnosed episodes of venous thrombosis and pulmonary embolism was carefully recorded and detailed post-mortem studies were performed in a search for venous thrombo-embolism in patients who died. The beneficial effect of prophylactic treatment was clearly demonstrated. Mortality was almost halved in treated patients. Pulmonary embolism did not occur in any patient under the influence of anticoagulation but occurred in 18 per cent of the control series and was considered to be the cause of death in 10 per cent. In life, clinical evidence of venous thrombosis was found in 29 per cent of the control series compared with only 3 per cent of those receiving treatment; in the post-mortem series 83 per cent of the control patients but only 14 per cent of treated patients were found to have venous thrombosis. There was an excess of post-operative wound haematomas in patients receiving phenindione but no patient died as a result of treatment and the authors drew the firm conclusion that prophylactic oral anticoagulation was practicable, safe, and capable of eliminating the risk of pulmonary embolism in these high-risk patients.

The method of randomization used in this trial has been criticized and it is possible that the significantly higher mortality in the control group may have been influenced by an excess of poor-risk patients within that group. However, the conclusion that prophylactic oral anticoagulation effectively prevented venous thrombo-embolism was incontrovertible and Sevitt and Gallagher's study provided evidence upon which orthopaedic surgeons might base a prophylactic policy. To what extent has Sevitt and Gallagher's work influenced ortho-paedic practice and is treatment being offered, sixteen years later, to patients who sustain hip fractures? This was a question recently posed by Morris and Mitchell who conducted a postal survey, throughout the United Kingdom, of current practice in the diagno-sis and prevention of deep venous thrombosis in elderly patients with hip fractures. They obtained replies from 411 orthopaedic surgeons (a response of 64 per cent) and found that, apart from a commonly expressed aim to make patients ambulant as soon as possible, only 13 per cent of the surgeons were sufficiently con-vinced of the risk of venous thrombo-embolism to offer any form of prophylaxis, whether of proven value or not. Only 3 per cent of the surgeons routinely prescribed prophylactic anticoagulants. Further-more, the great majority (85 per cent) relied on clinical signs in the diagnosis of venous thrombosis despite the fact that such signs are notoriously unreliable. Three reasons can be postulated for the failure of current practice to reap what appeared to be a clear-cut benefit from a line of prophylactic treatment. First, that orthopaedic surgeons are unaware of Sevitt and Gallagher's findings; second, that they are aware of them but consider that the patients used in the study are unlike the patients they normally treat, and third, that they consider that the Sevitt and Gallagher trial was not convincing. To clarify the last two points Morris and Mitchell therefore re-evaluated anticoagulant treatment in a controlled trial similar to that of Sevitt and Gallagher but using the patients presenting in a busy District General Hospital, achieving a more satisfactory method of randomization and using the ^{125}I-fibrinogen uptake test to diagnose venous thrombosis in life in addition to undertaking detailed post-mortem studies in patients who died. Their findings confirmed that treatment effectively prevents venous thrombo-embolism both diagnosed isotopically in life and revealed at post mortem. The death-rates in the two groups differed but were, how-ever, not statistically significant (23 out of 80 in the control and 16 out of 80 in the anticoagulated group), showing that in these elderly and ill patients causes of death other than pulmonary embolism are making a major contribution. A strong case for prophylactic anti-coagulation can, however, be made out on their data in those patients who are medically fit before their injury and in whom death from pulmonary embolism would therefore be untimely.

Sixteen years after Sevitt and Gallagher we are therefore able to say that although the benefit in terms of survival may be more limited than was first suggested, help rather than harm will result from prophylactic anticoagulation. How should these findings be incorporated into the routine practice of orthopaedic surgeons?

References

1. SEVITT, S., and GALLAGHER, N. G. (1959). 'Prevention of venous thrombosis and pulmonary embolism in injured patients: A trial of anticoagulant prophylaxis with phenindione in middle aged and elderly patients with fractured necks of femur', *Lancet*, ii, 981.
2. MORRIS, G. K., and MITCHELL, J. R. A. (1976). *Q. Jl Med.* (in preparation).

Postscript and prospect

Postscript and prospect

GORDON McLACHLAN

1. The co-ordination of the field

The organization of modern society is complex, and public policies
to ensure justice and equality and to safeguard the citizen are a
result of several evolutionary processes, empirical as to effect. The
ideal of democracy assumes an understanding of such processes
and how they knit together. Medical care which touches each
individual in one way or another during his life span demonstrates
uniquely the many facets of reconciling the problems of the individual seeking relief from the many-headed hydra of suffering and
ill-health with those of large-scale public organizations providing
the interrelated services of relief and subject to those checks involving public and professional action.

The complexity of the panorama of quality assurance and the
various methods entailed to check it which are set out in this
publication indicate the need for all concerned with health services
as well as the public at large to be aware and understand the implications of a number of ongoing activities which relate to quality
and taken together go some way to place the many issues which are
involved in perspective. Some of these are on-going, and are checks
taken for granted; some follow the drama of events, and are sometimes inevitably part of them; some involve special efforts.

The 'disaster' approach is exemplified by the maternal mortality
inquiry, by the experience of the Hospital Advisory Service which
has the potential for extension, and to some extent by the malignant
hypertension study which has of course wider implications. All of
these indicate special roles for professional assessment groups
operating within a recognized administrative policy with the

objective of improving professional processes. The same can be said to apply to the procedures for surgical evaluation and medical self-assessment—indeed for all accreditation processes. The potential for monitoring with occasional selective inquiries is clear from the essay on SCRIPS, the mechanism for which is centralized although it does not include the means for authoritative comment, far less action. Experience of the surveys of laboratory perform-ance suggest what is possible by continuous external assessment, although again it is not currently a mandatory requirement. Any procedures to effect this would need the development of special mechanisms within the administrative structure which raises the spectre of bureaucratic imperatives.

Questions of quality have a habit however of arising outside specially designed mechanisms and from the essay from Wessex a special art in planning and informed management seems to be an absolute necessity at executive level. Institutional practice at the operational level has a special place in the models and the essay from the Western Infirmary, Glasgow, and that on autopsy rates raise issues about the processes of the sub-system which is hospital practice. The difficulties of placing quality control and its information base in the authority structure is brought out in the essay on the Medical Executive Committee. The first priority to cover the special problems of general practice would seem to be a more satisfactory educational base.

The main implications of these essays for the reader may how-ever lie specially in illuminating the scope and complexity of the problems and in distinguishing the mechanisms which are capable of being developed operationally in relation to the assessment of quality and to the various roles identified.

2. *The over-riding principles and lessons to emerge*

But there are matters of principle which though touched upon only occasionally in the essays, are bound to have a dominant effect on the conduct of any system for the maintenance of quality and which never should be far away from the thread of the debate.

A basic long-established concept which continues to rule in

modern society is the special relationship between doctor and patient, but nowadays there is superimposed on it the organization of health care institutions at various levels and a range of professional and technical services all of which depend on separated educational systems each of which is itself controlled in some way or other as to standards. The question of quality of care related to certain not too closely defined standards depending on a variety of elements has complicated the issue of care. The doctor/patient relationship has to be harmonious and balanced if effective care is to result; harmonious because the morale of both must be protected, balanced because though there is a primary responsibility for aspects of the relationship upon one partner, the doctor (and where appropriate his back-up), its discharge can only be effectively performed with the help of the other in a *consensus in idem* and on certain assumptions as to the application of skills, knowledge, and techniques.

Brook and **Avery** refer to the objective of compassionate care for the patient and **Cochrane**'s essay etches a picture of such compassion. Whatever the system of health care and its controls and however far technology advances, nothing will change the fact that the medical and other caring professions have a special role and responsibility in the exercise of humanity in all their dealings with patients, and their dedication and motivation in this role will be a major determinant of quality whatever the excellence of the facilities available, and whatever the standard of professional practice.

The quality of health care is highly sensitive to the *morale* of those who work in health services, and all those (politicians, bureaucrats, and public) who deal with the caring professions have to recognize that fact. No one can yet estimate what damage may have been done to the special character of quality which has been a feature of the NHS since its inception by the events of 1975.

It is a natural assumption, as well as a hypothesis that explains some of the findings reported here, that the standard of professional practice is dependent not only on factors such as education and morale but also on human variability springing from the fact that one man may have special gifts in practice different from his neighbour's. The monitoring of medical practice can rarely be

profitably directed to the observation of such differences. Perhaps
it is for this reason that one of the most important principles is
stressed in the chapters by **Dollery, Godber, McColl,** and **Yates**
that the maintenance of confidentiality in the study of an individual
doctor's performance is fundamental to its effectiveness in assessing how practice may be improved through the modification of
procedures or the further education of those involved. **McColl's**
description of how it was a teaching hospital tradition that an
informal assessment of quality was constantly practised within a
closed society of senior consultants, will illustrate the special
climate which human beings need for this sensitive exercise in
personal questioning. Nobody outside the medical profession can
cavil at this, for few professions practice such heart-searching.
Management therefore has to recognize and provide for this
confidentiality.

Brook and **McColl** have made the point that in earlier days
when there was much less at the technological level which could be
done for the benefit of the patient, the assessment of quality by the
consideration of outcome was relatively simple; but with the
development of technological and pharmacological methods, there
has been a swing over to more complicated monitoring practice
presumably because of a belief that a satisfactory outcome was
certain if the right procedures were followed at the right time. This
however has certain limitations as Cochrane has demonstrated (1).

Today there appear signs on a political level of an interest in the
assessment of the effectiveness of health care policies and how
effectively resources are being utilized. **Brook** in commenting
upon this subject has noted that despite the lack of any systematic
delivery of health care in the US, there has been a deliberate
attempt there to create the means for such assessment. **Godber**
explores the possibility of the development of a mechanism in
Britain.

Yet there is a major factor which may be unique to the UK and
certainly gives an extra dimension to quality assurance in the NHS
while defying measurement, though not sense nor sensibility. This
is the 'hidden contract' which protects the consultant's responsi-

bility to the particular patient. This historically is fundamental to an understanding of the acceptance of the NHS, between the profession at the highest level (and particularly that part of it concerned with higher and continuing education) and those acting for the common good, entrusted with the setting up, maintenance, and development of the Services. The existence of this must be acknowledged as a major factor in the acceptance of the NHS with all it implies by the medical profession and the consensus preserved; for it is the basis of self-disciplinary measures on which the professions concerned with such a personal service must operate; and the application of undue bureaucratic means of control however worthy their objectives can only be self-defeating.

In considering the lessons to be learnt from the essays in this publication, the basic problem is how, in a complex environment where different mechanisms each will have their place, and where there will be many different roles to be played by those who practise the means to reach the ultimate end, there can be established a strategy which will pull together all these strands into a coherant attack, the aim of which is to raise the quality of medical care.

The application of the results of the different forms of monitoring is attained by implementations of actions following publication or by their adoption as part of the subject matter for educational programmes. It is an indication of how attitudes change to note in **Godber**'s essay that the decision to publish the results of the confidential inquiries was at the time considered daring, although acknowledged now as reasonable practice. A question posed by **Dollery** is in effect one of general policy: how many other studies of such a nature may exist or could be initiated, and finally published with significant effect on the quality of care? In the long term, the greatest effect from the monitoring process may be achieved through the adoption of the results or their acceptance as educational subject matter, for in this way future doctors will be permanently influenced and those already qualified, though with less certainty, changed in their traditional attitudes. Yet as **Cochrane** points out, there is no natural response to indications how matters may be improved.

The connection between the quality of care and communication particularly through medical education at every gradation of the spectrum (from undergraduate to the continuing education of the specialist) is basic to the whole debate. In his wide-ranging essay, **Irvine** stresses that the medical profession through the means of raising the standards of professional and specialty education of its own initiative, is continuously striving to raise the quality of care to higher levels. The establishment of the Royal College of General Practitioners and its adoption of a specialist training programme can be seen as a conscious response to a realization of the indifferent quality of practice as it was and difficulties in monitoring it. One has not to look far for other examples—in the creation, for instance, of the Faculty of Community Medicine which will certainly be involved in the development of population medicine and in the development of criteria on which quality in all aspects can be judged. Indeed the role of the community physician is crucial and theirs is a heavy responsibility. The whole process of specialist training, even if now traditional in the older colleges and faculties, is a conscious and deliberate programme aimed at raising and maintaining standards of care, which though it can never be the sole assurance of quality has a fundamental part in its attainment.

An important element, although most usually it is not established with the intention of directly affecting quality, is the creation of an awareness of an external interest in the quality of practice. In research generally the 'Hawthorne effect' is well-known and it appears from the references in the essays by **McColl** and **Yates** that the establishment of a record-keeping of the effects of different patterns of care is sufficient in itself to vary that pattern in a favourable direction. One can hardly doubt also that the existence of the confidential inquiries into maternal mortality have favourably affected the standard of care quite apart from the publication of the results of the inquiries. It seems a matter for further debate whether it may be possible to create this awareness of interest as a continuing feature of health care practice not dependent upon spasmodic studies following disasters, carried out often for quite different purposes.

The most widely established system created for the purpose of monitoring, and certainly the most expensive, is Hospital Activity Analysis and the more elaborate forms of information systems such as the Oxford Record Linkage Study and the Scottish Hospital In-Patient Statistics. **Heasman**'s essay reports on the uses of the Scottish system and its possible development. The question remains however, on whose initiative? It seems apparent that without the use of 'exception reporting' as advocated in **Yates**'s essay and the explicit acceptance that someone, very possibly the community physician, must have the major role as broker in determining criteria for such reporting, the full value of these large information systems will not be exploited. The difficulty of organizing large enough samples at district level to show significant variations in outcome for specific diagnoses is a problem with some ramifications. But all this in no way devalues the importance to be attached to the establishment of these information systems because, as **Doll** has indicated (3), without them there can be no beginnings to an assessment of quality. The debate should therefore now turn to proposals for the best mechanism of exploitation.

Efficiency and effectiveness, whether of facilities or of practice have in the end to be judged by their outcome. For this the controlled clinical trial is one of the most important techniques. The implications of **Cochrane**'s essay concern the method by which such trials may be established on a continuing and deliberate basis rather than through the sudden demands by Government for answers to questions concerning the validity of new techniques or through the initiative of individuals curious about the validity of established practice. Whether the responsibility for this should rest with the Department, the Medical Research Council, some specially constituted research council (4), or the regional health authorities is a matter for careful debate and further exploration. It is relevant to note that, apart from controlled clinical trials inquiries of the nature of those reported by **Godber** and **Dollery** often broaden clinical knowledge in addition to clarifying the variability of practice. Studies of the outcome of care are therefore of research value besides being a tool for the control of quality. An example of this is given by **Cochrane** in the note appended to his essay which raises questions too, about communication and applications.

Finally there is one skill which is of supreme importance—that of management which can be exploited to affect any strategy or system. **Revans**'s essay provides a clear-cut illustration of how a comparatively amorphous and badly capitalized system can be improved in terms of quality by planned development and a deliberate strategy of structural improvement. It confirms that in respect of 'structure' the improvement of quality depends upon the state of the art of planning and information and upon a special quality of sympathy and understanding health service managers need, whether or not medically qualified, in formulating policy options and presenting them in such a way that politicians and public may come to considered judgements upon them. In the debate about the achievement of quality of care it is performance in those areas which should be scrutinized whenever an issue about 'structure' is brought to the forefront of discussion. Although it has to be recognized that 'good institutional practice' is necessary at all levels and in different ways. It is evident in **Wilson**'s account of the history of the Health Services Research Unit at the Western Infirmary, Glasgow, that the establishment of such units may be of the greatest importance in the fostering of an atmosphere of on-going inquiry. 'Good' practice with a bearing on quality may take many forms however. Thus another mechanism in the realm of good institutional practice is that of the autopsy. **Waldron**'s essay indicates that there has been an apparent decline in the use of this well-tried mechanism for the monitoring of quality in diagnosis and therapy. The study is continuing in order to discover the significance of this decline and whether and how it should be arrested.

There can also be external means of control, the initiative of which is primarily in the realm of management. Thus **Baker**'s belief that the HAS, which it should be recalled was in effect born out of a disaster inquiry, is effective as an already established technique and could with advantage be extended, supports

Dollery's earlier thesis (2). It is a matter for the supreme command of the NHS, presuming there is one for such matters, whether this should be done. Indeed the various means for assessing quality needs an over-all appreciation at the highest possible level and poses the need for the establishment of some mechanism designed for intelligent and eventual action.

3. The changing climate of professional and public opinion

It is interesting how discussion about the assessment of medical care has developed rapidly over the last few years. A study of the major medical journals in the English-speaking world in the last eighteen months is impressive in the change of attitude especially in the UK displayed not only by the content of many of the contributions relating to the need for quality assurance regarding medical care, but also in the sympathetic view of the editorials to the need for some means of assessment (5). This is a healthy, welcome development on which a public policy sympathetic to professional endeavour could be built if the maximum political benefit is to be got, both on the professional and on the political-bureaucratic fronts, since it would seem only a matter of time before it becomes a matter for wider public debate.

Yet it is evident from the current literature that while there is some anxiety to try to meet the very real variations in quality, there are real fears about the possible effect of the application of any control system.

There is general feeling that critical self-examination should be encouraged to avoid professional isolation but there is a certain nervousness when it comes to the use of experimental methods to develop criteria in case its use, even experimentally, leads to a suggestion for the development of some form of external audit of clinical practice. Yet fears will only be allayed by discussing ways and means, however unpromising the prospect.

An editorial in the *British Medical Journal* is startlingly frank about the relationship of process and outcome.

No external audit of medical treatment can control its quality effectively while individual opinions differ so widely in what should be included in a standard protocol even in common acute disorders . . . Much of what is accepted treatment rests on no more than widely held judgements. Validation—or refutation—of its judgements by objective tests is needed if there is to be any prospect of effective control of the quality of medical care in the future. [6]

Nor are the real problems seen as confined to traditional medical issues, since doctors are having to learn to comprehend and manage the sociological and psychological environments in which they practise (7).

In general it seems clear that effective monitoring of 'process' has probably in the UK little future other than an educational exercise and of course therein lies its probable value. It is in the educational field that much can be achieved but a policy and plan has to be developed going beyond the traditional educational arrangements.

In the first instance it is evident there has to be a major educational effort to create an atmosphere of self examination not only of process and practice generally but of the results of therapies. The reaction to Cochrane's much-praised book (8) has been too overwhelming to dismiss the feeling that scientific medicine has not hitherto adopted the scientific approach to the outcome of therapies as comprehensively as it ought.

This line of speculation also leads to the question of how best to develop arrangements to ensure a reasonable degree of surveillance without curbing the legitimate demands for clinical freedom having regard to the present state of medical science, in order to try to maximise what society acting as a group can do for the individual. There are, however, currently well-founded doubts about the adequacy of reasonable criteria, or of understanding. To complement this approach therefore it must surely be of the essence to consider what official policies are now necessary in order to put the position in a sensible perspective and to encourage initially a reasonable level of professional self-examination. It is in fact the failure hitherto to develop comprehensive concepts to give perspective to what is required by way of arrangements to monitor quality, which gives rise to much of the confusion.

4. To the horizon and beyond

It is relatively easy to reach the conclusion that the development of such concepts must be precedent to the institution of a credible policy which should also embrace a reasonable programme of approach which avoids putting a straitjacket on the development of medical practice, either through a mass of restrictive rules or through the almost certain increase in costs occasioned by organizational requirements to put indices on quality assurance.

What should the main features be of such a policy and programme? There is probably a number of distinct approaches to the final goal for it is evident that there is a number of models applicable to quality control, not exclusive nor alternative but interrelated. As a general policy, however, some strategic direction of the advances along each path is needed, and one or two deliberate approaches chosen as priorities for action. The immediate priority is probably towards the creation of confidence amongst those primarily involved the front-line clinicians, and the development of the facilities required, but a programme for a comprehensive attack on the problem is a necessary complement.

Above all to get anywhere it must be a cardinal principle that the medical profession itself has to be closely involved in any scheme involving evaluation of therapies. It will no doubt be a matter for debate whether they should be exclusively involved, and only time, continuous experiment and experience of their performance will tell whether they should be so. They certainly should be urged to develop their own approaches, for if the profession does not show itself active, they might be required to be so by public pressures (9). An authoritative lead is probably necessary from the Royal Colleges but the question is how the initiative on the policy front towards a strategy can be begun and sustained.

The US approach is both interesting and instructive. Thus, Senator Bennet in introducing the PSRO amendment to the Social Security Act 1972 said

physicians, properly organised and with a proper mandate are capable of conducting an ongoing effective review program which would eliminate much of the present criticism of the profession and help enhance their

stature as honourable men in an honourable vocation willing to undertake necessary and broad responsibility for overseeing professional
functions. [10]

In the event the medical profession is primarily involved in the
organizations set up to develop professional standards and the
review of programmes. In the UK the embryo organizations
already exist in the divisional system and executive committees at
ground level but there being no requirement or incentive there is
little or no action in the area of quality. There is of course no
conceptual framework on which to build. There is still a major
requirement for a comprehensive analysis of the criteria and of the
way in which medical care organizations in all societies should
operate to monitor health quality in order to bring out clearly
where the functions of the managers lie as distinct from those of
the professionals. It is part of the duty of the management to
provide within reason the mechanisms to enable the system to
work effectively, but clearly there has to be some central prompting,
though desirably not by Statute. In the UK as has been pointed
out there is no General Staff organization for the NHS (11) and it
is difficult to see what the catalyst will be.

The essays of **Godber** and **Heasman** describe particular aspects
of the part played by medical administration in supporting and
co-ordinating monitoring programmes, but to be effective these
are basically dependent upon the goodwill and initiative of the
clinicians. **Revans's** essay indicates the crucial importance to
quality of care of good management of resources in an organized
health care system with good goals and policies, including personnel management. It also must lead to speculation about the
facilitating functions of management. Thus at the institutional
level to take the question of deaths and complications meetings, if
these are considered clinically or educationally important in
individual institutions or in groups of institutions working to
provide services for specific populations, it is a fault of administrative policy if conditions, say because there is not enough staff,
prevent their being held as a routine process. It is part of the
political/managerial function to ensure the provision of necessary
facilities. It is part of the professionals' to formulate how they

should be conducted. Again **McColl**'s suggestion for the use of accreditation procedures to implement policies recognized as important to quality assurance is worthy of serious and urgent consideration by the higher educational bodies. Similarly if for example there is something concrete by way of principles to be learnt from the well-established confidential maternal mortality survey as a method of surveillance, what is the administrative initiative and the procedure required to see if it can be applied to other problems, say neonatal deaths? In the case of the UK, because of the numbers of deaths involved, it probably could not be applied at national level. But as is remarked by **Godber** there may be a case for applying the inquiry procedure at regional, area, or even district level; and is it worth developing a special system to arrange for this? Should not each division or Medical Executive (Cogwheel) Committee have a sub-committee on quality anyway? The provision and development of the system will be Caesar's even if its working must be God's.

Of course this line of speculation need not be wholly confined to questions relating to outcome. It is also applicable equally to general policies in relation to social acceptability and levels of service and how to achieve these. It has been part of general policy in health for more than twenty years to seek to devote more resources to the 'maintenance medicine' groups including the aged, the mentally ill, and the mentally handicapped. Yet successive governments till today have hardly followed through their general statements about the need for these groups to get priorities for more resources. There is surely a case for an identifiable monitoring mechanism for this. Indeed it has been announced (12) that a British political party is setting up a group to monitor the progress of the declared policy of successive governments in the case of the mentally ill and mentally handicapped. Had a monitoring system been developed to check this aspect of political performance, the picture might have been very different now. The function of both the political and management authorities is relatively clear in such cases. What is not so clear is the effectiveness of the follow-through.

Again, how far should monitoring go and at what level should it be developed? Is it necessary for example to include special mechanisms at the institution, district or area level first of all to establish evaluation criteria, then to apply these on an ongoing basis to services? There is a special function revealed here for the community physician working closely with clinicians to develop the intra-professional confidence necessary to establish a reasonable mechanism. Have the ways and means to achieve such results been conceptualized in any realistic way? It is of course just as important to ensure that there is not an over-enthusiastic approach to develop evaluative systems, which while having some use are expensive in relation to what is produced. The real problem is how to put all the obvious requirements together sensibly.

A feeling of confidence on all sides, based on a real understanding is of course an absolute prerequisite for action. The current emphasis on assessment is a challenge to enable resources to be deployed and the benefits of medical science made available to the greatest number of people in the most acceptable way. Yet it raises questions about medical education and the role of educational bodies at all levels as leaders in conceptual development.

In the Introduction it was stressed that the direction of this publication was to the better development of the debate about the role of the medical profession in maintaining and raising the quality of care. It has been necessary in order to create a balanced picture to include in it the responsibilities of the administration and to illustrate the complexities inherent in consulting the public and the profession about structure and in making the best use of information systems. It is however consistent with the primary aim of the publication to return finally to the responsibilities of the medical profession.

A careful reading of the essays will emphasize how important is the role of that special feature in the British medical scene, the Royal Colleges and their faculties. It is their traditional function to maintain and raise the professional standards of their members. The younger colleges and faculties such as the Royal College of General

Practitioners and the Faculty of Community Medicine are fully engaged at the present time in establishing themselves, thus. At their beginning the Royal College of Obstetricians and Gynaecologists set a notable example and the point has been made of the important role they played in the confidential inquiries into maternal mortality: they were also early users of the accreditation principle. More recently still the Royal College of Physicians with the support of the Nuffield Provincial Hospitals Trust have begun an experiment to discover how best to encourage their members in self-assessment (13) and are known to be interested in the field under review. In Scotland the Royal Colleges and faculties jointly are engaged in an important initiative in assessing the outcome of care in particular clinical fields which link the hospital and the community (14). **Whitehead**'s report on quality control in the pathological laboratory illustrates not only how units are accepting this service both inside and outside the NHS and can group themselves in a joint effort inspired by a responsibility to the profession and public they serve, but it illustrates also the role played, in this case, by the Royal College of Pathologists in supporting such an effort and developing it further.

Wilson's report about the Research Unit in the Western Infirmary, Glasgow, and in a lesser key, **Yates**'s survey of the use of information at divisional level, show how the universities and clinical divisions in teaching hospitals can also assume a responsibility to create a climate of opinion favourable to quality assessment as well as for providing the working base for using and extending information systems. While the Western is a teaching hospital the principle is equally true for other wholly service-orientated hospitals. No doubt other examples could be found of this kind of operation, although the difficulty in establishing such efforts and even more in communicating their lessons widely should not be under-estimated.

Yet it must be questioned whether the multiplicity of individual educational and other efforts by Royal Colleges, universities, and service institutions do not require some more central focus and a co-ordinating potential, for which the advocates of a Royal Academy of Medicine have often argued. It is a too-common complaint of our times to bemoan the lack of leadership and yet to give little thought to how it can be encouraged. It might well be that the creation of an institute on the lines of the Institute of Medicine (15) of the National Academy of Sciences in Washington, having as its prescribed aim the maintaining and raising of the quality of patient care in every sphere in the NHS, in the other organized medical services, and in the independent medical groups, might be the way in which leadership might be able to be exercised since there are certainly a number of major issues in medicine which need to be faced. Indeed a multidisciplined national institution operating responsibly and independently on a national basis could well provide the intellectual counter-balance necessary to the weight exercised by what is in effect the public monopoly in health policy. Yet any additional bureaucracy, however well-intentioned its establishment, is suspect and above all costly—certainly beyond being financed out of professional subscriptions which precariously finance the specialist bodies. Again the general debate is not just a private matter for the medical profession, the press and media are clearly embroiled in quality. The whole question of health at the moment is deeply scored too by the general issue of the impact of health policies on the health of the population as a whole and what can be afforded. The latter is easy, but the former is a very difficult political matter to grasp, for not only are the criteria few but it is now widely accepted the effect of personal health services is minimal compared to the influences of the environment and of behaviour on the individual.

The fact however does pose the need for the careful development of concepts which will not only lead to a better political understanding of the major influences on health as a whole, but also to policies in the interim period designed to make for the firm establishment of high morale through better-educated health care professions and a better-educated public. What is therefore required first is the adoption of a sensible comprehensive policy to analyse what is involved in the assessment and monitoring of health services in all its aspects, a programme for the implementation of such a policy, the resources to develop such a programme and a continuous review of it. The initial part of such a programme could profitably be devoted to the structured discussion in a series of forums of the major issues which should first be tackled. It should also not be too difficult to draw up a preliminary list where concepts and criteria could be the basis of further education of all health care professionals, not just the clinicians, since nowadays the whole question of health policies including the development and the deployment of resources is a matter for discussion and decision by others than politicians and the professionals.

On the professional side without claiming exclusiveness a credible programme of approach involving a variety of bodies to certain of the many complex problems extant and which would raise most of the questions about initiatives, financing, co-ordination, policies on priorities, etc., might include the following.

1. Investigations into certain certified causes of deaths in people below the age of 55 where there is a possibility that the quality of care may considerably influence the outcome. They might be conducted along the lines described in Chapter 1 by Godber and in Chapter 2 by Dollery and organized by the Royal Colleges. Suggestions may be made of suitable topics such as:
(*a*) Diabetic and hypoglycaemic coma.
(*b*) Asthma.
(*c*) Self-poisoning by drugs.
(*d*) Meningitis.
(*e*) Haematemesis.

2. Development of quality control in other fields in addition to biochemical laboratories following the example given in Chapter 5 by Whitehead. Activities under this head might be:
(*a*) Sample quality control check of accuracy of diagnoses entered on official hospital returns to check the reliability of the system and to keep it under review (cf. Chapters 8 and 9).
(*b*) Sample quality control of communications between general practitioners and hospital doctors—both ways. The lack of

information given in letters referring patients to hospital is often gross, such as no note of prescribed drugs. There are also often deficiencies in the replies from hospital.

3. Encouragement of Higher Training Committees to take account of extent of checks of standards of care in the hospitals in which they approve posts. They might inquire about:

(*a*) Regular meetings to review deaths and percentage of post mortems.

(*b*) Availability of data on promptness of writing discharge letters and so on.

(*c*) Review of quality of case-records.

(*d*) Review of waiting times for appointments, examinations, etc.

(*e*) Performance of controlled clinical trials in the hospital.

(*f*) Comparison of clinical statistics both between similar units in the hospital and with other hospitals in relation to length of stay for various conditions, outcome, etc.

(*g*) Check on number of drugs prescribed per patient and frequency of adverse reactions.

4. Use of newer methods to decide on the most efficient and economic use of clinical data and laboratory tests in the establishment of a diagnosis. Use of decision trees as described by Knill-Jones (see Chapter 8).

And in an attempt to stimulate interest in the younger element.

5. The establishment of prizes for:

(*a*) Undergraduate projects on quality of care.

(*b*) Postgraduate awards open to registrars to encourage production of MD and PhD theses on quality of care.

5. *Epilogue*

The quality of health services probably depends on four main human instincts:

1. Service to fellow man, the 'compassion' which exists in every walk of life but peculiarly necessary for a high level of patient care and sensitive therefore to the state of morale.

2. Professional pride, raised by group loyalty and identity, as evidenced by the long and distinguished history of the Royal Colleges.

3. Search for knowledge, the drive to research and find the truth even if it is disturbing to personal interest.

4. The political instinct, to decide policy and organize society in the interests of society. The drive for better organization of health services of which the establishment of the NHS is an outstanding example.

These instincts vary in intensity in man. An increased understanding of their place in health affairs and a gearing of policy to this end gives the best assurance of health services quality.

Yet the pursuit of quality is not an esoteric subject for it has to be stressed that the objective is positive—the improvement of medical care. **Brook** and **Avery** have expressed succinctly the real objectives in the USA where the issue is seen as major and are leading to better practice and thus to improvements in care.

The United States is engaged in implementing a series of quality assurance activities. In the short run, the success of these programs depends on rigorous program evaluation and feedback of results so that deficiencies can be corrected and improvements made. Without such feedback, these programs may be extremely costly yet produce no demonstrable improvements in health.

The biggest threat to the success of quality assurance programs, whether or not they benefit from advances in methods, lies with the failure to use the results of quality assessment studies to correct and improve medical care. Most studies have described deficiencies in care but have done little else with the information. This luxury can no longer be afforded. [17]

Similarly in the UK the ultimate aim of the many activities described or speculated about in this book is a better service to the patient and an assurance of quality.

To achieve such assurance there is a need for the better education of the profession, of management, of politicians and of the public at large and each of these groups presents different problems with regard to approach. There is also a prior need for the development of better mechanisms and criteria on which credible judgements can be made and decisions taken with regard to the improvement of quality of performance as well as in the selection and implementation of priorities. This poses the serious question of whether the existing system can effectively satisfy those needs, or whether the times call for an independent agency capable of delivering authoritative judgements on such issues which will lead to better policies. What has to be avoided is the creation of mechanisms as part of the bureaucracy of the NHS for the analysis and measurement of quality, which while intent on better quality might destroy the assurance of it.

References and notes

1. COCHRANE, A. L. (1972). *Effectiveness and Efficiency*. Rock Carling Monograph (London: Nuffield Provincial Hospitals Trust).
2. DOLLERY, C. T. (1971). 'The quality of health care', in McLachlan, G. (ed.), *Challenges for Change*, p. 1 (Oxford University Press for the Nuffield Provincial Hospitals Trust).
3. DOLL, SIR RICHARD (1974). 'Surveillance and monitoring', *Internat. J. Epidemiol.* **3**, 305.
4. McLACHLAN, G. (ed.) (1971). 'Editorial', *Portfolio for Health. Problems and Progress in Medical Care*, Sixth Series, p. ix (Oxford University Press for the Nuffield Provincial Hospitals Trust).
5. Some one hundred articles concerned with the subject have been identified in a bibliography based on the *Lancet, British Medical Journal*, and *New England Journal of Medicine* from January 1974 to January 1976.
6. 'Editorial', *Br. med. J.* **1** (1974), 255.
7. JONSEN, A. R. (1975). *New Eng. J. Med.* **292**, 1126.
8. COCHRANE, A. L. (1972). *Effectiveness and Efficiency*. Rock Carling Monograph (London: Nuffield Provincial Hospitals Trust).
9. There have been various articles in the press on quality. For example, Christine Doyle, *Observer*, 1 February 1976. The most recent, David Loshak, *Daily Telegraph*, 18 March 1976.
10. 118*th Cong. Rec.* **32** (1972), 478. (Remarks of Senator Bennett.)
11. NUFFIELD PROVINCIAL HOSPITALS TRUST (1975). 'Introduction and perspective', *Ninth Report*, p. 14 (London: Nuffield Provincial Hospitals Trust).
12. *The Times*, 24 April 1975.
13. NUFFIELD PROVINCIAL HOSPITALS TRUST (1975). *Ninth Report*, p. 109, Grant no. 78 (London: Nuffield Provincial Hospitals Trust).
14. *Proceedings of the Annual Community Medicine Conference* (September 1975).
15. Institute of Medicine, National Academy of Sciences, Washington DC.
16. For the Institute of Medicine project on Quality an extensive bibliography has been accumulated.
17. Brook and Avery, pp. 221–52.

Appendix

Trust activities relevant to quality of medical care

A bibliography of Trust grants relevant to quality of care

Trust activities relevant to quality of medical care

Questions of quality have long been a prime interest of the Nuffield Provincial Hospitals Trust as a body concerned with improvements in service. Indeed its position represents an aspect of private as distinct from publicly financed effort in the monitoring of medical care and its history in this respect reflects the increasing sophistication of views among those involved in health services about the priority steps required to improve medical care. Since one of its purposes has to do with organization, its work has spanned 'structure', 'process', and 'outcome' and it has progressively been concerned with each over the years.

Thus it was founded with the express purposes of working for ... the co-ordination on a regional basis of hospital, medical and, associated health services ... (1).

Subsequently, to this purpose was added 'and the promotion of improved organization and efficient development of hospital, medical and associated health services throughout the provinces' (2). This latter became the major purpose after the 1946 Act, which introduced arrangements for the regionalization of hospital service planning and organization.

To achieve these objectives the Trust adopted at an early stage a policy of study, experiment, and demonstration (3); and through the first of these became actively committed to a continuous review of critical aspects of the health services in the UK. Studies carried out under this policy can be divided, as will be seen from a scrutiny of the two attached bibliographies, between identifications of need and so of aims for health service policy often by means of an investigation of 'outcome', as well as inquiries into the 'structure' and 'process' of specific services. The two approaches are frequently interconnected and there has been an increasing focus upon outcome and policy. The same trend becomes apparent from the increasing and now very substantial monitoring carried out by the Departments of Health and Social Security and by the health authorities (4).

In response to the call for better studies to fit the scientific and social developments of this time, the Trust instituted in 1948, the Investigation into the Function and Design of Hospitals (5). While primarily concerned with better-designed hospitals this study posed questions beyond design, which stimulated studies of other elements fundamental to planning (6), which are of the very essence of considerations of improving the quality of 'structure'. Thus the need in any system to attempt scientifically to match facilities to 'demand' for services was revealed at an early stage as an important issue. This in turn raised questions about the relationship of 'demand' and 'need', but above all its challenge of accepted beliefs about the numbers of beds required for any given population had their effect on planning to make the best use of resources which is an element in the raising of quality. The studies detailed in the chapter 'Planning to Meet Demand' of the IFDH report were specifically alluded to in the first official Hospital Plan in 1960, when for the first time realistic bed requirements were urged to be taken as one of the bases for planning hospital services.

Again, when the Trust in 1951, instituted the study by Dr Stephen Taylor (now Lord Taylor) into general practice, the report eventually published was entitled *Good General Practice* (7), to reflect the fact that there were certain characteristics in practice that could be identified to indicate good quality in general practice. The study itself had come into being because of the dismay at the Collings Report (8) which was scornful of the standards of general practice in England, and Stephen Taylor in his study, during which he visited many general practitioners, concentrated on and distinguished those measurable elements which he and his distinguished steering committee felt added up to the basic definable requirements for good general practice. What has now come to be known in the jargon of the debates on quality of care as 'structure' and to a lesser extent 'process' was very much what Lord Taylor concentrated on in his study, while recognizing of course that it is not too easy to distinguish what in fact constitutes the personal factor in general practice to give the extra dimension to 'structure' and to 'practice' or 'process'.

Subsequently, the Trust's most important policies in pursuance of improving efficiency, included the development of comparisons between authorities to highlight the range of structural differences which existed (9). The hospital costing studies (10) and the studies of the work of nurses (11) were specifically designed to this use. The operational research work on the centralization of syringe services (12) and on central sterile supply (13), on hospital outpatients (14) and radiological services (15), grew out of the IFDH studies and also had the objective of promoting efficiency. Similarly the studies of 'casualty services '(16) and of 'food in hospitals' (17) were designed to highlight certain problems as a preliminary to correcting faults. Its specific interest in postgraduate medical education (18, 19) arose out of the need to improve the quality of services in the provinces in the key area of education, and its support of accreditation schemes of the Royal Colleges (20) can be seen too as in furtherance of this policy. This particular book however owes its origin to questions raised by work commissioned by the Trust at the other end of the spectrum of analysis of quality, namely 'outcome' which is after all the significant test of service. More than twenty years ago the disturbing observations in *Hospital and Community* (21) pointed the way to this important area but the most recent interest has been stimulated by the reception given to two books published by the Trust. The first of these was *Screening in Medical Care* (22) published in 1968 which raised questions about the effectiveness of a number of screening procedures in common use, and the second was the Rock Carling Monograph published in 1971 *Effectiveness and Efficiency* (23) by Professor A. L. Cochrane who was a member of the Screening Group.

When the Trustees invited Professor Cochrane to write a monograph on his views about effectiveness of care, there were few clues to the interest the book eventually stimulated (24). Leaving aside the technical difficulties involved in the use of randomized controlled trials advocated by Professor Cochrane, quite clearly the general conclusion that a great deal of therapeutic practice had never been assessed scientifically as to effect, had crystallized the anxieties of many people not just in the UK but throughout the world on this score.

If health services are assumed to have as the major objective the effective outcome of therapy, it is that end of the spectrum which must be studied.

It was to follow up this monograph that in 1972 the Trustees convened a small group under the Chairmanship of the late Lord Rosenheim to look at the general questions of quality of care and this publication is a result of the group's considerations. It is probably also appropriate to note that the Trust has in the mean-time also supported a number of projects in the general area of quality assessment (25).

References and notes

1. Trust Deed of setting up Nuffield Provincial Hospitals Trust dated 25 June 1940.
2. Supplementary Scheme for Nuffield Provincial Hospitals Trust dated 15 August 1962.
3. NUFFIELD PROVINCIAL HOSPITALS TRUST, *First Report, 1939–1948*.
4. —— *Eighth Report, 1967–1970*, and *Ninth Report, 1970–1975*. McLACHLAN, G. (ed.) (1971). *Portfolio for Health, Problems and Progress in Medical Care*, Sixth series (Oxford University Press for the Nuffield Provincial Hospitals Trust). McLACHLAN, G. (ed.) (1973). *Portfolio for Health 2, Problems and Progress in Medical Care*, Eighth Series (Oxford University Press for the Nuffield Provincial Hospitals Trust).
5–25. References to the Cumulative Index in the *Eighth* and *Ninth Reports* of the Trust: (5) VIII, 97. (6) VIII, 93. (7) VIII, 43. (8) VIII, 43. (9) VIII, 93–94. (10) VIII, 94. (11) VIII, 95. (12) VIII, 52. (13) VIII, 53. (14) VIII, 50–51. (15) VIII, 48. (16) VIII, 52. (17) VIII, 56. (18) VIII, 81–86. (19) IX, 131–5. (20) VIII, 84, 86 and IX, 133–4. (21) VIII, 92–93. (22) VIII, 23. (23) IX, 16, 33, 67–68, 79. (24) The book has had four printings and there are Polish, French, Spanish, and Italian translations. (25) IX, 33–34, 85–86, 108–9, 142–3.

A bibliography of Trust grants relevant to quality of care

Monitoring the service (structure and process)

The references in the right-hand column are to the cumulative index in the *Eighth* and *Ninth Reports* of the Trust.

1941	Studies of hospital services (Domesday Book)	VIII, 91
	1964 Use of medical resources in the Liverpool Region	VIII, 93; IX, 140
	1965 Supporting beds	VIII, 54
	1965 Medical records at ward level	VIII, 78
1949	Study of general practice (Collings)	VIII, 43
	1950 Good general practice (Taylor)	VIII, 43
	1961 Diagnostic facilities for the GP (Macaulay)	VIII, 45
	Prescribing in general practice	VIII, 50
	1963 Appointment systems in general practice	VIII, 45
	1966 Prescribing in Northern Ireland	VIII, 50; IX, 121
	1967 Survey of care in rural areas	VIII, 91; IX, 137
1949	Investigation of function and design of hospitals	VIII, 97
	1956 Central sterile supplies	VIII, 52, 53
	1959 Hospital engineering and supporting services	VIII, 100, 101
	1968 Study of the hospital supply system	VIII, 92
1949	Investigation of hospital costing	VIII, 94
	1968 Refinement of cost-benefit analysis in medicine	VIII, 95; IX, 140
1952	Services for the handicapped	VIII, 55
1952	Surveys of administration (Acton Society)	VIII, 91
	1968 Evaluative studies in health service administration	VIII, 102; IX, 137
	1971 Review of the divisional structure in action	VIII, 92; IX, 137
	1973 Case-study of Humberside reorganization	IX, 84, 138
1954	Maternity services in the SW Region	VIII, 59
	1966 Studies of maternity services	VIII, 60–62; IX, 123–4
1958	Casualty services	VIII, 52
	1969 Accident services	VIII, 52

1974 Study of effectiveness of rehabilitation services   IX, 123

1958 Study of day-hospitals for mentally handicapped   VIII, 65
    1959 Scottish mental health services   VIII, 66
    1960 Studies of community mental health services   VIII, 67
    1961 Mental health services in Devon   VIII, 68
    1963 Follow-up of psycho-geriatric discharges   VIII, 69
    1964 Effectiveness of hostels for the mentally ill   VIII, 69
    1968 Care at home of mentally subnormal   VIII, 70; IX, 125

1959 Study of X-ray departments   VIII, 48

1959 Group of studies of out-patient departments   VIII, 50–51

1959 Survey of geriatric services in Barrow-in-Furness   VIII, 63

1957 Social work in Rochdale   VIII, 74

1959 Hospital administrative staffing structure   VIII, 96
    1960 Study of nurse recruitment   VIII, 96

1962 Dental services   VIII, 57

1963 Survey of book and journal services   VIII, 76
    1966 Nursing libraries   VIII, 77

1964 Waiting-lists for child guidance   VIII, 73
    1968 Newcastle studies of child development   VIII, 62; IX, 124

1965 Oxford Record Linkage Study   VIII, 101; IX, 129
    1969 Computer development in Scotland   VIII, 80
    1973 Regional Medical Information Unit   IX, 130

1965 Review of postgraduate educational facilities in Scotland VIII, 85
    1967 Postgraduate medical education in UK   VIII, 86

1967 Deployment of medical manpower in Hull   VIII, 97

1968 Quality control in haematology   VIII, 49
    1974 Assessment of performance of clinical chemistry
            laboratories   IX, 143

1967 Screening in medical care   VIII, 49
    1973 Study of autopsy rates   IX, 143

1969 Voluntary services in Scottish hospitals   VIII, 58; IX, 123

1973 Quality of care, various projects   IX, 143

Identification of need and demand
(objective and outcome)

1942 Child health in Newcastle   VIII, 58
    1953 Morbidity records in childhood   VIII, 59
1947 Hospital and community studies   VIII, 92
    1956 Further studies in hospital and community   VIII, 93

1960 Studies for a community health service in
    Birmingham   VIII, 98

1952 Study of elderly in lodging houses   VIII, 63
    1957 Survey of the needs of the aged   VIII, 63

1955 Causes of accidents in the home   VIII, 52
    1956 Accident proneness among bus-drivers VIII, 48

1956 Caseload studies of Barrow and Tees-side VIII, 93

1958 Sudden death in infancy   VIII, 60

1959 Prevalence of mental illness in community VIII, 65
    Emotional disorders in schoolchildren   VIII, 72
    Survey of mental health needs in Anglesey VIII, 66
    Epidemiological studies of mental health in
      (Scotland)   VIII, 66; IX, 125
    1962 Regional survey of mental subnormality VIII, 68
    1964 Psychiatric case-register at Aberdeen VIII, 66; IX, 125

1959 Study for a student health service   VIII, 75

1959 Incidence of diabetes in the community   VIII, 76
    Study of epileptics in colonies   VIII, 76

1960 Social casework in general practice   VIII, 44–45
    1964 Ancillary work in general practice   VIII, 46; IX, 120
    1970 Priorities in general practice   IX, 87, 120
    1973 Experiments in the improvement of standards
      in general practice   IX, 120

1960 Nutritive value of meals   VIII, 56

1962 Survey of dental health   VIII, 57

1959 Studies of out-patients   VIII, 50–51

1965 Survey of disturbed adolescents   VIII, 71; IX, 127

1966 Study of low birth-weight   VIII, 61; IX, 123
    Study of spina bifida survivors   VIII, 62; IX, 124

1968 Information for divisions   VIII, 92; IX, 137–8
    1973 Information for district management   IX, 130

1969 Problems of the 1970s   IX, 138

1971 Study of self-poisoning as cause of admission IX, 126